GW00381273

BRIGHT RED

BRIGHT RED

THE LIVERPOOL – MANCHESTER UNITED MATCHES

MARK METCALF, TONY BUGBY
& LESLIE MILLMAN

AMBERLEY

First published 2012

Amberley Publishing
The Hill, Stroud
Gloucestershire, GL5 4EP

www.amberleybooks.com

Copyright © Mark Metcalf, Tony Bugby & Leslie Millman, 2012

The right of Mark Metcalf, Tony Bugby & Leslie Millman
to be identified as the Authors of this work has been asserted
in accordance with the Copyrights, Designs and Patents Act 1988.

All rights reserved. No part of this book may be reprinted
or reproduced or utilised in any form or by any electronic,
mechanical or other means, now known or hereafter invented, including
photocopying and recording, or in any information
storage or retrieval system, without the permission in writing
from the Publishers.

British Library Cataloguing in Publication Data.
A catalogue record for this book is available from the British Library.

ISBN 978 1 4456 0623 1

Typesetting and Origination by Amberley Publishing.
Printed in Great Britain.

Contents

Introduction

You would be mistaken in thinking the rivalry between Liverpool and Manchester United is only something that has existed in recent times.

Obviously there was considerable hype as United equalled and then overtook Liverpool's previous record of eighteen League titles, something the Merseyside club and its fans had cherished. And to lose it to your biggest rivals was something which was especially hard to palate. Liverpool fans in turn counter by continually taunting United over the five European Cups they have won to United's three.

United's success in 2011 was the latest sequel to a rivalry which began in 1894 when the two teams met for the first time in a game as important as any which subsequently has taken place ... and there have been some massive ones. It was a 'Test Match' which was to determine the status of both clubs.

United, then Newton Heath, had finished bottom of the First Division while Liverpool were champions of the Second Division, having gone through the whole campaign unbeaten. Test Matches, which were more like today's play-offs, were introduced when the Football League was expanded to two divisions. They featured the bottom three clubs in the top flight playing the top three in the second tier.

Liverpool won the initial meeting 2-0 to gain promotion, which meant Newton Heath were relegated. It was only the briefest stay, however, as the Merseysiders were immediately relegated as the two teams met for the first time in a League fixture in 1895.

Those first two League matches, played within three weeks of one another, also underlined how unpredictable the form book was, something which has invariably still been the case more than a century later. Liverpool won the first League meeting 7-1, which still to this day remains the record margin of victory between the two teams. In the return three weeks later, Newton Heath were no-hopers yet pulled off a 5-2 win.

It was not long before both Liverpool and Newton Heath, who became Manchester United in 1902, were both gracing the top division and achieving success. They each won the First Division title twice between 1901/11 as the rivalries intensified. United were given a helping hand in their title triumph of 1911 as it was Liverpool's win against Aston Villa at Anfield which presented them with the championship.

Liverpool were also United's first-ever opponents at Old Trafford and, true to form, spoilt the party by winning 4-3 after a terrific match. Ironically Liverpool had never previously won at Bank Street, the former home of Newton Heath/United.

There was also controversy when players from both clubs were involved in a betting scandal in 1915, resulting in three United players and four from Liverpool being found guilty of trying to fix the outcome of a game. They were all banned for life but later told the suspension would be rescinded if they signed up to fight in the First World War, which they all did with the exception of United's Enoch West, who never played again, and Sandy Turnbull, who was killed on the Western Front.

The fortunes of the two clubs could not have been further removed as Liverpool were crowned champions in 1920/21, the first of back-to-back titles, while United were relegated that same season. Then a decade later, United were relegated again from the First Division, their fate sealed following a 1-1 draw against Liverpool at Anfield. The 1930s were a difficult period for United and at one stage their survival was under threat. And on the field they struggled and one season only just staved off relegation to Third Division North.

United's fortunes improved after the Second World War and coincided with the appointment of Matt Busby as manager. Ironically, he arrived from Liverpool having turned down a coaching role at Anfield for the chance to become a manager.

Though Liverpool won their fifth League title in 1947, striker Albert Stubbins proving a costly but astute buy, it was United who would become a force under Busby. They won the FA Cup in 1948 and the League title success of 1951/52 came at a time when the post-war team was being dismantled and the 'Busby Babes' were beginning to emerge.

The fifties were a time when the fortunes of the two teams could not have been further removed as United's young team won back-to-back titles in 1955/56 and 56/57 and looked set to conquer Europe for years to come. Liverpool, by contrast, had lost their First Division status in 1954 and would not win it back until 1962 as they endured some lean times in the wilderness of Division Two.

The end of the decade saw both teams in the process of rebuilding – United after so many of their bright young stars perished in the Munich air disaster and Liverpool, whose appointment of Bill Shankly as manager in December 1959 proved a pivotal point in the club's history.

United and Liverpool both re-emerged and during the mid-sixties they were the nation's top two teams. Liverpool won titles in 1963/64 and 1965/66 and United in 1964/65 and 1966/67 and the rivalry was intense, but friendly. They were the heady days of Best, Law and Charlton at United while Liverpool were never short of goals with Roger Hunt and Ian St John as their strike-force.

While Liverpool continued to be a force and were nigh untouchable during the seventies and eighties both domestically and in Europe under Shankly, Bob Paisley, Joe Fagan and Kenny Dalglish, United went into decline after becoming the first English club to win the European Cup in 1968. They were relegated from the First Division six years later.

United rebuilt under Tommy Docherty, Dave Sexton and Ron Atkinson and enjoyed the odd moment of success in the knockouts. Indeed, United's FA Cup final victory against Liverpool in 1977 prevented them achieving the treble of League, FA Cup and

The Shankly Gates at Anfield.

European Cup, which United became the first club to ever achieve twenty-two years later, creating a piece of football history. How different it might have been!

While Liverpool were stacking up silverware, results did not always follow the form book, something which has happened since those early meetings in the 1890s. United, for example, did not lose a League match at Anfield between 1979 and 1988, which was remarkable bearing in mind Liverpool's home ground was for most of that time an impregnable fortress.

It was not until United appointed Alex Ferguson as manager that the shift in power flowed upstream along the Mersey to Manchester in the most dramatic manner imaginable. When Liverpool won their eighteenth League title in 1990, United's total was five. However, after two decades of United dominance in English football, they have edged nineteen-eighteen ahead.

Yet trying to forecast the results of Liverpool/United games is impossible as they rarely follow the form book and continue to this day to throw up surprises. United won seven times at Anfield between 1992 and 2005. Indeed; when Liverpool beat United 2-1 at home in September 2008, it was their first home League win against them since 2001.

Liverpool won three times in four seasons at Old Trafford between 2000–4, winning 1-0 with Danny Murphy scoring the match-winning goal each time. There was also a magical 4-1 away victory in March 2009 towards the end of another title-winning campaign for United.

Yet even the greatest have toiled in these fixtures. Liverpool legend Ian Rush is a classic example as he failed to find the net in almost ten years against United. Then; when he did, he scored in three successive games, the second of which smashed

J. McQUE.   J. McCartney.   A. Hannah.   S. H. Ross.   M. McQueen.   D. McLean.   J. McBride   A. Dick (*Trainer*).
        T. Wyllie   J. Smith,   J. Miller   M. McVean,   H. McQueen

The Liverpool team from the 1892/3 season.

Hunt's record of 286 goals for the club. He would eventually amass 348 goals in 660 appearances, yet so few were scored against United.

So what does the future hold in these fixtures? How long will the Ferguson dynasty remain, and will they be able to sustain their incredible success once he finally retires? The question for Liverpool is whether Brendan Rogers, who arrives at Anfield with fairly limited managerial experience, can bring back the glory days. Only time will tell, but one thing is for certain; there will be further dramatic twists when the two teams play one another in the coming years.

LET BATTLE COMMENCE

The first competitive*match between Liverpool and Manchester United, known then by their original name of Newton Heath, took place on the final day of the 1893/94 season.

---

* Newton Heath and Liverpool had played each other four times during the 1893/94 season, Liverpool winning [1-0 and 3-0] back-to-back Friendly matches in September 1893 in which Hugh McQueen was the first scorer. On 1 March 1894 Liverpool won [3-0] for the third consecutive match, before on 2 April Newton Heath recorded their first victory, 2-0. Friendly matches, which raised much-needed revenue, continued between the sides for a good number of seasons until they faded away once Division One and Two were permanently established.

Like many of the games that were to follow it was a big one – a Test Match or play-off to decide which of the two sides would be in the First Division the following season. Introduced when the Football League was expanded to two divisions at the start of the 1892/93 season, these were to run until 1898 when automatic promotion and relegation was introduced.

Under the rules the bottom three clubs in the top flight played the top three from the lower League. With Newton Heath having finished rock bottom in Division One, with just six wins from thirty League games, they found themselves facing a Liverpool side which had ended their inaugural Football League season in Division Two unbeaten in the League, with 50 points from 28 matches.

The previous season Newton Heath, in their debut Football League season, had survived after spending heavily on three new players – Joe Cassidy, James McNaught and Joe Peden, the first Irishman to appear in the Football League – in the week leading up to their successful encounter against Small Heath (Birmingham City) in the Test Match.

The match against Liverpool was, however, certain to be a much tougher encounter.

TEST MATCH SPECIAL

28 April 1894
Test Match
Liverpool 2 (Gordon, Hugh McQueen), Newton Heath 0.

The following is the match report taken from *The Manchester Guardian* on 30 April 1894. The match itself was played two days earlier at Ewood Park in front of a 6,000 crowd.

> There was not a breath of wind to affect play which was of an even and exciting kind during the first quarter of an hour, both sets of backs doing an enormous amount of work.
>
> Then from a free-kick in midfield McLean, with a huge kick, sent the ball right under the crossbar and Gordon headed through. In the next minute McCartney struck one of the posts with a terrific shot, and Liverpool proceeded to press. Falls saved splendidly from a bully, but a judicious centre by Gordon gave McQueen an opening, and he scored with a lightning-like shot. After this Newton Heath had a couple of chances, which were spoiled by bad shooting.
>
> At half-time the score stood Liverpool 2 Newton Heath 0.
>
> On resuming Liverpool attacked determinedly, their play being much superior to that of their opponents. At length Newton Heath forged ahead, and gained a couple of free kicks for 'hands' close to the Liverpool goal, but the danger was cleared.
>
> The excitement, which had previously been manifested, subsided and though Liverpool continued to have the best of matters the play on both sides was moderate, the players suffering from excitement. Towards the finish Newton Heath made an effort to score and

Donaldson had a clear run, but proffered to shoot and sent the ball wide of the posts. On the play Liverpool deserved their victory showing greater smartness all round and a far superior combination.

Patrick Gordon, who scored the first of many goals in games between the sides, had joined Liverpool at the beginning of the season from neighbours Everton after playing in the 1893 FA Cup final, which was won by Wolves 1-0.

Liverpool: M. McQueen, Hannah, McLean, McCartney, McQue, McBride, Gordon, McVeon, Henderson, Bradshaw, H. McQueen.
Newton Heath: Fall, Mitchell, Erentz, Perrins, McNaught, Davidson, Clarkin, Farman, Donaldson, Hood, Pelton.

1
The Second Division Encounters: 1895–1905

The Test Match result saw Liverpool replace Newton Heath in Division One but when the Merseysiders subsequently finished bottom of the League the following season, and lost to Bury in the Test Match, it meant that the first League games between Liverpool and Newton Heath took place in 1895/96. Both were memorable matches, with the first seeing Liverpool achieve their record victory against their foes.

LIVERPOOL IN SEVENTH HEAVEN

12 October 1895
Second Division
Liverpool 7 (Becton 2, Bradshaw 2, Geary 2, Ross), Newton Heath 1 (Cassidy).

Newton Heath arrived at Anfield in confident mood having started the season with three wins and two draws. Liverpool, however, were four points ahead having won six and lost one in seven so the stage was set for a thrilling occasion. The match had created great interest in both cities and it was widely rumoured in the press beforehand that the away side had been promised a bonus from the club if they were victorious.

When the two teams entered the arena, it was clear that a significant number had journeyed to see the game from Manchester, such were the cheers for 'the Heathens'. However, long before the end these same cheering supporters were very quiet, and one or two may well have headed for home long before the end of the game.

The margin of the victory, however, had been manifestly unjust. Newton Heath, especially in the first period, had been just as good as the home side and were slightly unfortunate to go in at half-time 3-1 down after Frank Becton, playing his finest game in the Liverpool colours, Tom Bradshaw and Fred Geary had made it 3-0 before a free kick from Joe Cassidy, back for his second spell with the Manchester club, reduced the arrears.

In the second period the away backs were accused by the papers of being too slow in getting the ball away and, after three further goals from Geary, Bradshaw and Becton, the ex-Preston North End man Jimmy Ross, who was the first man to hit four League goals in a game, scored a marvellous effort, sending the ball flashing past Bill Douglas in the Heath goal from a narrow angle to make it 7-1. It was one of twenty-three goals the Scotsman was to score for Liverpool that season and was probably his finest.

Ross was a star performer for almost twenty years, during which he helped Preston to become the first side to complete the League and FA Cup double in 1888/89. It had cost Liverpool £75 when they bought him from Preston in July 1894.

Liverpool: H. McQueen, Curran, Dunlop, McCartney, McQue, Holmes, Geary, Ross, Allan, Becton, Bradshaw.
Newton Heath: Douglas, Dow, F. Erentz, Perrins, McNaught, Cartwright, Clarkin, Kennedy, Cassidy, R. Smith, Peters.

Despite the margin of their victory there was a warning for Liverpool from the match reporter in *The Cricket and Football Field*, which possibly provided the best coverage of football affairs in England with reporters at every match. He said: 'The Heathens, although they lost by seven goals to one, will require some beating on the return visit.'

That is exactly what transpired three weeks later at Bank Street, Clayton. This was Newton Heath's second ground, the club having vacated North Road, Newton Heath, in the summer of 1893. It was not to be until February 1910 before Manchester United, as they had become known, played the first match at Old Trafford against, guess who? Yes, Liverpool.

HEATH HAT-TRICK HERO PETERS

2 November 1885
Second Division
Newton Heath 5 (Peters 3, Clarkin, R Smith), Liverpool 2 (Becton, Ross).

Liverpool were weakened by injuries to key players – William Dunlop, the versatile Matt McQueen and John Holmes – but nevertheless established a 2-0 lead after just four minutes, with Frank Becton and Jimmy Ross the scorers.

The Newton Heath left flank in James Peters and Dick Smith, both former Heywood Central players, was in fine form though and Peters reduced the arrears and by half-time the home side were in front after Peters added to his earlier effort and John Clarkin cut inside to beat John Whitehead, making only his third and subsequently final appearance for Liverpool.

The fourth goal arrived soon after the break when Joe Cassidy squared the ball and Smith was on hand to push the ball home. At the end Newton Heath had recorded their first ever victory against Liverpool. Peters had also become the first man ever to score a hat-trick in the matches between the sides. His goals that day were among a total of 14 in 51 first-team games he played for Newton Heath and the game was his finest ninety minutes on a football pitch.

Despite their revenge in the return match, Newton Heath were by the season's end well behind Liverpool, who by finishing top of Division Two again participated in the play-offs. These had been converted into a mini-league rather than a one-off match. With two wins and a draw from four games, Liverpool again returned to Division One and this time were to stay there until 1903/04. During that spell they were to win the first of their eighteen League titles.

Newton Heath: Douglas, Dow, F. Erentz, D. Fitzsimmons, McNaught, Cartwright, Clarkin, Kennedy, Cassidy, R. Smith, Peters.
Liverpool: Whitehead, Goldie, Wilkie, Keech, McQue, M. McQueen, Hannah, Ross, Geary, Becton, Bradshaw.

The next time the two sides were to meet in the League was again back in Division Two in 1904/05. By this time Newton Heath had, as it was now many years since they had last played in the area from which they had drawn their name, become Manchester United.

FIRST FA CUP MEETINGS

Newton Heath and Liverpool did, however, play each other three times in the FA Cup between 1898 and 1906. The first was a 0-0 draw at Clayton in a second-round match which attracted a crowd of 11,000 paying £289 in gate receipts.

12 February 1898
FA Cup, Second Round
Newton Heath 0, Liverpool 0.

Liverpool, lying twelfth in Division One, had pressed in the first half. Yet it was Newton Heath, managed by Alf Albut, who would have taken the lead if the referee, Mr A. J. Barker, from Newcastle, had been quicker as he failed to get out of the way of a goal-bound shot by James Collinson.

Collinson was a big crowd favourite as he was the first local player to play regular League football for Newton Heath.

Liverpool were constantly denied scoring opportunities by the hard work of the Erentz brothers, Fred and Harry, and centre half James McNaught, who ensured the teams went off goalless at half-time.

Newton Heath did come more into the game during the second period. Joe Cassidy and Collinson both went close but Abraham Hartley and Becton kept up the Liverpool momentum, forcing fine saves out of Frank Barrett, a Scottish international goalkeeper.

Newton Heath: Barrett, H. Erentz, F. Erentz, Draycott, McNaught, Cartwright, Bryant William, Collinson, Boyd, Cassidy, Dunn.

Liverpool: Storer, A. Goldie, Dunlop, McCartney, McQue, Cleghorn, Cunliffe, McCowie, Hartley, Becton, Lumsden.

16 February 1898
FA Cup, Second-Round Replay
Liverpool 2 (Wilkie, Cunliffe), Newton Heath 1 (Collinson).

The replay at Anfield attracted a sparse crowd of 6,000, which was far removed from the sell-outs of recent times.

And just like their first meeting four days earlier, it proved another tightly contested match, with precious little separating the teams. In the end an eighty-fifth-minute goal from England international Daniel Cunliffe proved decisive as Liverpool edged through to a third-round meeting against Derby County, to whom they lost 5-1 in a replay.

Liverpool's opener was scored by Thomas Wilkie, one of his two goals for the club, while Newton Heath's consolation came from James Collinson.

Liverpool: Storer, Wilkie, Dunlop, McCartney, McQue, Cleghorn, Cunliffe, Finnerham, Hartley, Becton, Lumsden.
Newton Heath: Barrett, H. Erentz, F. Erentz, Draycott, McNaught, Cartwright, Bryant William, Collinson, Boyd, Cassidy, Gillespie.

7 February 1903
FA Cup, First Round
Manchester United 2 (Peddie 2), Liverpool 1 (Raybould).

On the third occasion that these sides met in the FA Cup, the renamed Manchester United gained their revenge for the earlier defeat at Anfield when they won 2-1 at Bank Street in front of a 15,000 strong crowd.

Having made it to the first round after playing their way through four qualifiers against Accrington Stanley, Oswaldtwistle Rovers, Southport Central and Burton United, United's victory, as a Second Division side, was something of a shock.

The game itself was not much of a spectacle for the crowd, who saw Jack Peddie score in the twenty-fifth and twenty-seventh minutes to ensure a half-time lead of 2-0. Peddie had a decent scoring ratio during his time at the club, scoring 58 times in 121 first-team appearances.

Sam Raybould reduced the arrears for Liverpool shortly after the restart, following which the match became keenly and in some cases roughly contested. As United were missing a number of key players, the result raised hopes of a good Cup run but in the following round another Liverpool side, Everton, beat them 3-1 at Goodison Park. Bury, however, were to go on to win the FA Cup that season and their 6-0 defeat of Derby County remains the record victory in the final.

Sam Raybould was the first Liverpool player to score a hat-trick against Manchester United. In the 1902/3 season, Raybould was the top scorer in Division One with 31 goals.

United: Birchenough, Stafford, Rothwell, Downie, Griffiths, Cartwright, Street, Pegg, Peddie, Smith, Hurst.

Liverpool: Perkins, Glover, Dunlop, Parry, Raisbeck, Goldie, Goddard, Livingstone, Raybould, Chadwick, Cox.

ANOTHER PROMOTION TUSSLE

24 December 1904
Second Division
United 3 (Arkesden, Roberts, Williams), Liverpool 1 (Parkinson).

It was on Christmas Eve when the sides next met, in a game which would go a long way to deciding who would win promotion to Division One.

Liverpool had been relegated with West Bromwich Albion at the end of the previous campaign. This ended an eight-year spell of top-flight football during which, in 1900/01, Liverpool had become the second side from Anfield to capture the League title, Everton having done so in 1890/91 before moving to Goodison Park.

Success meant that Tom Watson, appointed to replace John McKenna as Liverpool manager in 1896, captured his fourth title as a manager having previously led Sunderland to successes in 1891/92, 1892/93 and 1894/95.

There had seemed little likelihood of Liverpool winning the title when, with twelve games left, they travelled to Roker Park in February nine points behind leaders Nottingham Forest and seven adrift of Sunderland. But a magnificent run, in which ten matches were won, including at Sunderland, and two drawn, proved just enough to pip Watson's one-time charges and bring the trophy to Anfield.

While Liverpool had been playing First Division football, United had also been looking to eventually challenge for the highest honours. Armed with money from new owner John Henry Davies, manager Ernest Mangnall, recruited from Burnley in 1903 to replace James West after his three years in charge, had been scouring Britain for new talent that would eventually see them win the title for the first time.

At Christmas, United were in third place and only two points behind second-placed Liverpool with a game in hand. Liverpool had only lost once in fifteen matches, a 2-0 reverse at top-of-the-table Bolton Wanderers in their previous away game. The stakes were therefore high for both sides.

> A victory was to both teams a matter of vital importance, and the strongest available sides were paraded … the enthusiasm was infectious, and when the teams appeared the reception each received at the hands of their respective followers presented a sight not to be forgotten.
> Taken from the *The Football Field*.

Such was the interest in the game that one of the then largest football crowds ever to assemble in England arrived, as 40,000 were packed into Bank Street.

The huge crowd saw a fine game. Liverpool 'keeper Ted Doig, rated among the best goalkeepers ever produced by Scotland and a man who had helped Sunderland to four League titles in 1892, 1893, 1895 and 1902, kept his side level in the first period with a series of thrilling saves, especially from Charlie Roberts and Alex Bell.

However, he had no chance after thirty-five minutes when Harry Williams scored from a Jack Allan cross. The tumultuous cheers of the home fans were however swiftly silenced when Jack Parkinson, Liverpool's dashing, fearless forward, headed an equaliser to make it 1-1 at half-time.

Liverpool would have taken the lead but Harry Moger, the United 'keeper, pulled off a tremendous diving save to deny Sam Raybould. After fifty-five minutes though Roberts, the United captain, struck his side back into the lead, a goal that was celebrated deliriously by their followers with hats, caps and all sorts of missiles hurled high into the air. With Liverpool pressing, towards the end Thomas Arkesden added a third from the penalty spot and the home crowd were ecstatic in their praise of their side.

United: Moger, Bonthron, Hayes, Downie, Roberts, Bell, Schofield, Allan, Peddie, Arkesden, Williams.
Liverpool: Doig, West, Dunlop, Parry, Raisbeck, Fleming, Goddard, Robinson, Raybould, Parkinson, Cox.

RAYBOULD TREBLE CLINCHES PROMOTION

22 April 1905
Second Division
Liverpool 4 (Raybould 3, Cox), United 0.

When the two sides met on Good Friday in the penultimate game of the season, United knew they had to win to give themselves any chance of pipping either Liverpool or Bolton for promotion. With two games left, third-placed United were three points behind both sides. A draw would take Liverpool back up, and the match's attraction resulted in a then record Anfield crowd of 28,000. The clamour to see the game from a decent vantage point meant that even the press box was invaded, forcing some journalists to seek an alternative location.

Ernest Mangnall, having seen his side lose at Chesterfield the previous day, chose to play Alf Schofield and Dick Duckworth down the right rather than John Beddow and Allan. The match was refereed by Mr Lewis, of Blackburn. Back in 1894 he had been in charge of the Test Match at Ewood Park, which had seen Liverpool gain promotion at Manchester United's expense. Would history repeat itself?

Initially at least, the importance of the occasion clearly got to both teams and the match was a scrappy affair. Gradually Liverpool began to play in the fashion their supporters had become accustomed to, having seen their side win thirteen and draw two of their last sixteen League games.

Then, after forty-one minutes Jack Cox opened the scoring after a fine run and, when Sam Raybould added a second almost immediately afterwards, United probably realised they were set to play at least another season in Division Two.

In the second period, Raybould added to United's misery by adding two more to complete his hat-trick, becoming the first Liverpool man to achieve such a feat in games between these two sides.

By winning 4-0, Liverpool gained promotion. At the end many of the crowd, which had during the game spilled at least twice on to the pitch, forcing the referee to halt proceedings, ran onto the field and there was great rejoicing among those who had seen their side gain a famous victory. The result saw Liverpool clinch the Division Two title with Bolton runners-up and United missing out in third place.

Liverpool: Doig, West, Dunlop, Parry, Raisbeck, Fleming, Chorlton, Robinson, Parkinson, Raybould, Cox.

United: Moger, Bonthron, Fitchett, Downie, Roberts, Bell, Schofield, Duckworth, Peddie, Arkesden, Wombwell.

2
Clubs Reunited in Top Flight

The 1905/06 season brought success for both clubs. United finished in second place behind the Second Division Champions Bristol City to gain promotion. Liverpool, meanwhile, became the first promoted side to go on and capture the First Division title the following season, finishing four points clear of Preston North End in second place. Only four sides have equalled Liverpool's feat – Everton in the thirties, Spurs in the fifties, Ipswich Town in the sixties and Nottingham Forest in the seventies. Whether anyone will ever do so again must be a real doubt.

For Tom Watson, it was his fifth First Division title as a manager and it looked like he might equal Preston in 1889 and Aston Villa in 1897 by recording the League and FA Cup double. That dream was ended by neighbours Everton, who won their FA Cup semi-final at Villa Park. Everton went on win the Cup for the first time by beating Newcastle in the final.

Liverpool had signed a world-class goalkeeper in Sam Hardy from Chesterfield, who the Sunderland and Arsenal legend Charlie Buchan rated 'the finest goalkeeper I played against. By uncanny anticipation and wonderful positional sense he seemed to act like a magnet to the ball.'

LITTLE FESTIVE CHEER

25 December 1906
First Division
United 0, Liverpool 0.

The clash on Christmas Day was between sides in the bottom half of the table, with Liverpool in eleventh place and Manchester United thirteenth.

The make-up of the United team was to change significantly in a week's time. Ernest Mangnall had acted swiftly to secure the services of four players who were to play an important part in United's success over the following years, bringing in Billy Meredith, Sandy Turnbull, Jimmy Bannister and Herbert Burgess after Manchester City had been forced to offer for sale all their players following the exposure of 'under the counter payments' during an era when the rules restricted players' wages to a maximum

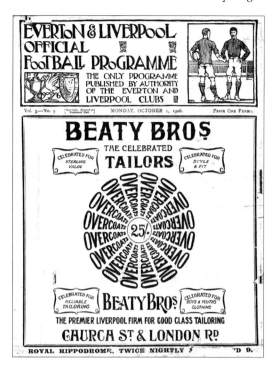

of £4 a week. The players, all suspended until 1 January 1907, were to bring United up to Liverpool's level on the pitch while off it the club was making plans to move to a new state-of-the-art ground in Stretford. The rivalry was set to intensify.

The match was not exactly great fare for the Bank Street holiday crowd of 20,000, ending 0-0. United should have won but Sam Hardy was at his best, saving numerous efforts, especially from centre half Charlie Roberts.

United: Moger, Holden, Blackstock, Duckworth, Roberts, Bell, Schofield, Berry, Menzies, Picken, Wall.
Liverpool: Hardy, Saul, Chorlton, Lathom, Raisbeck, Hughes, Goddard, Robinson, Raybould, McPherson, Lipsham

By 1907, Bank Street had undergone considerable improvements so that its capacity had risen to 50,000, although only 5,000 watched the final First Division fixture there on 22 January 1910. The ground was typical of Football League grounds of its time, being set among densely populated working class terraced housing, from which many of the club's supporters were drawn, and close to smoky factories.

The Bank Street pitch itself was nothing like the fabulous billiard table-like surfaces of the Premier League today and had little grass on it, especially in the winter. At the same time periods of heavy rain often meant there were mud patches and puddles for the players to overcome. The site is now the car park of the Manchester Velodrome, with a plaque on a house wall indicating the presence of the former ground.

UNITED'S FIRST WIN AT ANFIELD

6 April 1907
First Division
Liverpool 0, United 1 (Turnbull).

By the time of the return on Easter Monday, United had leapfrogged Liverpool to establish a five-point gap over their rivals, having won five and drawn one of their previous six matches.

Herbert Burgess, Sandy Turnbull and Billy Meredith all played for United and their appearance helped their club record their first ever win at Anfield. It was, however, a fortunate two points as Liverpool, thrashed 4-0 the day before at Aston Villa, missed a hatful of chances.

Charlie Roberts, so often the playmaker, was forced to show his defensive skills and Harry Moger in goal played heroically. Sam Raybould, so often a key player in previous seasons for Liverpool, played poorly and was soon to leave the club to sign for Sunderland after scoring 128 goals in 225 first-team appearances. He is the tenth-highest goalscorer in the club's history. In the event Alex 'Sandy' Turnbull scored United's winning goal.

United finished eighth in the table while Liverpool, the reigning League champions, languished in fifteenth place at the season's end.

Liverpool: Hardy, Saul, Dunlop, Parry, Raisbeck, Bradley, Goddard, Hewitt, Raybould, McPherson, Carlin.

United: Moger, Bonthron, Burgess, Duckworth, Roberts, Bell, Meredith, Williams, Menzies, Turnbull, Wall.

SANDY'S THE MAN

7 September 1907
First Division
United 4 (S. Turnbull 3, Wall), Liverpool 0.

Sandy Turnbull became the second Manchester United player to score a hat-trick against Liverpool when the two sides met in the second game of the 1907/08 season.

Large numbers of Liverpool fans had made the trip to Manchester and they cheered their side onto the pitch, but once goalkeeper Sam Hardy was beaten in the thirty-third minute by Turnbull there was no way their side was going to create history by beating their rivals away for the first time. In fact, if it hadn't been for Hardy the score would have rivalled that of Anfield in 1895, when United had been trounced 7-1.

Liverpool were missing their inspirational leader, Scotsman Alec Raisbeck, but even with him in the side it would have been difficult to have seen them cope with a United forward line which now contained the most creative wingers in the country in Billy

Meredith and George Wall, an England international whose ability to run at pace and cut inside before shooting was a lethal part of his game. It was Wall who scored the second just before half-time, while Turnbull added two more after the restart to make the final scoreline 4-0.

This was one of United's thirteen victories from the first fourteen matches of the season that provided the platform for the club's first ever Division One title.

United: Moger, Holden, Burgess, Duckworth, Roberts, Bell, Meredith, Bannister, Menzies, A. Turnbull, Wall.

Liverpool: Hardy, West, Saul, Parry, Lathom, Bradley, Goddard, C. Hewitt, J. Hewitt, Bowyer, Cox.

FIRST OF UNITED'S NINETEEN LEAGUE TITLES

25 March 1908
First Division
Liverpool 7 (McPherson 3, J Hewitt 2, Robinson 2), United 4 (Wall 2, Bannister, J Turnbull).

When the two teams next met in March, Liverpool were in twelfth place while United, despite a dip in form in the New Year, were still six points clear of second-place Newcastle United with two games in hand. Liverpool, fourteen points behind the leaders, had lost five games at home including their previous game 1-0 against Manchester City. However, and not for the last time in matches between the sides, the form-book was torn apart. So too, on this occasion, was the United defence, especially in the first half.

It took only three minutes for Liverpool to take the lead, Joe Hewitt fastening onto a centre from Arthur Goddard to crash home a magnificent shot that caught the underside of the bar before flying into the net. Nine minutes later Billy McPherson, with only his third goal of the season, was onto another Goddard centre to make it two; Robbie Robinson then knocked home the third after nineteen minutes before McPherson drilled in the fourth on the stroke of half-time. United had conceded more goals in forty-five minutes than in any single game in the season. Could Liverpool equal or even better their 7-1 win in 1895?

Goalkeeper Ted Doig, standing in for the injured Sam Hardy, gave United a lifeline at the start of the second period, dropping a Charlie Roberts free-kick to a grateful George Wall to make it 4-1. The 'keeper then miskicked to present the outside left Wall with his and his side's second, which made it 4-2. Was a famous comeback now on?

Not so when McPherson, with his third goal of the match, made it 5-2, and Robinson added a sixth. However, United were determined to go down fighting and despite being four goals down they pinned the home side back around their penalty area, with James Turnbull and Jimmy Bannister reducing the arrears to 6-4 with quarter of an hour left.

It was now a game which no spectator – and with it being an afternoon kick-off during a working day the crowd was a much-reduced 10,000 – could take their eyes off. Doig made a marvellous save from Meredith, before Joe Hewitt, who had been outstanding during the game, finally ended any doubts about who would win by making it 7-4 and when the final whistle sounded, 'the enthusiasm equalled anything seen on the ground for many a long day. Absentees may think United were not trying too hard,' reported *The Football Field*.

It had been a truly marvellous match, one which must go down as one of the finest ever between the two sides.

Despite the result Manchester United, as expected, went on to win the First Division at the end of the season, finishing with a record points total of 52, 9 clear of Aston Villa in second. Liverpool were well back in eighth place.

Liverpool: Doig, West, Saul, Harrop, Raisbeck, Chorlton, Goddard, Robinson, J. Hewitt, McPherson, Cox.
United: Moger, Stacey, Dalton, Duckworth, Roberts, Downie, Meredith, Bannister, J. Turnbull, Picken, Wall.

WIN TAKES UNITED TOP

26 September 1908
First Division
United 3 (Halse 2, J. Turnbull), Liverpool 2 (Cox, Raisbeck pen.).

United won the inaugural Charity Shield as they beat QPR 4-0 at Stamford Bridge in late August to add to their earlier title triumph. Ernest Mangnall's side had started the League season in thrilling fashion, and had won all four games, scoring thirteen goals. Liverpool had also done well and stood level on points, having lost once in their first five fixtures. After some very mixed weather in the lead-up to the game, it started in blazing sunshine.

The hopes of a large away following were raised by Liverpool's start as they pushed United back and forced Charlie Roberts into some hasty clearances. It was therefore something of a surprise when from their first serious attack United scored in the thirteenth minute when Sandy Turnbull headed down Billy Meredith's cross for Harold Halse to beat 'keeper Sam Hardy.

Hardy then showed that even the best 'keepers can make a mistake, failing to collect a poor shot from Halse and gifting the United forward and his side the second to give the home side a comfortable lead at half-time.

Liverpool pulled a goal back when, following an Arthur Goddard cross, Jack Cox was left with plenty of time to make it 2-1 after fifty-four minutes. It took United five minutes to restore their two-goal lead when Hardy was unable to hang on to Wall's shot and James Turnbull scored. The home side was not finished and Hardy was able to make some amends for his poor performance by making good saves from Wall and Meredith.

Liverpool reduced the arrears after the ball landed in the penalty area and, as each side tried to force it forward, George Stacey was adjudged to have handled and Alex Raisbeck scored from the resulting penalty.

This was the start of some serious pressure by Tom Watson's side but, in their anxiety to get an equaliser, they gave away too many fouls and United ended up hanging on to a just about deserved victory. As leaders Newcastle lost, United went to the top of the table.

United: Moger, Duckworth, Stacey, Downie, Roberts, Bell, Meredith, Halse,
    J. Turnbull, S. Turnbull, Wall.
Liverpool: Hardy, Saul, Rogers, Chorlton, Raisbeck, Bradley, Goddard, Parkinson,
    Hewitt, Orr, Cox.

LIVERPOOL PILE ON MISERY

30 January 1909
First Division
Liverpool 3 (Goddard, Chorlton pen., Hewitt), United 1 (S. Turnbull).
By the time the two teams met again in January, Newcastle had restored themselves at the top of the League, United were fourth and Liverpool sixth. In their previous away game at Middlesbrough, League champions United had suffered their heaviest defeat in two years, losing 5-0.

It was, nevertheless, United who started the more brightly and the only surprise was that it took until the twenty-second minute for them to take the lead. George Livingstone sent over a cross that Sandy Turnbull only just missed but, when Wall collected and returned the ball, Turnbull was up swiftly to dive and head home.

Billy Meredith had yet to score so far in the season, but against a lesser 'keeper than Sam Hardy he may have had two in as many minutes, the home custodian earning the cheers of his side's followers with two great diving saves. The England international was lucky, however, just before half-time when Richard Duckworth's shot beat him but cannoned back into play from the crossbar. If that had gone in the away side would surely have rested a little easier in their dressing room at half-time with a two-goal advantage. Instead, after largely outplaying their hosts, there must have been a fear that one goal was not going be enough.

There was moment of real controversy in the first minute of the second period when Alex Downie appeared to have handled in the area, with the referee consulting his linesman, Mr Watson, who decided the United player had not handled intentionally. Stung by this perceived injustice, the home crowd got behind their side and they

George Stacey made 267 first-team appearances for Manchester United and was a member of the League championship winning sides of 1907/8 and 1910/11 and the FA Cup winning side of 1908/9.

were cheering in the fifty-fifth minute when Arthur Goddard headed home Jimmy Bradley's corner to equalise. It was one of 80 goals Goddard scored for Liverpool in more than 400 first-team appearances.

The game was now a very even affair but, with twenty minutes left, Liverpool took the lead. The goal came when Goddard, after taking the ball off George Wall, beautifully found Joe Hewitt who was tripped by George Stacey and Tom Chorlton converted the resulting penalty.

Hewitt thought he had made it 3-1 when Vince Hayes cleared his shot from the line with Harry Moger beaten, but the Liverpool centre forward was not to be denied and after eighty minutes he hit an unstoppable shot to give the home side a two-goal cushion that they never looked like losing. Hewitt had been the Man of the Match and by the end Liverpool had recorded their fourth home victory in five games against their rivals.

United went into free-fall in the League for the rest of the season, winning just one game in fourteen as they finished thirteenth. Liverpool were three places below them after a disappointing campaign. United's slide may have had something to do with their minds being concentrated on winning the FA Cup, which they did by beating Bristol City 1-0 at Crystal Palace through a Sandy Turnbull goal.

Liverpool: Hardy, Saul, Chorlton, Parry, Raisbeck, Bradley, Goddard, Robinson, J. Hewitt, Orr, Cox.
United: Moger, Stacey, Hayes, Duckworth, Roberts, Downie, Meredith, Livingstone, Halse, A. Turnbull, Wall.

DAWN OF A NEW ERA

9 October 1909
First Division
Liverpool 3 (Parkinson 2, Stewart), United 2 (S. Turnbull 2).

The 1909/10 season would bring a magnificent new venue for these increasingly competitive games to be played at in the construction of Old Trafford, expected to open early in 1910, with United's home game against Liverpool expected to be one of the first to take place there. However, before then there was the little matter of Cup holders United again visiting Anfield. Liverpool were in ninth place and United four places higher although, with only a handful of games having been completed, there was still plenty to play for.

There were 30,000 to watch what turned out to be another excellent game between the two sides. With Moger ruled out through a damaged thigh Elijah Round, the ex-Oldham 'keeper, made his first of what proved to be only two appearances for United. There was a debut on the home side for Jimmy Speakman, a local Liverpool lad, standing in for the injured Arthur Goddard. Joe Ford, who had played well in a 1-1 draw at Newcastle United the previous weekend, was preferred to George Wall at outside left for United. Ronald Orr, in Goddard's absence, captained Liverpool.

The match started at a hectic pace, and before seven minutes had been played Liverpool had taken the lead. John McDonald passed to Orr, whose ball behind the United defence sent the wide man hurtling down the wing, and when he cut the ball back, Jack Parkinson turned it into the net to enormous cheers from the crowd.

McDonald had joined Liverpool during the summer from Glasgow Rangers after playing in two drawn Scottish Cup finals at Hampden Park against Celtic, at the end of which around 6,000 followers of both clubs invaded the pitch when it was announced that, in contradiction to earlier newspaper reports, no extra time would be played. Rumours had spread that the Scottish FA were fixing games to ensure replays took place, resulting in another set of gate receipts. Rioters tore out the goalposts, ripped up the nets and smashed down fencing. Bonfires were made out of the broken barricading. Firemen were attacked and only more than two and a half hours later did police force rioters from the ground. Nobody seriously considered holding a third match and thankfully Rangers and Celtic did not meet again in the Scottish Cup final until 1928.

When United sought an equaliser at Anfield, Liverpool's Bob Crawford, a splendid tackler, battled with Billy Meredith down the away right to prevent a breakthrough. For once Roberts, the immaculate performer, was finding it difficult to tame his opposing centre forward Parkinson, who constantly took him on, shooting from every angle. Fortunately Elijah Round was in fine form as the away side clung on. But with five minutes of the first half remaining, Liverpool finally made it 2-0. Jack Parkinson did the damage, rushing in from the right to give Round no chance with a twenty-yard shot. It was one of the Liverpool centre forward's thirty League goals during the season, a record which saw him become the second (after Sam Raybould in 1902/03) of six Liverpool players to finish as top scorer at the end of a Division One or Premier League season.

Parkinson might have got his side's third and his hat-trick seconds later, but Round saved his shot from the edge of the area. United, whose backs were the strongest part of the side, had taken a rare chasing and were glad to go off just 2-0 down.

Sam Hardy had hardly been troubled in the first half but he showed his talent by saving superbly from Sandy Turnbull at the start of the second period. Round then produced the save of the match by diving across his goal to keep out MacDonald's effort, which brought great applause from the crowd.

United were given a lifeline back into the game when Crawford brought down Harold Halse, with Sandy Turnbull scoring the resulting penalty as the deficit was halved. Would Liverpool pay for missing so many chances? The answer, at least initially, was yes when Sandy Turnbull scored his second and the game's equaliser from a Meredith corner on the hour. It was a position no-one could possibly have predicted just fifteen minutes earlier.

Liverpool were not to be denied, though, and MacDonald, showing the sort of wing play that delighted audiences, wriggled his way down the line before hitting a superb ball from close to the corner flag that floated over the outstretched hands of Round for Jimmy Stewart to roar in and head home. The cheers of the crowd would have been heard from miles away, but for the next fifteen minutes their silence told its own story. United pressed, Liverpool were frantic but somehow they hung on to a deserved victory from a game that had thoroughly entertained those lucky enough to have witnessed it.

Liverpool: Hardy, Chorlton, Crawford, Robinson, Harrop, Bradley, Speakman, Stewart, Parkinson, Orr, McDonald.
Manchester United: Round, Stacey, Hayes, Duckworth, Roberts, Bell, Meredith, Halse, J. Turnbull, S. Turnbull, Ford.

OPENING OF OLD TRAFFORD

19 February 1910
First Division
United 3 (Homer, S. Turnbull, Wall), Liverpool 4 (Goddard 2, Stewart 2).

By a remarkable coincidence the first game at Old Trafford turned out to be the match with Liverpool. It had been planned to open the stadium a month earlier against Tottenham Hotspur, who were making their debut season in Division One, but building delays forced it back. Only 7,000 were present at Bank Street to see United beat Spurs 5-0, around one sixth of the number that turned out for the Liverpool game. This saw 45,000 crowd onto the new terraces of a ground that the United directors had declared would eventually be big enough to hold 100,000 spectators. Perhaps, but it would certainly not be in their lifetime.

DAILY SKETCH, THURSDAY, FEBRUARY 17, 1910.

MANCHESTER UNITED'S NEW HOME AT OLD TRAFFORD

General view of the Manchester United Football Club's new ground, which will be opened on Saturday.

Mott and George Wall inspecting their new pitch at the private view yesterday.

Today if either United or Liverpool opened a new ground it would attract worldwide attention, but not so in 1910. Attention that weekend was fixed on the third round of the FA Cup and *The Manchester Guardian* even managed to list the game as having been played at Anfield.

The previous weekend both teams had experienced mixed emotions. Liverpool had lost to Merseyside rivals Everton while United had won a marvellous match at St James' Park, defeating the League champions Newcastle 4-3 with Sandy Turnbull scoring the winner and Harry Moger saving a penalty from Bill McCracken. It was probably the best performance of the season so far from Ernest Mangnall's side.

Liverpool had never managed to win at Bank Street, losing five and drawing twice. With the United men in the press declaring their liking for the new pitch all week then, it was going to be difficult for the away team. Liverpool were backed, though, by a considerable number of their own followers, who poured off the trains from Merseyside. After half an hour of the game many must have wished they had stayed at home. Yes, it was great to see this fabulous new arena, but United were 2-0 up.

Old Trafford's first goal came when Sam Hardy saved Harold Halse's powerful shot but was helpless to prevent Tom Homer netting the rebound. The second was worthy of the occasion, Dick Duckworth's free-kick dropping over the Liverpool defence where

Sandy Turnbull hurled himself headlong, just a foot off the ground, to head it past the Liverpool 'keeper. The hundreds of home fans who had brought bells with them and who were wearing red and white suits were overjoyed.

It was Arthur Goddard who reduced the arrears early in the second half after a fine, flowing Liverpool move left him in the clear. However, this looked to be a mere consolation when George Wall, in trademark fashion, cut in from the left to hit the ball across the goal and into the net at the far side with his right foot to make it 3-1.

If United thought they were home and dry they were mistaken, as Liverpool staged a spectacular recovery to snatch a dramatic victory. Goddard cut the deficit to 3-2 before Jimmy Stewart got his second of the season against United to make it 3-3. Moments later Stewart scored his third and Liverpool's fourth of this particular game as they triumphed for the first time away to United.

United would have to wait till they beat Sheffield United 1-0 in the next home game for a first victory at their new ground. And to show they really did like the place, they went on to win the remaining six homes games of the season. In fact, they were to lose only once at home over the next eighteen months. Old Trafford, from the very start, had become a fortress.

United: Moger, Stacey, Hayes, Duckworth, Roberts, Blott, Meredith, Halse, Homer, S. Turnbull, Wall.

Liverpool: Hardy, Chorlton, Rogers, Robinson, Harrop, Bradley, Goddard, Stewart, Parkinson, Orr, McDonald.

'POOL PEER THROUGH FOG TO WIN

26 November 1910
First Division
Liverpool 3 (Goddard, Parkinson, Stewart), United 2 (S. Turnbull, Roberts).
United were level on points with leaders Sunderland when they travelled to Anfield at the end of November, while Liverpool were struggling in seventeenth place, just one point above the relegation zone. United had won five and drawn one of seven away fixtures, whereas Liverpool had lost four from six at home. On paper it looked a banker away win and this, plus dense, heavy fog which would have prevented spectators at one end seeing the goal at the other during the first half, meant there were less than 10,000 at the match. Those who were absent, and even some of those inside the ground, missed a cracking game in which form went out of the window.

It was United who started the more brightly, and it was no surprise when they went ahead after Sandy Turnbull was on hand to turn the ball past Gus Beeby after it rebounded from the bar following George Livingstone's shot.

Jack Parkinson, who seemed to revel in games against United, thought he had equalised but his shot hit the bar, but then after twenty-four minutes Oscar Linkson, who was later killed during the Somme offensive during the First World War, fouled him. Arthur Goddard converted the resulting penalty to make it 1-1, which is how it remained at half-time.

The fog lifted after the restart to allow the paying public to see all the game. They witnessed United 'keeper Harry Moger making a brilliant save from Goddard as the home side swarmed all over their opponents and, with fifteen minutes of the game remaining, Harold Uren centred and Parkinson ran through to make it 2-1. It was one of twenty goals the dashing and fearless Liverpool centre forward scored that season and followed his thirty the previous season. His total for the club was 128 goals by the time he left to join Bury in July 1914.

The disbelieving Liverpool fans were ecstatic with eleven minutes left when their side went 3-1 up, Jimmy Stewart prodding home a loose ball from twelve yards. At no time during the season so far had United conceded more than two goals – they had now! With five minutes remaining, Robbie Robinson was thought to have headed Arthur Hooper's cross into his own goal, but afterwards the goal was credited to Charlie Roberts. The scorer, whoever it was, couldn't alter the fact that Liverpool had won 3-2 and deservedly so in a match where Goddard and Uren had been the stars, with Jock McConnell winning praise for his defensive duties that had even included marking Meredith for part of the game.

Liverpool: Beeby, Langworth, Crawford, Robinson, Harrop, McConnell, Goddard, Stewart, Parkinson, Orr, Uren.

United: Moger, Linkson, Stacey, Livingstone, Roberts, Curry, Meredith, Halse, Hooper, S. Turnbull, Wall.

TWO TITLE TRIUMPHS APIECE

1 April 1911
First Division
United 2 (West 2), Liverpool 0.
By the time of the return match on April Fool's Day, United had lost only three in eighteen games and were top of the table, with Aston Villa at the head of the chasing pack. Liverpool were in twelfth place, but in a tight League they were only four points ahead of nineteenth-placed Manchester City with six games left.

United had lost 4-3 at Old Trafford the previous season. There was to be no slip-up this time, even without the services of the injured Dick Duckworth and George Wall, Arthur Whalley and John Sheldon taking their places.

The crowd was not even half that of the previous season for this match but those present saw a scintillating performance from Billy Meredith, with the Welsh wing wizard at his imperious best. Fortunately for Liverpool, so too was that marvellous custodian Sam Hardy, whose athleticism was needed to deny Enoch West, signed in June 1910 from Nottingham Forest after previously finishing as the First Division top scorer in 1907/08. Hardy also enjoyed a touch of good fortune when Sandy

Turnbull's header, from another of Meredith's numerous crosses, flashed narrowly wide and Turnbull then completely missed the ball in front of goal after being set up by Meredith.

With Liverpool looking like they may even go in at half-time level, United scored in the forty-fourth minute, West beating Hardy with a fine left foot.

Arthur Goddard was injured following a tackle by Leslie Hopton and unable to resume after half-time, and as Liverpool were down to ten men, the match as a contest looked over. It was by now an entirely one-sided affair as Harold Halse shot narrowly wide, West was too slow to knock home a loose ball, Roberts dragged a shot wide, Robbie Crawford kicked away Turnbull's shot, Halse again shot just over before finally West added his, and his side's second and decisive goal. It was Meredith who made it, beating those who dared to challenge him for the ball before setting up his colleague for an unmissable opportunity.

Meredith, one of the all-time greatest footballers, would have been a star in whatever era he played. Manchester City signed him from Northwich Victoria in 1894, beginning a thirty-year association with Manchester that delighted supporters. Having helped City to the Second Division title, the Welshman was part of the side that beat Bolton Wanderers in the 1904 FA Cup final, at which he scored the only goal of the game. His first spell with City was to come to an end in December 1906 when he and three other players transferred across the city to United. After collecting two Division One titles along with another FA Cup winner's medal, Meredith moved back to play for City in 1921 and even appeared in an FA Cup semi-final three years later in his fiftieth year. Meredith won an incredible forty-eight caps for his country during a period when matches with the other home nations were the only staple fare.

The result saw Liverpool drop to fourteenth place and left United two points ahead of Aston Villa at the top. Hopes of a second Championship looked to have been dashed, however, in United's next game when Villa beat them, only for the West Midlands side themselves to be pipped when they took only a point in their penultimate match before the final Saturday of the season saw Ernest Mangnall's United beat third-placed Sunderland 5-1 at home while Aston Villa lost 3-1 at, guess where? Yes, Anfield! As a result, United had drawn level with Liverpool in lifting their second Division One title. Both, however, were a long way behind Aston Villa, with five championships. In between were Sunderland with four.

United: Edmonds, Hofton, Stacey, Whalley, Roberts, Bell, Meredith, Halse, West, S. Turnbull, Sheldon.
Liverpool: Hardy, Longworth, Crawford, Robinson, Harrop, McConnell, Goddard, Gilligan, Bowyer, Orr, McDonald.

BOTH SIDES DESPERATE FOR POINTS

18 November 1911
First Division
Liverpool 3 (Bovill 2, Parkinson), United 2 (West, Roberts).

United had beaten Swindon Town, Southern League Champions, by a remarkable 8-4 scoreline to capture the FA Charity Shield only weeks before playing Liverpool mid-way through November. Both sides had started the League season in poor form, with only six wins between them from twenty-three matches. It was Liverpool, having only won one from five home games so far in the season, who were the most desperate for points.

United, in their changed kit of blue shirts, were the first to show, with Billy Meredith beating Robbie Crawford before crossing for Enoch West to head over. Arthur Goddard then hit the side-netting as Liverpool pulled themselves into the match, and the home side looked to have taken the lead when Jock Bovill headed Harold Uren's cross towards goal but with Hugh Edmonds beaten, Alex Bell raced back to hack the ball away from the line.

The match was now proving a thriller for the Anfield crowd, Sam Hardy earning their applause for a magnificent save from a Sandy Turnbull effort. Just before half-time Crawford was flattened and knocked unconscious from a rough aerial challenge by West. The referee spoke to him whereas today it would have been a straight red and possibly further punishment from the Football Association. Football was tougher then, but so too, of course, was life in general. At half-time the score remained goalless.

When play resumed, Hardy again foiled Turnbull with another diving save. It was then the turn of the Liverpool fans to hold their hands in despair when Sam Gilligan thundered a shot past goalkeeper Hugh Edmonds only to find Tony Donnelly, who had started out as a 'keeper, on the line clearing.

United took the lead after fifty-seven minutes after a low shot from West appeared to catch Hardy off balance. Hardly had the game restarted before Liverpool were level, James Harrop and Bovill combining together to set up Jack Parkinson for an easy chance.

With both teams determined not to lose, a battle ensued. Some rough challenges were given and taken but after seventy-three minutes Liverpool roared into the lead for the first time, 'keeper Edmonds miskicking Bovill's shot to enormous cheers. Inside left Bovill made it 3-1 two minutes later, running onto a Parkinson pass before beating the 'keeper. Roberts' consolation goal in the eighty-eighth minute was a fine long-range effort but when the referee sounded the final whistle, Liverpool had beaten United 3-2. It was also Liverpool's fourth consecutive victory at home against their neighbours.

Liverpool: Hardy, Longworth, Crawford, Robinson, Harrop, Lowe, Goddard, Bovill,
    Parkinson, Gilligan, Uren.
United: Edmonds, Donnelly, Stacey, Duckworth. Roberts, Bell, Meredith, Halse,
    West, Turnbull, Blott.

PRECIOUS POINT FOR 'POOL

23 March 1912
First Division
United 1 (Nuttall), Liverpool 1 (Parkinson).

Injuries had decimated United when they resumed hostilities with Liverpool in the second game of the 1911/12 season and only five of those who had played earlier were on view at Old Trafford.

Liverpool started the game in real danger of being relegated. Having not won since January, only four points separated them from Manchester City, who were in the relegation zone. Reigning champions United had also experienced a poor season and were in thirteenth place. It was hardly surprising, therefore, that the match was a poor one, and at half-time it was fitting, following a scrappy affair played in blustery, squally conditions, that the score sheet should be blank.

Even the great Billy Meredith was off his game, kicking three corners straight out of play just after half-time. Only towards the end did the small crowd witness anything that might have compensated them for having parted with their hard-earned cash.

Firstly, a big kick by James Harrop left Jack Parkinson with a clear opening and he promptly beat United's debutant goalkeeper Ezra Royals. It was his fifth League goal against United. From the restart, United attacked and, when the ball ended up at the feet of another debutant, Tom Nuttall, he hit a great shot that not even the great Sam Hardy could stop to make it 1-1. Mickey Hamill and Freddy Capper shortly after missed great opportunities to win the match for United. In truth neither side had done enough to merit a win. The point was to prove invaluable to Liverpool as at the end of the season they finished just one point above Preston North End, who were relegated along with Bury.

United: Royals, Linkson, Donnelly, Duckworth, Roberts, Hodge, Meredith, Hamill,
   West, Nuttall, Capper.
Liverpool: Hardy, Longworth, Pursell, Robinson, Harrop, MacKinlay, Goddard,
   McDonald, Parkinson, Miller, Lacey.

ONLY 8,000 AT OLD TRAFFORD

23 November 1912
First Division
United 3 (Anderson 2 (1 pen.), Wall), Liverpool 1 (MacKinlay).

There were only 8,000 inside Old Trafford to watch two teams well off the top, with Liverpool in eleventh place and the hosts three spots lower. In almost ideal conditions it was United who were first into their stride and Ephraim Longworth, in one of his

371 peace-time appearances for Liverpool, was forced to clear a Billy Meredith shot that looked like it might open the scoring.

Jack Parkinson was being well contained by Charlie Roberts but it left little time for the United playmaker to get forward and support his forward line. The result was a match that seemed unlikely to produce a goal. That all changed following a free-kick just outside the box which George Wall drove and when Kenny Campbell – who had replaced Sam Hardy as the regular between the posts at the start of the season – saved, the outside left was first to the loose ball to make it 1-0. It was Wall's fifth goal against Liverpool.

Roberts now began to show what a marvellous player he could be, finding his forwards with deadly accurate passes and pulling the Liverpool defence in every direction. There was dismay when he was allowed to join Oldham at the end of the season, and in 1914/15 he almost took them to title glory, Everton piping them by a point.

George Anderson, dashing into the box, was brought down and, dusting himself off, he fired home the resulting penalty to make it 2-0 after half an hour. Liverpool's attempts to get back into the match were constantly frustrated by the determined efforts of the United backs and at half-time the score remained 2-0.

It became three when Anderson, after a powerful run, left Campbell to pick the ball out of the net as he turned to acknowledge the cheers of the sparse crowd. Although Don McKinlay did pull a goal back with fifteen minutes remaining, any hopes Liverpool might have had of grabbing an unlikely point disappeared when Arthur Goddard drove well wide a penalty awarded for a foul on McKinlay by Nuttall. In the event the miss of an open goal by Parkinson in the last minute only added to Liverpool's frustrations.

United: Beale, Duckworth, Stacey, Knowles, Roberts, Bell, Meredith, Nuttall, Anderson, West, Wall.
Liverpool: Campbell, Longworth, Crawford, Lowe, Ferguson, Peake, Goddard, MacKinlay, Miller, Parkinson, Metcalf.

UNITED KEEP ALIVE TITLE HOPES

29 March 1913
First Division
Liverpool 0, United 2 (Wall, West).
With Liverpool in twelfth place and United fifth, the second match involving these sides in 1912/13 attracted only 12,000 fans to Anfield. They saw the away side take control from the start and, after racing into a 2-0 lead before half-time, United comfortably collected both points to give themselves an outside chance of again capturing the Division One title.

Liverpool had played poorly in the previous game at home to Chelsea and manager Tom Watson had brought in James Speakman at outside right for his first home appearance of the season, and also preferred Henry Welfare to Jack Parkinson. Billy Meredith and Dick Duckworth were both missing for United through injuries.

The programme for the 29 March 1913 game between Liverpool and Manchester United at Anfield.

Although there was plenty of energy from both sets of players the first thirty minutes was poor, with neither 'keeper coming under any serious threat of conceding a goal. It was George Wall who opened the scoring after thirty-two minutes when, with the Liverpool defence drawn towards John Sheldon, the ball was switched across to the left-winger, who curled the ball round John Tosswill and beyond the despairing dive of 'keeper Ken Campbell. Seven minutes later it was 2-0 when Enoch West headed home Sheldon's corner and the score was to remain that way until the end. The season ended with Liverpool twelfth, with Manchester United in fourth place behind the champions Sunderland, winners of the title for the fifth time.

Liverpool: Campbell, Longworth, Pursell, MacKinlay, Ferguson, Peake, Speakman, Metcalf, Tosswill, Miller, Welfare.
United: Beale, Hodge, Stacey, Hamill, Whalley, Bell, Sheldon, Turnbull, Hunter, West, Wall.

UNITED TOP THE TABLE

1 November 1913
First Division
United 3 (Wall 2, West), Liverpool 0.

Before the match, United stood ten points and sixteen places above their local rivals, who were way down in eighteenth place after nine matches of the season. At the end, the gap had increased to seventeen places as the home side's easy victory pushed them to the top after Blackburn lost for the first time that season.

Any hopes that Liverpool fans might have harboured of a shock victory must have disappeared when United took the lead after only a couple of minutes, Ephraim Longworth's miskick being eagerly seized upon by George Wall, who swerved inside and with a great shot beat 'keeper Ken Campbell to the delight of the 20,000 crowd.

There must have been a good number who thought this would be the first goal of many, but it was not to be until the second half before United asserted their superiority and Liverpool were only denied a deserved first-half equaliser when Robert Beale dived full-length at the feet of Bill Lacey and when the 'keeper emerged with the ball he received enormous cheers from the crowd.

United's second and third goals both came in the final five minutes of the game, Wall's corner being headed past Campbell by Enoch West before George Stacey put the ball over the Liverpool defence for Wall to run through to score his second goal of the match.

United: Beale, James Hodge, Stacey, Gipps, Whalley, Hamill, Meredith, Woodcock, Anderson, West, Wall.
Liverpool: Campbell, Longworth, Pursell, Fairfoul, Lowe, Ferguson, Goddard, Dawson, Miller, Mackinlay, Lacey.

15 April 1914
First Division
Liverpool 1 (Dawson 30), United 2 (Travers, Wall).

By becoming the first side to win four of these games in a row, United completed their second double against a Liverpool side whose minds were clearly occupied with their big day in ten days' time. This was to be the club's first FA Cup final, a match against Burnley, and the side that ran out at Crystal Palace was to contain only five of those who played against United. Tom Watson's side had beaten renowned Cup fighters Barnsley, finalists in 1910 and winners in 1912; Gillingham; West Ham; QPR; and in the semi-final Aston Villa to qualify for what was at the time the biggest football game in the world.

With only 33 points from 35 games, Liverpool were lying in sixteenth place. Yet this was two places and three points above their opponents, who were desperate for a win to avoid relegation having last tasted victory on New Year's Day, fourteen matches previously. United had suffered the indignity of being thrashed 6-0 at Old Trafford by Aston Villa in March, a result that remains the club's record home defeat, although in 1961 Sheffield Wednesday scored one more goal in a 7-2 win in the fourth round of the FA Cup.

Liverpool took the lead on the half-hour mark, Jim Dawson sweeping home a fine move in which Jimmy Nicholl, scorer of both goals in the FA Cup semi-final, was prominent. Five minutes later United were back level when George Travers, signed in

February to boost their attack in the struggle to avoid relegation, scored after which the 28,000 crowd watched a dull, largely uneventful game.

The winner came when the limping Wall took advantage of some slack marking to score in the eighty-fifth minute. This was his ninth goal against Liverpool, drawing him level with Sandy Turnbull at the top of the United scoring charts against the Merseysiders. Jack Parkinson, with five, was Liverpool's leading marksman against United. The result ensured United's survival in Division One, with Preston North End and Derby County relegated. Liverpool moved forward to the Cup final, which they lost to a single Bert Freeman goal against a fine Burnley side.

Liverpool: Campbell, Grayer, Speakman, Fairfoul, Lowe, Ferguson, Dawson, Banks, McDougall, Nicholl, Lacey.

United: Royals, Hudson, Stacey, Knowles, Hunter, Hamill, Meredith, Travers, Anderson, Woodcock, Wall.

UNITED IN RELEGATION BATTLE

26 December 1914
First Division
Liverpool 1 (Pagnam), United 1 (Stacey pen.).

There was little to split these teams before kick-off on Boxing Day 1914, with United lying in the relegation places in nineteenth and Liverpool just two places and points higher.

Many believed it was ridiculous that football was continuing to be played while men were dying for king and country on the battlefields of Europe. In light of the fact that when the First World War kicked off, the Government had proclaimed hostilities would be short and 'sweet', the Football Association had taken the decision to play on. Then, when it became obvious that the war might be 'long and dangerous', the organisation came under pressure to maintain games as they were proving to be ideal locations for the military to recruit urgently needed personnel. In the event, when the players themselves started to sign up there was no option except to suspend competitive matches at the start of the following season.

The day after it has now been widely reported that English and German troops played a game of football during a Christmas Day ceasefire, around 25,000 people made their way to Anfield. Although the first half was not the best, the second more than made up for it, especially in light of the laughs the spectators enjoyed from seeing players go head over heels before falling face-first into the knee-deep mud patches which covered the pitch. There was also a moment of unimaginable excitement with the first goal of the match.

John Sheldon, the ex-United man who moved to Liverpool after finding it impossible to replace Billy Meredith in the side, almost opened the scoring for Liverpool but just as he was about to shoot, the ball got stuck in the mud. It was a sign of things to come.

John Hodge, the United right-back, was injured and forced to limp through the second half at outside left. Enoch West took up Hodge's defensive role but continued to demonstrate his usual combative style by shortly afterwards flattening Fred Pagnam who, unconscious, needed to be revived by the Liverpool trainer. Merry Christmas!

And ten minutes later Liverpool centre forward Pagnam was again off the pitch when West, again, clattered into him, leaving him face down in the mud and requiring a washing down in order to be able to see to continue. Yet if West had hoped to intimidate the Liverpool man, he clearly failed as after seventy minutes Jimmy Nicholl pushed the ball between him and George Stacey, and Pagnam raced past both to hammer home a fine goal, bringing one of the largest roars ever heard at Anfield. Pagnam might have even made it 2-0 within a minute of the restart, only to be denied by a goalmouth clearance from Stacey.

The right-back's clearance became even more important when George Anderson, who had been almost anonymous during the game, was brought down by a double challenge from Bob Pursell and Ephraim Longworth as he dribbled into the box. If the referee had waited just a few seconds it would have been 1-1 as the ball rebounded off Anderson and into the net, but blowing the whistle meant a penalty needed to be taken. This was calmly converted by Stacey to give both sides a point at the end of the game, although with Notts County winning, it failed to prevent United falling to last place in the League.

Liverpool: Scott, Longworth, Pursell, Fairfoul, Lowe, Ferguson, Sheldon, Pagnam, Miller, Lacey, Nicholl.
United: Beale, Hodge, Stacey, Cookson, O'Connell, Gipps, Meredith, Potts, Anderson, West, Norton.

CONTROVERSY AND CORRUPTION

2 April 1915
First Division
United 2 (Anderson 2), Liverpool 0.

It might have been the day after April Fool's Day but no-one was laughing later when it became clear there had been some dark goings-on before the match to seriously affect what followed during the ninety minutes.

At kick-off, United were only one point above Chelsea, who occupied bottom spot, and just above Tottenham Hotspur, who were also in the relegation zone. With three away games to follow in four days, things looked bleak for the Old Trafford side, especially as Ernest Mangnall's men had failed to win away from home so far this season and the final away fixture of the season was at Stamford Bridge. This, therefore, was a must-win game for the home side.

Liverpool weren't that much better off in terms of points, with just five more, but barring a late season collapse, they were safe from relegation. The away side were on a decent run, winning four and drawing three of eleven, so it should have been a difficult afternoon for United.

Initially that looked to be the case, with John Sheldon in particular being a thorn in United's side until Walter Spratt got the measure of the ex-United player, after which Liverpool were rarely an attacking threat.

United took the lead after forty minutes when George Anderson swept his shot past Elisha Scott. It could have been 2-0 just after half-time but Pat O'Connell dragged his penalty wide.

Any hopes Liverpool supporters had of seeing their side even advance into the United half were to be unfulfilled and midway through the second period Anderson scored his second by bundling home Joe Norton's cross from close quarters.

Liverpool then missed a glorious chance to pull a goal back when Sheldon failed to convert a penalty, after which there was never any prospect of a Liverpool revival. 'Mancunian' in *The Football Field* in his following day's column wrote that 'Beale had a very easy afternoon, and scarcely a shot worth mentioning reached him'.

There may have been bigger scores in previous encounters between these two sides – after all, Liverpool had once won 7-1 at Anfield – but none had been as easy. The result was to prove crucial to United, who lost four and drew one of the next five before beating Chelsea away and Aston Villa to stay up with relegated Chelsea and Spurs only one and two points respectively below them. Even a draw against Liverpool would ultimately have resulted in United finishing in the relegation zone as their goal average was poorer than Chelsea's.

However, when the First Division was extended to twenty-two clubs after the war, Chelsea were re-elected for the start of the 1919/20, where they were joined by Division Two's sixth-placed club, Arsenal, though Spurs stayed relegated.

There had been little action on the pitch during the game, but there was to be plenty off it once it ended. Almost immediately after the game ended handbills began appearing, alleging that a large amount of money had been bet at odds of 7/1 on a 2-0 win to United. A Football Association investigation was launched and found that 'a considerable amount of money changed hands by betting on the match and … some of the players profited thereby' rigging the match.

They included United players Sandy Turnbull, Arthur Whalley and Enoch West, though only West of the three had actually played in the game, and Liverpool's Jack Sheldon, Tom Miller, Bob Pursell and Tom Fairfoul, all of whom had featured in the match. It was later discovered that some players, such as Liverpool's Fred Pagnam and United's goalscorer Anderson had refused to take part. Pagnam had even threatened to score a goal to ruin the result, and later testified against his team-mates at the FA hearing.

All seven players were banned from playing for life in a decision handed down on 27 December 1915. The FA concluded that it had been a conspiracy by the players alone and no official from either club was found guilty of wrongdoing, and neither club was fined or had points deducted. West vociferously protested his innocence, even going so far as unsuccessfully suing the FA for libel. When it was suggested that if the men joined the armed forces their punishment would be rescinded, West refused. It meant that when all the rest of the players had their bans lifted in 1919 by the FA in recognition of their service to the country, he alone remained banned and he never played again. Neither did Sandy Turnbull, who was killed on the Western Front in 1917.

Tom Watson, the Liverpool manager, also never participated in another Liverpool/United duel as he died only weeks after the game at Old Trafford, going to his grave having managed five League title-winning sides. He was fifty-six years of age.

United: Beale, Hodge John, Spratt, Montgomery, O'Connell, Haywood, Meredith, Potts, Anderson, West, Norton.
Liverpool: Scott, Longworth, Pursell, Fairfoul, Bratley, MacKinlay, Sheldon, Banks, Pagnam, Miller, Nicholl.

FIRST WORLD WAR RESULTS

Non-competitive League football continued during the war. Liverpool and Manchester United participated in the Lancashire Principal Tournament.

1915/16

30 October	Liverpool 0 Manchester United 2
29 January	Manchester United 1 Liverpool 1
11 March	Manchester United 0 Liverpool 0
22 April	Liverpool 7 Manchester United 1

1916/17

7 October	Manchester United 0 Liverpool 0
20 January	Liverpool 3 Manchester United 3

1917/18

19 January	Liverpool 5 Manchester United 1
26 January	Manchester United 0 Liverpool 2

1918/19

25 January	Liverpool 1 Manchester United 1 (25,000 crowd)
1 February	Manchester United 0 Liverpool 1

3
The Inter-War Years

TWO TWENTIES TITLES FOR LIVERPOOL

Good as some tussles between the sides were during this period, the fact was that the outcome was rarely of importance in terms of title success. True, Liverpool did win the League championship in consecutive seasons in the early twenties, but with both sides finishing outside the top three in every other season the games at Anfield and Old Trafford meant more in terms of local pride, especially as Everton and City surpassed their local city rivals in the matter of winning trophies.

Liverpool, at least, managed to avoid relegation in this period, but not so United. They were relegated in 1921/22, but were back in the First Division by 1925/26, dropping down again at the conclusion of the 1931/32 campaign. Five seasons in the lower League were only briefly ended as, after winning the Division Two Championship in 1935/36, United fell straight back down the following season. At least this time the wait to come back up wasn't as long, and promotion ensured that the local games with Liverpool returned in the season prior to bigger hostilities resuming on the battlefield following the outbreak of the Second World War.

NEW-LOOK SIDES AS RIVALRY IS RENEWED

26 December 1919
First Division
United 0, Liverpool 0.

As more than four years had elapsed since the last time the sides had met in the League, it was hardly surprising that the composition of both sides had altered significantly since the infamous fixed match at the end of the 1914/15 season.

Running out at Old Trafford on Boxing Day 1919, only Billy Meredith had survived for United. The Liverpool side, however, contained four players, including three – Bob Pursell, John Sheldon and Tommy Miller – who had been involved in fixing the match, plus Ephraim Longworth at full-back.

Considering their respective positions of ninth and fifteenth in the League, there was a healthy crowd of 45,000 in attendance. A slippery ground, however, spoilt any chances of a good game in which two well-matched sides fought hard without success for what would have proved to be the winning goal. The best chance of the match fell to Henry Lewis but he hesitated in front of goal, giving United the chance to clear.

United: Mew, Moore, Silcock, Grimwood, Hilditch, Whalley, Meredith, Hodges, Spence, Meehan, Hopkin.

Liverpool: Campbell, Longworth, Pursell, Bamber, W. Wadsworth, MacKinlay, Sheldon, Lacey, Miller, Lewis, H. Wadsworth.

SECOND STALEMATE IN SIX DAYS

1 January 1920
First Division
Liverpool 0, United 0.

The return fixture at Anfield six days later was to also end goalless, although at least there was more action for the crowd to witness. Liverpool would have won the game if not for three good saves from Jack Mew in the United goal. Only once did the away side threaten, Wilf Woodcock bringing a fine save from Scotsman Kenny Campbell, who as always was ultra-reliable.

The first season after the cessation of hostilities saw Liverpool, with David Ashworth replacing Tom Watson as manager, finish fourth as West Bromwich Albion were crowned champions. United's new-look side, meanwhile, ended the campaign in twelfth place.

Liverpool: Campbell, Longworth, McNab, Bamber, Bromilow, MacKinlay, Sheldon, Lacey, Miller, Lewis, Pearson.

United: Mew, Moore, Silcock, Grimwood, Hilditch, Whalley, Meredith, Hodges, Spence, Woodcock, Hopkin.

FOUR MEETINGS IN ONE MONTH

8 January 1921
FA Cup, First Round
Liverpool 1 (Chambers), United 1 (Miller).

With the FA Cup being the biggest competition in the world at the time, there was no surprise to find 48,000 packed into Anfield for this eagerly awaited first round encounter. And it was Liverpool who made the stronger start, with United 'keeper Jack Mew forced to make a great save to deny Harry Chambers. When a series of corners and crosses followed, United were forced to defend deeply.

It was, therefore, a shock when with twenty-five minutes gone, Tom Miller took a pass from George Bissett, tricked a couple of defenders and ran through to find the net with a shot from the edge of the area. It was a fine solo goal, but Liverpool were level in the thirty-third minute when a Chambers volley left Mew with no chance to save.

Albert Pearson was unlucky not to make it 2-1 on the stroke of half-time when Mew was glad to see his shot hit the post with the 'keeper beaten. Liverpool's attacking was much less evident after the restart and United could have won the tie if their forwards had shown a bit more poise and composure in front of goal.

Liverpool: Scott, Lucas, MacKinlay, Bamber, W. Wadsworth, Bromilow, Sheldon, Chambers, Johnson, Lewis, Pearson.
United: Mew, Barlow, Silcock, Harris, Grimwood, Forster, Harrison, Bissett, Miller, Partridge, Hopkin.

LIVERPOOL WIN OLD TRAFFORD REPLAY

12 January 1921
FA Cup, First-Round Replay
United 1 (Partridge), Liverpool 2 (Lacey, Chambers).

The match was played in terrible weather, described in *The Manchester Guardian* as 'an example of Manchester's worst'. The Manchester End of Old Trafford was almost unplayable. It was the home side who struck first, Teddy Partridge defying the conditions to dance past the full-backs before somehow squeezing his shot beyond Elisha Scott, who had replaced Kenny Campbell as the regular 'keeper at Anfield, at the near post for a brilliant goal.

United 'keeper Jack Mew kept the scores level with a fine save from Chambers but, when Leslie Hofton conceded a free-kick, Bill Lacey shot home the equaliser. And it was another free-kick, this time from Chambers, which earned Liverpool their winner, thereby progressing to face Newcastle United in round two.

United: Mew, Hofton, Silcock, Harris, Grimwood, Albinson, Harrison, Bissett, Miller, Partridge, Hopkin.
Liverpool: Scott, Lucas, MacKinlay, Bamber, W. Wadsworth, Bromilow, Sheldon, Chambers, Lacey, Lewis, Pearson.

GAME ENDS IN GLOOM

5 February 1921
First Division
United 1 (Grimwood), Liverpool 1 (Chambers).

There was a fifteen-minute delay to kick-off at Old Trafford due to what was reported as 'the city authorities being unable to significantly increase the special car services at this time'. Trams were the most common mode of transport and, having taken workers home from the mills and factories on Saturday lunchtime, they were later used to ferry fans to Old Trafford.

Liverpool had chosen to give James Harrington his League debut at outside left, and were buoyed by the return of Ephraim Longworth from injury. Yet it was United who started the game in the ascendancy with Joe Myerscough and Teddy Partridge both missing decent opportunities. The Liverpool defence constantly struggled to cope with the attacking threat of United wingers Billy Harrison and Fred Hopkin, the latter having made his first appearance for United as a guest playing against Liverpool in a wartime fixture in March 1916.

When Miller was able to run beyond the Liverpool defence to square the ball for Partridge a goal seemed certain, only for the United inside forward to screw his shot horribly wide from six yards. Joe Myerscough was then unlucky with a shot that beat Elisha Scott only to flash narrowly wide. United continued to make and miss chances, William Harrison firing wide when well placed. In the final minutes two high corners from Partridge and Miller were fisted powerfully away by Scott.

The decision to start at 3.15 p.m. was questionable as the second period kicked off amid the gloomy Manchester skies in the days when there were no floodlights. At last Liverpool gave their supporters something to cheer, but Jack Mew did well to fist away shots from Harry Chambers and Harry Lewis. However, it was the home side who struck first after Scott did well under pressure to punch the ball far beyond the penalty area only to see John Grimwood stride forward and hit a beautiful shot that sailed over the heads of the defenders and the 'keeper to strike the back of the net. The sight of such a great goal brought with it tremendous roars from the home followers, but they were almost immediately silenced when Chambers headed home a fine John Sheldon cross from close in.

The game then became a desperate battle to the finish, with one major incident subsequently becoming the after-match talking point. It's one that modern-day fans are still arguing and debating about, only now it's whether goal-line technology should be used to clarify matters. It came when Mew fumbled Dick Forshaw's shot and when the ball dropped to the ground there were strident appeals from the Liverpool players for what would have proved the winning goal. Referee Mr Bayliss was equally adamant it wasn't a goal, and as his decision was final it remained 1-1 at full-time. The game ended in gloomy conditions, but had been well worth the admission price.

United: Mew, Barlow, Silcock, Hilditch, Grimwood, Forster, Meredith, Harrison, Myerscough, Miller, Partridge, Hopkin.

Liverpool: Scott, Longworth, Lucas, Bamber, W. Wadsworth, Bromilow, Sheldon, Forshaw, Chambers, Lewis, Harrington.

MARATHON VICTORY FOR LIVERPOOL

9 February 1921
First Division
Liverpool 2 (Lewis, Chambers), United 0.

The marathon finally came to an end with the fourth meeting in the space of one month. Liverpool gained most satisfaction as they emerged unbeaten. They had triumphed in the FA Cup after a replay and then collected three points from a possible four from their two League matches.

As Elisha Scott was ruled out with a heavy cold, Frank Mitchell made his debut for Liverpool in goal. News that Billy Meredith was to play for United was met with general approval by the large crowd, but it was Liverpool who were quickest into their stride.

After Harry Chambers shot just wide, it was no surprise when Harry Lewis opened the scoring after fourteen minutes for Liverpool. United 'keeper Jack Mew kept his team in the game with a great save from a Dick Forshaw goal attempt, but was well beaten after thirty-five minutes when Harry Chambers beat him and the two defenders on the line to double the home side's advantage. It was one they never looked like losing against a poor United side.

Liverpool would finish fourth in the table for the second successive season, while there was another mid-table spot for United.

Liverpool: Mitchell, Longworth, Lucas, Bamber, W. Wadsworth, Bromilow, Harrington, Forshaw, Chambers, Lewis, H. Wadsworth.

United: Mew, Barlow, Silcock, Hilditch, Grimwood, Forster, Meredith, Myerscough, Spence, Partridge, Hopkin.

CHRISTMAS COMES EARLY

17 December 1921
First Division
Liverpool 2 (Lacey, Chambers), United 1 (Sapsford).

As Liverpool were endeavouring to go to the top of the League, a big crowd had assembled, many of whom, the *Liverpool Echo* reported, had 'clearly had their Christmas spirits early!'

With Elisha Scott back in goal, Liverpool started at a cracking pace. Fred Hopkin, following his summer transfer, was playing for Liverpool against his old colleagues and he made the first chance, which Harry Chambers headed narrowly wide. It was United who had the first real shot at goal though, Scott reacting superbly to block George Sapsford's snap-shot. Danny Shone was guilty of a poor miss shortly afterwards for Liverpool.

United made the initial breakthrough when a mistimed clearance left Sapsford free to give United the lead after twenty minutes. The goal seemed to sap Liverpool's confidence, but Shone continued to batter away in what seemed to be a personal quest not to leave the field at half-time a goal down. He was to be disappointed but shortly after the restart, after a Chambers shot had been kicked off the line by John Silcock, the large crowd were cheering the equaliser. Don McKinlay drove a fierce shot which was blocked. The Liverpool front five charged through like a rugby pack as Bill Lacey smashed home.

The winner came when Chambers, having earlier forced two saves from Jack Mew, beat him with a low shot the 'keeper would have been disappointed not to have saved. The scorer and 'keeper then maintained their personal duel, with the 'keeper atoning for his earlier mistake by saving a number of efforts in a second half dominated by Liverpool.

Liverpool: Scott, Longworth, Lucas, McNab, MacKinlay, Bromilow, Lacey, Forshaw, Shone, Chambers, Hopkin.
United: Mew, Scott, Silcock, Hilditch, McBain, Grimwood, Gibson, Myerscough, Spence, Sapsford, Partridge.

LIVERPOOL CHAMPIONS, UNITED RELEGATED

24 December 1921
First Division
United 0, Liverpool 0.

League leaders Liverpool maintained the same starting line-up as for the previous meeting a week earlier. With the pitch soft and certain to cut up, the game started at a fast and furious pace, United being determined to take revenge for the previous weekend's defeat. Arthur Lochhead and Richard Gibson were prominent down the United right but the first chance in fact fell to Liverpool, when Harry Chambers' shot hit the side netting. Lochhead then thought he had scored just before half-time, only for Liverpool 'keeper Elisha Scott to fling himself to turn the ball over the bar.

The second period saw United step up the pace, Lochhead, Joe Spence and Teddy Partridge all having efforts at goal, but none failed to trouble Scott. He should, though, have been picking the ball out of the net when Tommy Lucas fouled Teddy Partridge but Neil McBain's penalty kick was too straight as Scott saved to keep the game goalless, to the delight of the Liverpool fans. It stayed that way until full-time in a match where over-anxiety had been the winner on the day, leaving United in the relegation zone and Liverpool top.

These positions were maintained until the end of the season, when United could only look on in envy as Liverpool were crowned champions for a third time as they finished six points clear of second-placed Sunderland, while the Old Trafford side finished bottom and were relegated.

United: Mew, Scott, Silcock, Hilditch, McBain, Grimwood, Gibson, Lochhead, Spence, Partridge, Robinson.
Liverpool: Scott, Longworth, Lucas, McNab, MacKinlay, Bromilow, Lacey, Forshaw, Shone, Chambers, Hopkin.

United finished runners-up in Division Two to Leicester City at the end of the 1924/25 season, so fixtures between the Liverpool and United resumed in the following campaign.

HIGH FIVES FOR LIVERPOOL

19 September 1925
First Division
Liverpool 5 (Forshaw 3, Chambers, Rawlings), United 0.

With only John Silcock and George 'Lal' Hilditch remaining from the side that had faced Liverpool four seasons earlier, United were hoping to beat their local rivals for the first time since 1915. Terrible weather had clearly affected the size of the crowd but, when the sides ran on to the pitch before kick-off, United were greeted with tremendous enthusiasm from the travelling support. And initially at least they seemed to have every right to be optimistic, with Frank Barson's traditional long, accurate throws looking certain to bring success as the ball bounced around the goalmouth. Yet it was Liverpool who struck first, Dick Forshaw controlling and hitting the ball almost in one move, a fine goal in the difficult conditions.

Harry Chambers doubled Liverpool's advantage with a fine shot after fifty-five minutes and then Forshaw's powerful drive quickly made it 3-0. When he got his third it left the home fans in the Bullens Road side chanting 'One, two, three, four' and after eighty-six minutes it became five when Archie Rawlings, running clear of a tiring United defence, finished confidently.

Liverpool: Scott, Lucas, MacKinlay, McNab, Cockburn, Bromilow, Rawlings, Chambers, Forshaw, Walsh, Hopkin.
United: Steward, Moore, Silcock, Hilditch, Barson, Mann, Spence, Smith, Lochhead, Rennox, McPherson.

LIVERPOOL LOSE THREE-GOAL LEAD

10 March 1926
First Division
United 3 (Hanson, Rennox, Spence), Liverpool 3 (Forshaw, Hodgson 2).

On a bitterly cold day, sixth against eighth was never going to bring in much of a crowd when just up the road Bolton Wanderers were playing Nottingham Forest in the quarter-finals of the FA Cup. The 9,214 fans who went to Old Trafford did, at least, see goals, whereas the Cup match finished goalless. After twenty minutes it seemed just a matter of how many Liverpool would score, the away forwards running through the United rearguard to score three times without reply through two goals from Gordon Hodgson and another from Dick Forshaw.

Even after Jimmy Hanson and Clatworthy Rennox had cut the lead to a single goal, Liverpool continued to look the more likely to score and a Cyril Oxley effort appeared to have crossed the line to make it 4-2, leaving the *Liverpool Echo* to state that 'the need for goal judges was made evident'. That's still to be decided more than eighty years later but, taking full advantage of their luck, United stole a point when Joe Spence shot home just before the end.

Liverpool finished seventh and United ninth as both finished on the same number of points. There was more satisfaction, however, for United in their first season back in the top division after a three-year absence.

United: Mew, Moore, Silcock, Bain, Barson, Mann, Spence, Smith, Hanson, Rennox, Partridge.
Liverpool: Scott, Lucas, MacKinlay, McNab, Cockburn, Bromilow, Oxley, Chambers, Hodgson, Forshaw, Hopkin.

FABULOUS FORSHAW'S TREBLE CHANCE

28 August 1926
First Division
Liverpool 4 (Forshaw 3, Hodgson), United 2 (McPherson 2 (1 pen.).

Dick Forshaw was the architect of Liverpool's win as he scored a hat-trick against United for the second successive season at Anfield. They were among 124 goals the centre forward netted in 288 appearances between 1919 and 1927 before he was transferred to neighbours Everton.

The game was played in bright sunshine, and there was a special cheer from the home supporters for a contingent of away fans from the Newton Heath Railway Works, home of United's club founders. When McKinlay won the toss he was more than happy to set the away side the task of playing into the strong sun.

Gordon Hodgson is number four in the list of all-time highest scorers in the top flight. He scored 287 goals for Liverpool in Division One.

The match was keenly contested and came to life when Liverpool scored two in three minutes during the first half. Firstly South African Gordon Hodgson headed home Fred Hopkin's cross – one of 287 goals he scored in Division One with Liverpool, Aston Villa and Leeds United – to make him fourth in the list of all-time highest scorers in the top-flight.

Then, in a repeat Forshaw headed another from another cross by ex-United man Hopkin. Alf Steward kept United in the game with a brilliant save, stopping Forshaw's well-hit shot from little more than eight yards, but the 'keeper then misjudged a forward ball and, as he dashed out, Liverpool centre forward Forshaw lifted the ball over him and into the net to make it 3-0 after thirty-two minutes.

United reduced the deficit shortly after the restart when Ronald Haworth, in his first of only two appearances for United, and Albert Smith combined for the latter to find Frank McPherson, whose powerful shot left 'keeper Elisha Scott helpless.

McPherson's seventy-third-minute penalty then appeared to have given the away side a chance of a point. However, Forshaw sealed victory with his third goal after seventy-five minutes, thus ensuring that for the second consecutive season he had recorded a hat-trick at Anfield against United.

Liverpool: Scott, Lucas, MacKinlay, McNab, Cockburn, Bromilow, Edmed, Hodgson, Forshaw, Chambers, Hopkin.
United: Steward, Inglis, Silcock, Hilditch, Barson, Mann, Spence, T. Smith, McPherson, Haworth, Thomas.

DYNAMIC DICK DOES IT AGAIN

15 January 1927
First Division
United 0, Liverpool 1 (Forshaw).
Dick Forshaw again grabbed the headlines with Liverpool's match-winning goal at Old Trafford. The centre forward certainly relished playing against United as this was his eighth goal against them in four matches.

A tight first-half midfield battle had kept chances to a minimum. United 'keeper Elisha Scott made a fine save from a Frank McPherson header before opposite number Alf Steward made a super stop after Gordon Hodgson touched on Harry Chambers' header and, with the ball spinning past him and towards the goal, the 'keeper spun backwards to somehow get his hand to it and push it round the post. Hodgson, already celebrating, stood with his hands on his head in disbelief.

Just before half-time Forshaw had a goal disallowed for offside but, in a second half played in pouring rain, the Liverpool centre forward was quickest to a loose ball when Hodgson's shot hit the inside of the post and dropped onto the line. Towards the end Dick Edmed might have made it 2-0 but, after being sent clear, he failed miserably with his shot.

It was another season of mid-table obscurity for both clubs, though ninth-placed Liverpool finished six spots ahead of United.

United: Steward, Moore, Jones, Bennion, Grimwood, Mann, Spence, Hanson, McPherson, Sweeney, Partridge.
Liverpool: Scott, Done, MacKinlay, McNab, Pratt, Bromilow, Edmed, Hodgson, Forshaw, Chambers, Hopkin.

GREAT SCOTT MAKES BREAKTHROUGH

24 December 1927
First Division
Liverpool 2 (T. Scott, Chambers), United 0.

As the weather was poor, there was only a small crowd inside Anfield, with the majority having gathered under the newly covered Kop end. With the pitch sodden, especially in the middle, it was a surprise to see the game start so quickly, but the only incident of note in the goalmouth areas was when a drive from United's Frank McPherson brought a good save from South African Arthur Riley.

The breakthrough came from Liverpool on the hour when Tom Scott's shot had just enough on it to beat Lance Richardson. Although United piled forward in search of an equaliser, it was Liverpool who finished off the scoring when just before the end Harry Chambers headed in from a corner taken by Dick Edmed.

Liverpool: Riley, Lucas, MacKinlay, McMullan, Jackson, Bromilow, Edmed, T. Scott, Devlin, Chambers, Hopkin.
United: Richardson, Moore, Jones, Bennion, Mann, Wilson, Spence, Partridge, Hanson, Johnston, McPherson.

SPENCE HELPS STAVE OFF RELEGATION

5 May 1928
First Division
United 6 (Spence 3, Rawlings 2 , Hanson), Liverpool 1 (Hodgson).

Knowing that only victory would be enough to keep them in Division One, United attacked from the start of the game. Gaining both points, however, would require them to beat Liverpool for the first time since 1915.

And with the backing of a noisy crowd, United took the lead after twelve minutes when Joe Spence scored from what seemed an impossibly tight angle as he somehow managed to squeeze the ball into the corner of the net. So pleased were they at this success that every United player, except 'keeper Alf Steward, came forward to shake the hand of the scorer who would go on to complete a hat-trick.

With the crowd urging United not to sit back, Liverpool 'keeper Arthur Riley made a fine save from a Jimmy Hanson effort before Billy Johnston hit the bar with a powerful drive. United inside left Johnston got his reward shortly after when his neat, incisive pass was swept home by Bill Rawlings to double the home side's lead. Five minutes later it got even better when Rawlings' shot beat Riley to make it 3-0. Though Gordon Hodgson reduced the arrears, Spence ensured the home side went into the break with a three-goal advantage when he scored with a beautiful first-time effort.

His hat-trick goal soon after the restart was a great effort; cutting inside, he beat Riley with a shot that crashed into the net off the underside of the bar. Then when Spence had his shot saved after eighty-six minutes, Hanson followed up to make it 6-1, leaving Tottenham Hotspur and Middlesbrough to suffer the drop into Division Two. United had survived, but only just as they finished only one point and three places above Spurs, who finished second bottom. Only two points separated the bottom nine teams and Liverpool, despite finishing sixteenth, were like United only two points clear of bottom spot.

United: Steward, Moore, Jones, McLenahan, Mann, Wilson, Spence, Hanson, Rawlings, Johnston, Thomas.
Liverpool: Riley, McBain, MacKinlay, McMullan, Jackson, Bromilow, Edmed, Hodgson, Murray, Race, Hopkin.

LIVERPOOL TWICE LOSE LEAD

15 September 1928
First Division
United 2 (Silcock, Hanson pen.), Liverpool 2 (Hodgson, Edmed).

There was a United debut for half-back Charlie Spencer, who had been signed from Newcastle United, but his side fell behind after just two minutes when Gordon Hodgson met a Fred Hopkin cross to power home a right-foot shot. 'No goalkeeper on earth would have stopped such a drive, such was its fierceness,' as one newspaper report described.

United equalised after forty minutes when Liverpool 'keeper Elisha Scott, coming out to collect a Jack Silcock cross, was unsighted by Bill Rawlings and the ball flew over both players into the back of the net. United, boosted by the goal, pushed forward in the second half but fell behind when Dick Edmed made it 2-1. However, when Dave Davidson handled, Jimmy Hanson ensured the game ended all square with a seventy-second-minute penalty.

United: Steward, Moore, Silcock, Bennion, Spencer, Wilson, Spence, Hanson, Rawlings, Johnston, Williams.
Liverpool: Scott, Jackson, Done, Morrison, Davidson, Bromilow, Edmed, Hodgson, Whitehurst, McDougall, Hopkin.

ANFIELD WIN KICK-STARTS CLIMB TO SAFETY

13 February 1929
First Division
Liverpool 2 (Hodgson, Done pen.), United 3 (Reid 2, Thomas).

United's victory at Anfield was bitter-sweet as, despite the two precious points picked up, they remained bottom of the First Division. It was their first win in sixteen League matches but, remarkably, it would act as the catalyst for a remarkable end-of-season run in which they lost only once in their last fifteen games to climb to twelfth place.

And United's improved fortunes coincided with the capture of forward Tom Reid from Liverpool in early 1929 as he scored fifteen goals in the remaining seventeen League games of the campaign, including two on his return to Liverpool, for whom he had scored 30 goals in 55 matches between 1925 and 1929.

Liverpool took the lead after twelve minutes when goalkeeper Alf Steward's attempt to kick clear the ball cannoned off the outstretched foot of Gordon Hodgson and back beyond the 'keeper and into the net. After missing a number of further chances, Liverpool paid the penalty when Reid equalised in the twenty-seventh minute, when after playing a lovely one-two with Joe Spence, he finished confidently. This success encouraged United, who took the lead when Reid met Harry Thomas's cross from the left to hit the ball beyond 'keeper Arthur Riley. And when Thomas netted not long after, United had scored three in five minutes to lead 3-1.

Bob Done reduced the arrears just two minutes later from the penalty spot but, hard as they pressed in the second half, Liverpool failed to find an equaliser to leave the handful of away supporters in the crowd jumping up and down at the end of the game, although the result still left their side at the bottom of the League and two points from safety. Liverpool would eventually finish fifth.

Liverpool: Riley, Jackson, Done, Morrison, Davidson, Bromilow, Edmed, Hodgson, Clark, Race, Salisbury.
United: Steward, Moore, Silcock, Bennion, Spencer, Mann, Spence, Hanson, Reid, Rowley, Thomas.

NEW BOY SMITH'S DREAM DEBUT

21 September 1929
First Division
United 1 (Spence), Liverpool 2 (Smith 2).

Jamie Smith, whose 66 League goals for Ayr United in the Scottish Second Division the previous season still remains a British record, scored twice in what was a dream debut at Old Trafford. Smith, who cost £5,500, only arrived in Lancashire the night before.

Joe Spence had given United a half-time lead, but on the hour the new man made it 1-1 and ten minutes later hit a scorching shot that 'keeper Alf Steward had no chance of saving. Smith's no-nonsense, never-say-die attitude had already won him the affection of the good number of Liverpool fans who had travelled down the East Lancs Road to see their side take both points. Smith was to finish as Liverpool's top marksman at the end of the season with 23 goals, and scored another 14 the following season.

United: Steward, Moore, Dale, Bennion, Spencer, Mann, Wilson, Spence, Hanson, Rawlings, Rowley, Thomas.
Liverpool: Riley, Jackson, Lucas, Morrison, McDougall, Davidson, Edmed, Hodgson, Smith, Race, Hopkin.

RACE ECLIPSES NEW SIGNING

25 January 1930
First Division
Liverpool 1 (Race), United 0.

Harold Race was Liverpool's match-winner in a game described as one of the poorest ever between the sides. Yet it was won with one move of quality as Dick Edmed slipped the ball beyond the United defence to leave Race in the clear to score on the stroke of half-time before a crowd boosted by a desire to see new signing Tom Bradshaw in action.

Known as 'Tiny' because of his strapping physique, Bradshaw cost Liverpool £8,000 for his services from Bury, where he had first been capped for Scotland at Wembley in 1928 when 'The Wizards' thrashed England 5-1. Bradshaw was to enjoy a long, successful career at Anfield, playing 219 times before being transferred to Third Lanark in September 1938.

Liverpool: Riley, Jackson, Lucas, Gardner, McDougall, Bradshaw, Edmed, Race, Smith, McPherson, Hopkin.
United: Steward, Dale, Silcock, Bennion, Hilditch, Wilson, Spence, Boyle, Reid, Rowley, McLachlan.

UNITED RELEGATED AT ANFIELD

3 April 1931
First Division
Liverpool 1 (Hodgson), United 1 (Wilson).

Having survived relegation by just two points at the end of the 1929/30 season, there was to be no reprieve for United in this campaign. Though United played Liverpool twice in four days over the Easter period, the results mattered little as, prior to kick-off at Anfield on Good Friday, United were twelve points behind third-from-bottom Blackpool with just six games remaining. So while a 1-1 draw wasn't too bad a result against eighth-placed Liverpool, it simply confirmed relegation.

These were troubled times for United and there was a serious threat to the survival of the Old Trafford club in that period. It was to be some time before they returned to the top flight.

Liverpool: Riley, Jackson, Lucas, Morrison, Bradshaw, McDougall, Barton, Hodgson, Wright, McPherson, Hopkin.
United: Steward, Mellor, Silcock, Bennion, Hilditch, McLachlan, Spence, McLenahan, Wilson, Rowley, Hopkinson.

UNITED GO DOWN WITH GUNS BLAZING

6 April 1931
First Division
United 4 (Reid 2, McLenahan, Rowley), Liverpool 1 (A Scott).

United at least showed some fight in the return at Old Trafford, where fans voted with their feet and stayed away. The crowd was a pitifully low 8,058.

A facial injury suffered at Anfield meant Jack Wilson's place was taken by Tommy Reid, who opened the scoring after three minutes when, following some lovely approach play by Hugh McLenahan, he finished in style from ten yards. Seven minutes later McLenahan doubled the lead, powerfully heading Joe Spence's cross past 'keeper Elisha Scott.

It could have been a lot worse for the away side as both scorers passed up great opportunities to add to United's total. It took until just before half-time for Liverpool to threaten, Tom Bradshaw bringing a smart save from Alf Steward.

United made the game safe five minutes into the second half when Harry Rowley headed a great goal from another Spence cross. Liverpool pulled a goal back with thirty minutes remaining, Alan Scott, with his second and final goal for Liverpool, scrambling the ball home from close in. But when Reid and Spence again combined well, Reid hit his second with two minutes remaining to make it 4-1.

United: Steward, Mellor, Silcock, Bennion, Hilditch, McLachlan, Spence, McLenahan, Reid, Rowley, Hopkinson.
Liverpool: E. Scott, Jackson, Lucas, Morrison, Bradshaw, McDougall, Barton, Hodgson, A. Scott, McPherson, Hopkin.

It was another five years before the sides met again, in late November 1936. In the intervening period United went through some desperate times, finishing as low as twentieth in the Second Division in 1933/34 and only avoiding relegation to Division Three North by one point. Liverpool, meanwhile, essentially remained a mid-table team, though there were a couple of season when they, too, flirted with relegation.

HOWE TO INFLICT DEFEAT

21 November 1936
First Division
United 2 (Manley, Thompson), Liverpool 5 (Hanson, Eastham, Howe 3).

In the week leading up to the game, a struggling United had strengthened their forward line with the purchase of centre forward John Thompson from Blackburn Rovers. Despite scoring on his debut, Thompson was unable to prevent United suffering their first home defeat of the season. While the margin was harsh, there was no doubt that Liverpool deserved the victory, especially after an impressive second-half display that blew the hosts away.

New man Thompson started well, back-heeling the ball into the path of Ron Ferrier, whose shot sailed just over. And it was Liverpool who were pinned back for the first twenty minutes, and they were grateful to Matt Busby when he made a fine tackle to bring to an end a dribbling run by George Mutch. Having failed to trouble 'keeper Roy John, it was something of a surprise when Liverpool took the lead, Fred Howe sending Jimmy Hanson away and he cut inside to fire a low shot past John's outstretched left arm.

Within two minutes United were level when Mutch, attacking down the left, found Thompson who, to the crowd's great delight, drove home a debut goal. It was a temporary reprieve as within three minutes Howe found Berry Nieuwenhuys and when the outside right's shot hit the post, John was helpless to prevent Harry Eastham putting Liverpool 2-1 ahead. The winger also made the third, taking on Busby's through-ball before beating George Roughton for pace. John made a fine save but was unable to keep hold of the ball and Howe had the simple task of slotting it home two minutes before the break.

United tried manfully to get back into the game in the second period. Billy Bryant thought he had reduced the deficit, only to have his effort disallowed for offside. The outside right at least had the pleasure of creating the home side's second on the hour, Tom Manley heading his cross past Alf Hobson.

It took Liverpool only four minutes to restore their two-goal advantage, a poor Hugh McLenahan pass being seized upon by Howe to make it 4-2. Howe again profited from a slip in the United defence to crash home a shot for his hat-trick to give Liverpool an emphatic victory.

United: John, Griffiths, Roughton, Brown, McLenahan, McKay, Bryant, Mutch, Thompson, Ferrier, Manley.
Liverpool: Hobson, Cooper, Dabbs, Busby, Bush, McDougall, Nieuwenhuys, Eastham, Howe, Balmer, Hanson.

RELEGATION LOOMS AGAIN

27 March 1937
First Division
Liverpool 2 (Hanson, Howe), United 0.

With United next to bottom and Liverpool just four places and four points above them, it was a match neither side could afford to lose. Liverpool had been thrashed 5-0 the previous day by championship-chasing Manchester City, who come the end of the season would win their first Division One title. The contrast between the two Manchester sides couldn't have been greater and City were certainly the top dogs.

United kept the same side that had played Everton the previous weekend, but Liverpool were forced to make four changes, with young South African Dick Kemp replacing fellow countryman Arthur Riley in goal for the home side on a beautifully sunny day.

The game started at a furious pace and United 'keeper Tommy Breen had to make a good save from a dangerous Ted Savage drive. George Mutch then fired over for United, who were grateful to Walter Winterbottom for a superb tackle on Fred Howe as the Liverpool centre forward threatened to burst clear.

United looked to have opened the scoring when Mutch fired his shot past 'keeper Dirk Kemp only to see the ball whistle agonisingly wide, and they continued to look the most likely to open the scoring.

However, midway through the opening period Liverpool went ahead when Fred Howe, in space, received a lovely pass from John Balmer and looking up, hit a great shot that 'keeper Tommy Breen did brilliantly to prevent entering the net, but when the ball ran loose Jimmy Hanson was the quickest to react and poked it into an empty net. The left-winger then almost grabbed a second, only for his shot to come back into play off the woodwork. United ought to have equalised shortly before half-time when centre forward Mutch wriggled clear of his marker but missed badly from eight yards.

It may have been that the furious start to the game had taken something out of the players because the second period was a timid affair. With less than one minute remaining, Liverpool wrapped the game up when Fred Howe scored from close in and sent United to the bottom of the League.

While they did overhaul Sheffield Wednesday by the end of the season, a twenty-first-place finish meant a return to Division Two. In the event the drop down lasted only one season and the fixtures between the sides resumed against the gathering storm-clouds of a Second World War.

Liverpool: Kemp, Cooper, Dabbs, Savage, Bradshaw, McDougall, Taylor, Eastham, Howe, Balmer, Hanson.
United: Breen, Griffiths, Roughton, Brown, Winterbottom, Whalley, Cape, Gladwin, Mutch, Baird, Manley.

BERRY GOOD DAY FOR LIVERPOOL

7 September 1938
First Division
Liverpool 1 (Nieuwenhuys), United 0.

Newly promoted United had made a moderately successful return to the top flight, winning one and drawing one of the three League fixtures which preceded their visit to Anfield.

A freak goal decided the outcome of the September game, a high ball from South African Berry Nieuwenhuys getting caught in the wind and eluding United 'keeper Jack Breedon.

Neither side looked like scoring after that and the only entertainment came in the form of Willie Fagan's fabulous dribbling skills. Towards the end, Liverpool full-back Jim Harley was badly injured with a depressed cheekbone that kept him out action for a lengthy period.

The final game of the 1938/9 season saw Manchester United beat Liverpool 2-0. The Second World War was to end competitive League football for the next seven years.

Liverpool: Riley, Cooper, Harley, Busby, Rogers, McInnes, Nieuwenhuys, Taylor, Fagan, Balmer, Kinghorn.

United: Breedon, Griffiths, Redwood, Gladwin, Vose, Manley, Bryant, Craven, Smith, Pearson, Rowley.

HANLON HITS THE HEIGHTS

6 May 1939
First Division
United 2 (Hanlon 2), Liverpool 0.

It was the last match of the season and all those who saw it did not need reminding; it was a non-event, with neither side having anything to play for.

Liverpool ended the season in eleventh place, finishing three spots ahead of United, who stayed up comfortably having been immediately relegated the last time they were promoted.

Jimmy Hanlon was United's match-winner as he scored twice in three minutes to seal victory in the latter stages of the opening period. The Manchester-born Hanlon scored 22 goals in 70 first-team appearances, including the shot and header which accounted for his goals against Liverpool.

United: Breedon, Redwood, Roughton, Warner, Vose, McKay, Bryant, Wassall, Hanlon, Carey, Rowley.

Liverpool: Riley, Cooper, Bush, Busby, Rogers, McInnes, Nieuwenhuys, Eastham, Fagan, Balmer, Van Den Berg.

SECOND WORLD WAR RESULTS

After a twenty-year break, the non-competitive League football returned in 1939/40. Football was regionally organised and Liverpool and Manchester United participated in War League North.

1939/40

18 November	Liverpool 1 Manchester United 0
16 March	Manchester United 1 Liverpool 0

1940/41

23 November	Liverpool 2 Manchester United 2
30 November	Manchester United 2 Liverpool 0
26 April	Liverpool 2 Manchester United 1
5 May	Manchester United 1 Liverpool 1 (at Maine Road)

1941/42

22 November   Liverpool 1 Manchester United 1

29 November   Manchester United 2 Liverpool 2

1942/43

10 October   Manchester United 3 Liverpool 4

17 October   Liverpool 2 Manchester United 1

1943/44

23 October   Liverpool 3 Manchester United 4

30 October   Manchester United 1 Liverpool 0

1944/45

4 November   Liverpool 3 Manchester United 2

11 November   Manchester United 2 Liverpool 5

1945/46

9 February   Manchester United 1 Liverpool 2 (32,993 crowd)

16 February   Liverpool 5 Manchester United 0 (37,197 crowd)

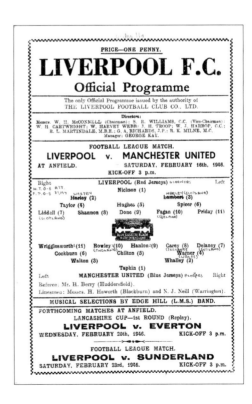

4
Busby Sparks United Revival

United's board of directors went with a radical change of policy when football resumed after the end of the Second World War and they were quickly vindicated in the decision to give Matt Busby total control of team affairs. That persuaded Busby to turn down the offer of a coaching role at Liverpool in favour of a move to Old Trafford. Starting work on 1 October 1945, the Scot almost immediately began to take the club back towards a place at the top of English football last enjoyed before the First World War.

STAN'S THE STAR MAN

11 September 1946
First Division
Manchester United 5 (Pearson 3,Mitten, Rowley), Liverpool 0.
(at Maine Road)

Old Trafford was out of action after being heavily bombed by the Luftwaffe so the first competitive League match between the two teams since May 1939 took place at Maine Road. City's willingness to allow their rivals the chance to play at their home ground was generous and in keeping with the spirit of the times.

With four points from the first six and an impressive 7-4 beating of Chelsea the previous weekend, Liverpool, fresh from a successful summer tour of North America, were looking to continue the domination they had enjoyed against their near neighbours during the inter-war years. Missing ace striker Billy Liddell through injury, Liverpool suffered a further blow when 'keeper Cyril Sidlow was unable to get leave from the Army to play. Charlie Ashcroft, deputising in goal, was to endure a difficult afternoon, especially from Stan Pearson, whose hat-trick was reward for a fabulous performance.

Three up by the break, Matt Busby's side were never in trouble at the back, equalling their record margin of victory against Liverpool to ensure a fourth straight win and confirm their place at the top of the table. It was early days but was a first title since 1911 in the offing?

If all the games had been played at Maine Road then almost certainly, but United were indifferent away from home and when the sides again clashed late in the season,

Manchester United crushed Matt Busby's former side 5-0 at Maine Road in September 1946.

it was their opponents who were showing the form of champions after winning eight and losing just the once in eleven matches.

United: Crompton, Carey, McGlen, Warner, Chilton, Cockburn, Delaney, Pearson, Hanlon, Rowley, Mitten.
Liverpool: Ashcroft, Harley, Ramsden, Taylor, Hughes, Paisley, Nieuwenhuys, Balmer, Jones, Fagan, Priday.

STUBBINS MONEY WELL SPENT

3 May 1947
First Division
Liverpool 1 (Stubbins), United 0.

Following the early-season debacle at Maine Road, the Liverpool directors had acted quickly to pinch Newcastle United striker Albert Stubbins from under the noses of neighbours Everton.

Liverpool paid a club record of £12,500 for Stubbins, but he paid them back as the goals he scored in his debut season helped them lift the First Division title. He would go on to score 83 goals in 178 appearances for them.

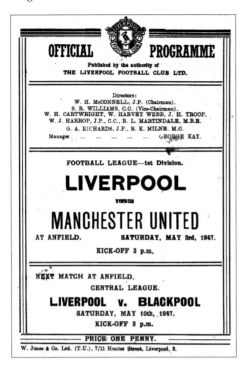

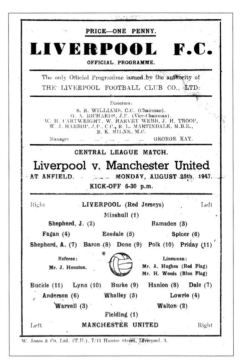

Stubbins scored on his debut against Bolton Wanderers at Burnden Park and he was also the match-winner against United. He and John Balmer, who earlier in the season became the only Liverpool player in the club's history to hit hat-tricks in three consecutive matches, each finished with 24 League goals and both hit 28 in all competitions.

Prior to kick-off Liverpool were in fifth place, four points adrift of second-placed United with a game in hand and five behind leaders Wolves with both having played thirty-seven League matches.

Liverpool's victory made it twenty points from a possible twenty-four. The home side scored early before resisting a fierce second-half onslaught. There were only twelve minutes on the clock when Billy Liddell's lightning pace and close control took him within five yards of the goal, and when he squared the ball back Stubbins swept it home for a priceless lead.

United seemed certain to equalise just before the break but Stan Pearson was left scratching his head when his shot towards the far post was saved by an out-of-position Cyril Sidlow. It was a lucky break and, when half-time brought news that Portsmouth were beating Wolves, the tension rose even higher.

There were few chances in the second half, the most significant moment coming when the referee ruled that Bob Paisley's foul on Pearson had taken place only inches outside the penalty area, rather than inside it as the United players and supporters claimed.

Victory pushed Liverpool to within three points of the leaders but all four of their remaining games were away, an indication as to how difficult it would be to finish top. In the event seven points out of eight, including a 2-1 victory in the title-decider at Wolves, proved just enough to pip both the Black Country club and United, who finished runners-up.

Liverpool: Sidlow, Lambert, Spicer, Jones, Hughes, Paisley, Palk, Balmer, Stubbins, Watkinson, Liddell.
United: Crompton, Carey, Aston, Warner, Chilton, McGlen, Delaney, Hanlon, Burke, Pearson, Rowley.

GREAT START FOR UNITED

27 August 1947
First Division
United 2 (Morris, Pearson), Liverpool 0.
(at Maine Road)

United were given an early chance to avenge the defeat at Anfield in May when the sides met early in the 1947/48 season at Maine Road. Goals twenty-five minutes into each half gave the home side a deserved victory.

After an hour, Liverpool were still very much in the game but an injury to Jim Harley as he prevented Charlie Mitten from doubling United's advantage was to reduce the Liverpool right-back to a passenger for the rest of the game. It was no great surprise, therefore, when Stan Pearson doubled the lead after sixty-nine minutes. John Morris had given the home side a deserved lead as United began the season in impressive form.

United: Crompton, Carey, Aston, Warner, Chilton, McGlen, Delaney, Morris,
    Rowley, Pearson, Mitten.
Liverpool: Sidlow, Harley, Lambert, Taylor, Hughes, Paisley, Watkinson, Balmer,
    Stubbins, Palk, Liddell.

LIVERPOOL BACK FROM THE DEAD

3 September 1947
First Division
Liverpool 2 (Stubbins, Balmer pen.), United 2 (Mitten, Pearson).

The return only a week later was a tighter affair, though when Charlie Mitten and Stan Pearson struck early to give Matt Busby's side a two-goal lead, there seemed little chance of a Liverpool comeback.

Cyril Sidlow was badly at fault with the second and the 'keeper continued his bad day by then giving away a penalty. Three down would surely have been too great a deficit to overcome so there was relief when Jack Rowley saw his effort well saved by

Sidlow. Nevertheless, having shown themselves superior in speed, craft and passing in the opening period, the only hope for Liverpool's supporters was that their side had shown great courage and determination to keep battling away.

So there was huge excitement when Albert Stubbins scored soon after half-time. Urged on by the home crowd, Liverpool pushed forward with even centre half Laurie Hughes coming forward to fire two shots narrowly wide. There was great rejoicing when Jack Balmer made it 2-2 from the penalty spot and, with over twenty minutes remaining, a famous victory looked on. Yet perhaps because of the effort of hanging on in the first period and attacking frantically in the second, Liverpool rarely threatened the United goal after that and the game ended in a deserved draw.

Having largely held the pacey Billy Liddell, United's Johnny Carey for his 'sins' was booed by the home crowd, while Mitten was the best forward on display in a game United should have wrapped up before half-time.

Liverpool: Sidlow, Jones, Lambert, Taylor, Hughes, Paisley, Watkinson, Balmer, Stubbins, Palk, Liddell.
United: Crompton, Carey, Aston, Warner, Chilton, McGlen, Delaney, Morris, Rowley, Pearson, Mitten.

BUSBY MAGIC STARTS TO PAY

24 January 1948
FA Cup, fourth round
United 3 (Mitten, Morris, Rowley), Liverpool 0.
(at Goodison Park)

With close to 75,000 inside Goodison Park and thousands outside, the gates were closed half an hour before kick-off to prevent a tragedy. Those fortunate enough to witness the match saw a magnificent United display. The result was further confirmation of how foolish Liverpool had been after the Second World War when they offered ex-player Matt Busby the job of assistant coach rather than the manager's job he craved, Busby deciding instead to apply and land the vacant manager's job at United.

Liverpool could, however, have made it more difficult for Busby's side but Jack Balmer's shot lacked pace, allowing John Aston to clear off the line in the first minute, and Cyril Done then shot wide from an easy position. But with Albert Stubbins being consistently thwarted, United's confidence gradually grew and at times the interchanging of their forwards bamboozled the Liverpool defence. All three goals came in a seven-minute first-half burst, Jack Rowley sweeping home a Charlie Mitten cross in the thirtieth minute, Johnny Morris hammering home from thirty yards before from the restart Rowley beat Ray Hughes in the air and Mitten raced on to place the ball coolly over the head of 'keeper Ray Minshull as he raced out.

Official Programme

FOOTBALL ASSOCIATION CUP

4th ROUND

GOODISON   PARK.

Manchester United

versus

Liverpool

AT GOODISON PARK

SATURDAY, 24th JAN., 1948

KICK-OFF 2-30 p.m.

Price : Twopence

W. Jones & Co. Ltd. (T.U.), 7-11 Hunter Street, Liverpool, 3.

With Old Trafford out of action and Manchester City at home, Manchester United played their 1947/8 FA Cup fourth round tie at Goodison Park.

Victory at Goodison continued the thrilling FA Cup run by Busby's side which, playing every game away from Old Trafford, wrapped up its first Cup win since 1909 when beating Blackpool 4-2 in a thrilling Wembley final that many still consider the finest match ever played at the famous stadium.

United also finished runners-up to Arsenal as they came within seven points of securing the historic double of League and Cup. Liverpool finished eleventh in the First Division.

United: Crompton, Carey, Aston, Anderson, Chilton, Cockburn, Delaney, Morris, Rowley, Pearson, Mitten.
Liverpool: Minshull, Jones, Lambert, Taylor, Hughes, Paisley, Liddell, Balmer, Stubbins, Done, Priday.

LIVERPOOL LACK FIRE-POWER

25 December 1948
First Division
United o, Liverpool o.
(at Maine Road)

Fourth-placed United were eight places higher than Liverpool prior to the Christmas 'double-header' in 1948.

Liverpool had struggled to score goals, with only 30 in 22 games, and with Billy Liddell and Albert Stubbins both missing, they were rarely to threaten Jack Crompton over the entire 180 minutes in the two games.

However, with Liverpool 'keeper Ray Minshull playing confidently and Charlie Mitten passing up the only serious chance of the game, Liverpool were well satisfied with the point they took back from the Christmas Day game at Maine Road.

United: Crompton, Carey, Aston, Cockburn, Chilton, McGlen, Delaney, Pearson, Burke, Rowley, Mitten.
Liverpool: Minshull, Shepherd, Lambert, Taylor, Jones, Paisley, Payne, Balmer, Done, McLeod, Brierley.

CHRISTMAS CHEER FOR UNITED

27 December 1948
First Division
Liverpool 0, United 2 (Pearson, Burke).

Two days later, before an Anfield crowd more than double that of the previous game against Aston Villa, the need for Liverpool to satisfy their supporters' needs by attacking the game proved their undoing.

Without playing particularly well, goals from Stan Pearson and Ronnie Burke gave Matt Busby's side a comfortable victory. Having won the FA Cup the previous season in a thrilling fashion, many critics had predicted United would walk away with the First Division title, but in the end Portsmouth won it fairly comfortably by finishing five points ahead of second-placed United, with Liverpool back in twelfth place.

Liverpool: Minshull, Shepherd, Lambert, Taylor, Jones, Paisley, Payne, Balmer, Done, McLeod, Brierley.

United: Crompton, Carey, Aston, Cockburn, Chilton, McGlen, Buckle, Pearson, Burke, Rowley, Mitten.

ANOTHER EARLY-SEASON CLASH

7 September 1949
First Division
Liverpool 1 (Stubbins), United 1 (Mitten).

Once again the fixtures pitched the sides against each other early in the campaign and in a hard-fought game that left both teams still unbeaten, Charlie Mitten gave United a deserved lead when he headed home Jack Rowley's centre on the stroke of half-time.

Liverpool, though, were the better side in the second half and got their reward after seventy-eight minutes when Albert Stubbins flicked Billy Liddell's cross home. Jimmy Payne had won the ball out on the right before sending it across the field to Liddell on the left and in the confusion the United defence had been unable to recover.

In a very good game, the highlight was the battle between Johnny Carey and Liddell, with the United defender largely winning the duel through a combination of power and pace but ultimately losing out in the creation of the equalising goal.

Liverpool: Sidlow, Lambert, Spicer, Taylor, Hughes, Paisley, Payne, Baron, Stubbins, Fagan, Liddell.

United: Crompton, Aston, Lowrie, Lynn, Chilton, Delaney, Pearson, Rowley, Buckle, Mitten.

UNITED v. ASTON VILLA, March 8th, 1950
The seven goals scored against Villa without reply sent United to the top of the table. This graphic picture shows inside right Downie lobbing the ball over Villa 'keeper Rutherford for United's fifth goal.

NICE ONE CYRIL

15 March 1950
First Division
United 0, Liverpool 0.

Liverpool 'keeper Cyril Sidlow had played the game of his life when he constantly denied his former team-mates at Molineux in May 1947, helping Liverpool achieve a 2-1 victory in their title-decider as they were crowned First Division champions. Sidlow had joined Liverpool from Wolves in February 1946 for a then club-record £4,000 fee.

Sidlow's performance at Old Trafford in March 1950 might not have meant as much but it was arguably just as good with three saves, two of which were from Jack Rowley, firmly in the great category. He was also constantly off his line as Charlie Mitten and Jimmy Delaney crossed accurately, preventing John Downie adding to the five he had notched up against Aston Villa in United's previous home game.

Sidlow did enjoy a touch of good fortune, with the home forwards twice hitting the woodwork, but cool, calm and confident, the 'keeper was not going to be beaten on this particular day.

After finishing runners-up in each of the previous three seasons, United were fourth this time and Liverpool eighth.

United: Crompton, Carey, Aston, Warner, Chilton, Cockburn, Delaney, Downie,
Rowley, Pearson, Mitten.
Liverpool: Sidlow, Lambert, Spicer, Taylor, Jones, Paisley, Payne, Baron, Stubbins,
Christie, Liddell.

NIGHTMARE FOR NEW KEEPER

23 August 1950
First Division
Liverpool 2 (Liddell, Allen (o.g.)), United 1 (Rowley).

With Manchester United certain to miss Charlie Mitten after the winger had chosen
to accept considerably more money to play for Santa Fe in Colombia, Matt Busby had
given Billy McGlen, better known as a left half, the chance to play on the wing while
he searched for a replacement. Meanwhile, a record fee of £10,000 had brought Queens
Park Rangers 'keeper Reg Allen to Old Trafford. Running out at Anfield was only the
second game between the sticks for the former commando. It didn't go well.

The game itself was a great one which at kick-off looked in doubt, but the heavy fog
lifted five minutes into the game, giving spectators a fine view of a game played on a
wet ground.

Afterwards the *Liverpool Echo* reckoned that for the home fans, it would be talked
about for years as one of the best games seen at Anfield. The opening goal saw Jimmy
Payne beat two defenders for pace before threading the ball down the line for Phil
Taylor to pull it back where Billy Liddell banged it home. United equalised after
twenty-five minutes, a close-range finish by Jack Rowley deservedly bringing them
level.

Allen made what proved to be the fatal mistake after thirty-seven minutes when,
attempting to punch Cyril Done's centre away from goal, he conspired to push the ball
into the net.

The second half was a frantic affair with both sides, through Liddell and Stan
Pearson, cracking shots against the woodwork before Jack Balmer appeared to ensure
both points with a fine header only for the 'goal' to be disallowed for handball in the
build up. Liddell's pace caused Johnny Carey major problems but it was Jimmy Payne's
trickery on the ball that had probably done the most to help Liverpool secure both
points on a day when United had displayed the more constructive football, but had
been undone by Liverpool's more direct approach.

Liverpool: Sidlow, Shepherd, Spicer, Jones, Hughes, Paisley, Payne, Taylor, Done,
Balmer, Liddell.
United: Allen, Aston, McIlvenney, Chilton, Cockburn, Delaney, Downie, Rowley,
Pearson, McGlen.

JOHN DOWNS LIVERPOOL

30 August 1950
First Division
United 1 (Downie), Liverpool 0.

After the excitement of the previous week, the return at Old Trafford was a disappointing affair with few thrills. The hopes of the large away following were dampened before kick-off when Billy Liddell was ruled out with a leg strain.

Liverpool rarely threatened to get back into the game once John Downie gave United the lead midway through the opening period. Only in the last ten minutes of the game did the Merseysiders manage to force United onto the defensive but at no time could they find the way to beat 'keeper Reg Allen.

United would go on to finish runners-up for a fourth time in five seasons as the main prize continued to elude them. Liverpool ended in ninth place.

United: Allen, Carey, Aston, Gibson, Chilton, Cockburn, Bogan, Downie, Rowley,
   Pearson, McGlen.
Liverpool: Sidlow, Shepherd, Spicer, Jones, Hughes, Paisley, Payne, Taylor, Done,
   Fagan, Brierley.

DEBUTS FOR 'BABES' BYRNE AND BLANCHFLOWER

24 November 1951
First Division
Liverpool 0, United 0.

Having missed out on a first title in forty years by finishing in second place at the end of the previous season, Matt Busby was slowing refashioning his side and in this game he gave debuts to full-back Roger Byrne and Jackie Blanchflower at right half. Liverpool, who were ninth and two places behind their visitors, had a new man in charge of first-team affairs with Don Welsh arriving from Brighton in March 1951 to replace George Kay as manager.

The crowd of just over 42,000 witnessed a poor game with little goalmouth action, with even the change of ball at half-time to a white one, more easily seen in the gloomy conditions failing to spice things up.

The new ball should have nestled in the Liverpool net within minutes but, rising unmarked, Jack Rowley headed Ernie Bond's cross well wide. Liverpool had appealed strongly in the first half for a penalty when their former player Allenby Chilton appeared to have elbowed Jack Smith off the ball inside the area, but the referee ruled it was outside. In truth neither side did enough to present a strong claim for both points.

Liverpool: Ashcroft, Jones, Lambert, Heydon, Hughes, Paisley, Jackson, Baron, Smith, Payne, Liddell.

United: Crompton, Carey, Byrne, Blanchflower, Chilton, Cockburn, Berry, Pearson, Rowley, Downie, Bond.

ASHCROFT A RIGHT LIVERPOOL CHARLIE

12 April 1952
First Division
United 4 (Byrne 2 (1 pen.), Downie, Rowley), Liverpool 0.

By the time of the return, Manchester United had suffered just two defeats in eighteen games since the sides had met at Anfield. The trouble was that they had both come in the last three games and, with the other match drawn, Matt Busby's lead at the top of the table had been cut such that, prior to kick-off, they were in a three-way tie with Arsenal and Portsmouth. Liverpool had also improved since November and, although unable to win the title, were only six points behind the leaders in fifth place.

Goalkeeper Charlie Ashcroft had been one of the stars of the Liverpool side during the season, relegating Cyril Sidlow to the reserves as he played 34 of his side's 42 League matches. Only weeks earlier he'd been considered good enough to play for England 'B' against Holland in Amsterdam but he was to blot his copybook this particular day

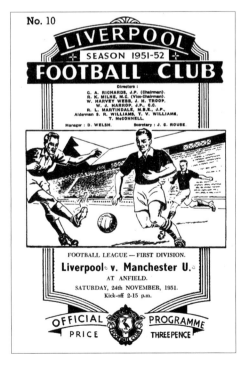

with a poor game. He'd had no chance with the first when Roger Byrne scored from the spot after Bill Jones punched out Stan Pearson's shot for a penalty. Liverpool might have gone in level only for Reg Allen to make a great save from Kevin Baron to keep his side ahead at the break.

The game was wrapped up in an eight-minute spell early in the second half. First Ashcroft dropped Byrne's cross to leave John Downie with a simple chance, and then Byrne followed up on an Ashcroft fumble to make it 3-0 before Rowley guided the ball beyond the 'keeper for the fourth. News that Arsenal had been beaten 2-1 at Bolton capped off a great day for United who, with seven points from the final four games of the season, captured the title by four points from the Gunners and thus entered the record books as the third United side to win the First Division title after previous successes in 1907/08 and 1910/11.

United: Allen, McNulty, Aston, Carey, Chilton, Whitefoot, Berry, Downie, Rowley, Pearson, Byrne.
Liverpool: Ashcroft, Lambert, Parr, Jones, Heydon, Paisley, Jackson, Baron, Smith, Payne, Liddell.

UNITED PILE ON MISERY

13 December 1952
First Division
Liverpool 1 (Liddell), United 2 (Aston, Pearson).

Liverpool were aiming to put an indifferent season behind them. There were less than 35,000 at Anfield but the majority were in a happy mood at half-time after Billy Liddell had given the home side an early lead against a side featuring Billy Foulkes for the first time.

However, five minutes after the restart, Stan Pearson headed the ball down to John Aston, who showed calmness as he drove a low shot no more than a couple of inches off the ground past the Liverpool 'keeper. Liddell then had a fine shot saved by Jack Crompton.

A fine run by Aston seconds later saw him round Bill Jones before pulling the ball back for Pearson to push towards the goal and, despite the frantic efforts of Ashcroft and Phil Taylor, the ball trickled over the line for the winning goal. Albert Stubbins drove a last-minute effort from outside the box just over the bar as United clung on for victory.

Liverpool: Ashcroft, Jones, Moran, Taylor, Heydon, Paisley, Payne, Baron, Stubbins, Smith, Liddell.
United: Crompton, Foulkes, Byrne, Carey, Chilton, Cockburn, Berry, Doherty, Aston, Pearson, Pegg.

LIVERPOOL RELEGATION THREAT

20 April 1953
First Division
United 3 (Pearson, Rowley, Berry), Liverpool 1 (Smyth).

Having long since dropped out of the title race, reigning champions United's last home game of the 1952/53 season drew less than 21,000. A good number had journeyed from Merseyside, desperate to see their side put behind them a terrible season by bringing to an end a six-match losing run away from home. As they only had one game left after their visit to Old Trafford, Liverpool faced dropping down to Division Two, where they last played in 1904/05.

It was going to be difficult. Though Billy Liddell returned after injury, Liverpool were weakened by the absence of regulars Jack Smith, Roy Saunders, Russell Crossley and Jack Balmer. It showed as United raced into a two-goal lead within ten minutes through goals from Stan Pearson and Jack Rowley.

And with no recovery in sight, the lead was extended after eighty minutes when Johnny Berry ran from beyond the centre circle to send the ball into the net and the few remaining away fans headed to the exits, thus missing out on Sammy Smyth's late consolation effort. Travelling home, they knew that Liverpool now had to beat Chelsea in their final game of the season in order to preserve forty-three years of top-flight football. Goals by Bill Jones and Louis Bimpson secured the victory, but a failure to improve the following season was to prove fatal.

United: Crompton, Aston, Byrne, Carey, Chilton, Whitefoot, Berry, Downie, Taylor, Pearson, Rowley.
Liverpool: Ashcroft, Jones, Lambert, Maloney, Taylor, Williams, Payne, Bimpson, Smyth, Rowley, Liddell.

LIVERPOOL LOSE TWO-GOAL LEAD

22 August 1953
First Division
Liverpool 4 (Bimpson 3, Jones), United 4 (Rowley, Lewis, Byrne (pen.), Taylor).

Anfield witnessed a thrilling game when United were early visitors as the two teams shared eight goals. Liverpool looked on it as a lost opportunity, though, as they held a 4-2 lead just short of the hour.

It looked bad for Liverpool when Jack Rowley gave United an early lead, but eleven minutes later 'keeper Jack Crompton's attempt to block Billy Liddell's shot saw the ball bounce down off the bar where the onrushing Louis Bimpson forced home the equaliser. If the United 'keeper was looking to forget his woes with a half-time cup of tea, it proved difficult as seconds before the break he failed to collect a Jimmy Payne cross and when Liddell pushed it across the goal, Bill Jones had no problems in hitting the empty net.

The equaliser, three minutes after the restart, was controversial as Tommy Taylor went down theatrically following a challenge from Ray Lambert for a penalty kick which Roger Byrne smashed home. Urged on by a noisy home crowd, Liverpool hit back with two goals in five minutes to lead 4-2 after fifty-eight minutes. Bimpson, by scoring both, became the first Liverpool player to score a hat-trick in the fixtures between the sides since Fred Howe in 1936. Liddell's corners had been perfectly flighted and Bimpson had done superbly to push the ball beyond Crompton.

If United were to get anything from the game then a quick reply was essential and they got one on the hour, Eddie Lewis lobbing the ball beyond Ashcroft. The equaliser took longer to arrive but with seven minutes remaining Tommy Taylor, after appearing to control the ball with his arm, bundled it home, flattening Ashcroft in the process.

Liverpool: Ashcroft, Lambert, Spicer, Taylor, Hughes, Paisley, Payne, Baron, Bimpson, Jones, Liddell.

United: Crompton, Aston, Byrne, Gibson, Chilton, Cockburn, Berry, Rowley, Taylor, Lewis, Pegg.

19 December 1953
First Division
United 5 (Blanchflower 2, Taylor 2, Viollet), Liverpool 1 (Bimpson).

Liverpool travelled to Old Trafford in desperate need of points. Don Welsh's side had lost 5-1 at Fratton Park the previous Saturday, establishing a record tenth consecutive away defeat since the season's start. The run was in fact seventeen, as the last seven away games of the previous season had also been lost. The result had left the Anfield side in twenty-first place, level on points with bottom club and big spenders Sunderland. United were in ninth place, eleven points behind joint-leaders West Bromwich Albion and Wolves. It was hardly surprising, therefore, that Old Trafford was only half-full, with just over 26,000 present.

For the second successive season, United won the fixture by a four-goal margin and it could easily have been more. Tommy Taylor put United ahead within a quarter of an hour of the kick-off following a defensive mix-up. If that wasn't bad enough, much worse was the fact that in trying to prevent the goal Eddie Spicer hurt himself clashing with Taylor and, with his legs bandaged together, he disappeared on a stretcher with a suspected broken leg. It was an injury Spicer never recovered from, retiring soon after at the age of thirty-one.

A goal up and with a man extra, United took full advantage. Liverpool 'keeper David Underwood made some good saves but could not prevent United doubling their advantage after thirty-four minutes, Jackie Blanchflower scoring the first of his two goals.

Dennis Viollet and Taylor doubled the home side's advantage. Four down, Louis Bimpson, who earlier in the season scored four times at Anfield against Burnley and a hat-trick against United, grabbed a consolation but United's fifth from Blanchflower with eleven minutes remaining restored the four-goal cushion.

With Sunderland drawing at home to Newcastle, Liverpool slipped to bottom place in the table. Though they finally brought to an end a dreadful run of away defeats by drawing their fourteenth away game at Turf Moor, they finished bottom of the League at the season's end and were relegated. It was to be sometime before the fixtures between United and Liverpool were to resume.

Liverpool's run of twenty consecutive away defeats, starting with the final seven games of the 52/53 season through to the fourteenth game of the 1953/54 season, is perhaps the club's most unwelcome record.

United: Wood, Foulkes, Byrne, Whitefoot, Chilton, Edwards, Berry, Blanchflower, Taylor, Viollet, Rowley.

Liverpool: Underwood, Lambert, Spicer, Saunders, Wilkinson, Twentyman, Jackson, Baron, Bimpson, Smyth, Liddell.

5
Both Clubs Rebuild

Liverpool's relegation in 1954 was to bring to an end the League games between the clubs until 1962. In the intervening period Matt Busby's rebuilding had created a brilliant side that would surely have become the first to complete the League and Cup 'double' in the twentieth century if it hadn't been for a vicious Roy McParland challenge that left United 'keeper Ray Wood with a fractured cheekbone. It proved a pivotal moment in the 1957 FA Cup final as Aston Villa triumphed 2-1 at Wembley. Having won the First Division in consecutive seasons, Busby's side was then advancing menacingly behind leaders Wolverhampton Wanderers with a third of the 1957/58 season remaining when a far greater tragedy occurred as the squad travelled back from a match with Red Star Belgrade after securing a European Cup semi-final encounter against AC Milan.

Stopping over in Munich to refuel, the plane crash that followed during an abortive take-off saw eight players and three key club officials among the twenty-three people killed. Johnny Berry and Jackie Blanchflower also suffered career-ending injuries, while youngsters Kenny Morgans and Albert Scanlon were never quite as good when they were able to return to action. Busby himself was given up for dead, and he was even read the last rites.

Following the tragedy, Liverpool, like many other clubs, offered Manchester United a chance to take some of their players as part of their rebuilding programme. Laurie Hughes, the former England centre half, was made available on a free transfer but in the event the offer was never taken up.

Amazingly, acting manager Jimmy Murphy, who'd only missed Belgrade as he was on international duty with Wales, utilised all the remaining players at his disposal and by adding a few experienced signings somehow got United to Wembley for another Cup final. In the circumstances, being beaten 2-0 by Bolton Wanderers was a truly remarkable achievement and, with Busby slowing resuming his role as manager, the spirit engendered during this time even took United as far as finishing as League runners-up the following season.

Liverpool, meanwhile, were doing their best to stay where they were. Successive promotion challenges were mounted but despite never finishing outside the top four the Anfield side was no nearer the top flight than the day they left it when Bill Shankly was appointed manager in December 1959.

The memorial plaque to the Manchester United players and officials who died in the Munich air disaster and (*inset*) a commemorative clock showing the date and time of the disaster.

One of his first games in charge was the FA Cup third round match against United at a time when Busby and Murphy were, once again, slowly rebuilding a new side to take them back to the summit of English football and a further challenge in Europe.

BOBBY DAZZLES IN CUP CLASH

30 January 1960
FA Cup, Fourth Round
Liverpool 1 (Wheeler), United 3 (Charlton 2, Bradley).

Bill Shankly could not possibly have had time to put his stamp on the club or side and Liverpool's defeat meant they would have to wait at least another season before recording their first FA Cup success, their best efforts having been in 1914 and 1950 as losing finalists to Burnley and Arsenal respectively.

The match was a personal triumph for Bobby Charlton, who in previous weeks had appeared to lack confidence, but his two fine goals set up a comfortable win for Matt Busby's side.

However it was new boy Maurice Setters, signed only weeks earlier from West Bromwich Albion, who proved the most influential player by breaking up a wave of home attacks in which Jimmy Melia and Roger Hunt were prominent. Indeed, if Hunt

had managed to push a first-minute shot round Setters on the line, the match might have proven a much more difficult affair for United.

Charlton opened the scoring twelve minutes later when, after dribbling round Johnny Wheeler and John Molyneux, his shot had just too much pace for Liverpool 'keeper Bert Slater. However, Liverpool were level after thirty-six minutes when Harry Gregg failed to collect Ronnie Moran's free-kick and, when the ball ran loose, Wheeler was in sharply and the ground erupted into a frenzy.

Just before half-time, United strode back into the lead when Warren Bradley's centre was swept home by Charlton, who was unlucky in the second forty-five minutes not to get his hat-trick when his cannonball shot struck the 'keeper, who knew little about it. Bradley, who United signed from amateur club Bishop Auckland soon after Munich, scored the third United goal and it was a fine effort, jinking inside to blast home the ball off the underside of the crossbar for what proved to be his only FA Cup goal during his four years at Old Trafford.

By the time the sides next met it was, again, in the First Division after Liverpool had run away with the Division Two title in the 1961/62 season when Roger Hunt scored 41 League goals to earn a first England call-up.

Liverpool: Slater, Molyneux, Moran, Wheeler, White, Leishman, Melia, Hunt, Hickson, Harrower, A'Court.
United: Gregg, Foulkes, Carolan, Setters, Cope, Brennan, Bradley, Quixall, Viollet, Charlton, Scanlon.

BOTH CLUBS IN RELEGATION SCRAP

10 November 1962
First Division
United 3 (Herd, Quixall (pen.), Giles), Liverpool 3 (St John, Melia, Moran).

Both sides were in desperate need of points prior to kick-off; Liverpool needed to avoid slipping back down into Division Two at the first attempt while United were just two places higher in the table at eighteenth.

Matt Busby's side had beaten League champions Ipswich Town 5-0 in the previous match and looked set for a further two points when they led 2-1 going into the final five minutes of the match against a Liverpool team with just two points from their eight previous away games.

The home side had struck first in windy conditions when Albert Quixall, who earlier had been denied by a fine Tommy Lawrence save, provided a superb defence-splitting pass for David Herd to run clear and the centre forward made no mistake from ten yards as Lawrence advanced.

Liverpool had rarely threatened during the first half but equalised on fifty-one minutes when following a miskick by Hunt, Ian Callaghan drove a powerful shot that

Harry Gregg did well to save but couldn't hang on to and Ian St John was the sharpest man around to push home the loose ball.

United though were soon back in front, Quixall scoring from the spot after Melia had upended Johnny Giles. The Liverpool man made amends on eighty-five minutes when he chased down a Ron Yeats header that seemed certain to go out for a goal kick and somehow managed to squeeze the ball into the net from an impossible angle. Four minutes later it seemed as if Liverpool had both points in the bag when Ronnie Moran's thirty-yard free-kick almost broke the back of the net.

There was bitter disappointment for Shankly's side when with only seconds to go Giles scored the equaliser, cutting between Moran and Yeats – both of whom appeared willing to leave the tackling to the other – and when the Irishman saw Lawrence closing him down he beat the 'keeper with a fine drilled shot to earn his side a valuable point.

United: Gregg, Brennan, Cantwell, Stiles, Foulkes, Setters, Giles, Quixall, Herd, Law, Charlton.
Liverpool: Lawrence, Byrne, Moran, Milne, Yeats, Stevenson, Callaghan, Hunt, St John, Melia, A'Court.

UNITED IN SURVIVAL BATTLE

13 April 1963
First Division
Liverpool 1 (St John), United 0.

Prior to kick-off, United were just three points clear of Birmingham City and the dreaded drop into Division Two. Winning at Anfield was going to be difficult as Liverpool had lost only three times in seventeen matches, and the previous day had hammered Tottenham Hotspur 5-2. Defeat followed by one point in a double-header with Leicester on Easter Monday and Tuesday threw Matt Busby's side into a desperate struggle to survive in the top flight.

The game itself was a poor one, enlivened only by its single goal which came after seventy-two minutes when Willie Stevenson made a fine defensive interception before moving forward to deliver a lovely pass to Roger Hunt, who stepped aside for Ian St John to advance and hit a fine shot into the net from twelve yards.

Earlier Liverpool might have had a penalty when Billy Foulkes barged over Hunt before Nobby Stiles annoyed the Kop by delivering what the *Liverpool Echo* described as a 'Churchillian gesture' and then added to their wrath when he, amazingly, bundled over the considerably larger Ron Yeats for a foul.

Only at the end did United look like scoring, when Bobby Charlton lobbed the ball over Allan Jones, in for the injured Gerry Byrne, before hitting a powerful shot that seemed net-bound only for 'keeper Tommy Lawrence to dive bravely and send the ball out for what proved to be a harmless corner.

Liverpool, in their first season back in the top flight, finished a highly respectable eighth while United ended fourth from bottom and only three points clear of the relegation places.

Liverpool: Lawrence, Jones, Moran, Milne, Yeats, Stevenson, Callaghan, Hunt, St John, Arrowsmith, Melia.
United: Gregg, Brennan, Dunne, Crerand, Foulkes, Setters, Giles, Stiles, Quixall, Law, Charlton.

YEATS THE DESTROYER

23 November 1963
First Division
United 0, Liverpool 1 (Yeats).

How fortunes had changed as United were three points behind top-of-the-table Liverpool, a contrast to the previous season in which both sides were at one stage battling relegation. Having played one game more than Liverpool, Matt Busby would

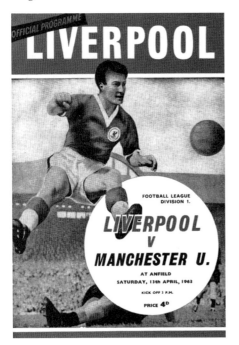

have realised beforehand that a win was a necessity if they were to give themselves a chance of overhauling leaders Liverpool at the top.

The match, which took place as the world came to terms with the assassination of American President John F. Kennedy in Dallas, proved to be a tight affair with few first-half chances. Peter Thompson floated over a corner and when Ron Yeats and 'keeper Harry Gregg smashed into each other in a determined rush for the ball, only a desperate Maurice Setters goal-line clearance, made at the expense of crashing into the post, prevented the opening goal. The United midfielder's brave intervention was not without repercussion, however, as he was knocked out, while lying close to him unconscious was Gregg, who had fractured his collarbone.

Setters was at least able to resume playing after the break, playing in front of centre forward David Herd, who had replaced Gregg in goal. The Irishman, who had pulled people out of the plane wreckage at Munich, was determined to go back on – although there was no chance of playing in goal!

Harry Gregg recalls that:

> After my collar bone was pushed back into place I insisted on having a shirt pulled over and my arm strapped up. By going back out and playing centre forward I ignored the pleading of the orthopaedic surgeon Mr Glass and afterwards I was told it could have pierced my neck or lung. Later I got the biggest rollicking of my whole career for going back onto the field.
>
> Big Ron Yeats broke my collarbone. Ron was a great header of the ball, but for a big lad he could also get it down and use it pretty well to bring other players into the game. The

games against Liverpool were a derby match twice over, and the atmosphere before each game either at Old Trafford or Anfield was something else.

Liverpool fans always gave the away players abuse, but none more so than the 'keepers and if you also played for United then it was a whole lot worse. On the pitch there would also be abuse. As I dived at the feet of Ian St John he would be telling me how he'd break my leg and I'd reply that if he did I would stuff it down his throat. None of the on-field animosities ever spilled over into after-match events, and like most United players I had a good relationship with many Liverpool players, especially St John.

Goalkeeping at the start of the sixties was different compared to today when they are much more protected. Nowadays the 'keepers also punch the ball. If you did that then, there would have been no contract at the end of the season. Goalkeepers were expected to catch the ball and deal with the consequences of forwards challenging for the ball. We'd also go down at attacking forwards' feet in an attempt to gather the ball, while nowadays the 'keepers try to spread themselves in a star shape.

Inspired by Gregg's never-say-die attitude, United worked to close down the Liverpool midfield but should have fallen behind when St John's weighted pass sent Roger Hunt clear only for the England international to lose his balance as he shaped to shoot, allowing Herd to gratefully collect the ball.

Liverpool finally scored after seventy-five minutes when Yeats rose to power Ian Callaghan's corner beyond Herd. It was the Scotsman's first goal since arriving from Dundee for a fee of £22,000 in the summer of 1961 and it was enough to seal victory. Yeats was to score 16 times for Liverpool; although ironically his most famous goal during his ten years at Anfield was one he put into his own net as it proved to be the winner for Borussia Dortmund in the final of the Cup Winners' Cup in 1966. Liverpool were bidding to follow Tottenham Hotspur and West Ham United by becoming the third English side to win the competition, which was absorbed into the UEFA Cup at the end of the 1998/99 season.

Liverpool: Lawrence, Jones, Moran, Milne, Yeats, Stevenson, Callaghan, Hunt, St John, Arrowsmith, Melia.
United: Gregg, Brennan, Crerand, Foulkes, Setters, Giles, Stiles, Quixall, Law, Charlton.

LIVERPOOL CLOSE IN ON TITLE

4 April 1964
First Division
Liverpool 3 (Callaghan, Arrowsmith 2), United 0.

By the time of the return, Liverpool were advancing on a first Division One title since the twenties. With Nobby Stiles replacing the injured Ian Moir, United were hoping to prevent Liverpool taking an early lead and Alf Arrowsmith, enjoying his finest season during his career at Anfield, was denied by a fine save from Harry Gregg as

United defended the Kop end. However, from the resulting corner the United 'keeper's attempted catch saw him lose possession and, following a delightful Roger Hunt back-heel, Ian Callaghan somehow managed to get the ball home from a tight angle.

With United showing little in attack it was no surprise when Liverpool doubled their lead after thirty-nine minutes when Arrowsmith headed home Callaghan's pull back. Arrowsmith's second, early in the second half, was a great goal after a slick passing move. The ball was fed to Roger Hunt who, from just outside the area, slipped it inside to Arrowsmith, who beat Gregg from ten yards.

There were still nearly forty minutes remaining and, with the Kop urging United to go home, there was never any likelihood of Matt Busby's side rescuing even a point, although Denis Law showed he wasn't prepared to go down without a fight as he earned a booking for flattening his fellow Scot Ian St John. On another day he might have been sent off, but the loss of both points was damage enough for a side that had also just lost in the FA Cup semi-final to West Ham United. Law's consolation was to come a few weeks later when he became the first, and to date, only Scotsman to be named European Footballer of the Year. By then Liverpool had won the First Division title in only Shankly's fourth full season in charge, with United finishing runners-up, a remarkable achievement bearing in mind their scrap against relegation twelve months earlier.

United: Gregg, Brennan, Dunne, Crerand, Foulkes, Setters, Best, Stiles, Herd, Law, Charlton.
Liverpool: Lawrence, Byrne, Moran, Milne, Yeats, Stevenson, Callaghan, Hunt, St John, Arrowsmith, Thompson.

UNITED TOP OF THE TABLE

31 October 1964
First Division
Liverpool 0, United 2 (Herd, Crerand).

After their title triumph the previous season, Liverpool started the 1964/65 campaign poorly and were struggling in eighteenth place when Matt Busby's side arrived after having thrashed Aston Villa 7-0 the previous weekend. Victory, with leaders Chelsea losing, saw United move proudly to the top of the League.

Two goals was, in fact, poor reward for a United side that, apart from a brief spell after half-time when Liverpool attacked the Kop, dominated throughout. United's speed constantly had Liverpool on the back foot and it was a surprise that it wasn't until the thirty-fifth minute that they took the lead. It was a fortunate goal and came when Bobby Charlton swung the ball into the middle and Denis Law's header glanced off Ron Yeats and bounced just right for David Herd to smash it into the net from close range.

With Liverpool failing to trouble Pat Dunne in the United goal, Charlton looked to have doubled his side's lead after fifty-five minutes only for his thirty-yard shot to

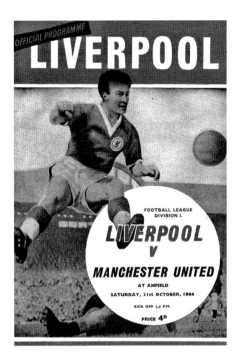

whistle just wide. Yet with Charlton and Paddy Crerand running the midfield, a second goal wasn't long in arriving. Charlton slipped the ball to Crerand, who played return pass with Law before calmly lobbing the ball over 'keeper Tommy Lawrence and into the net off the crossbar.

United's ability to strike with such directness was the difference between the sides and, although Bobby Graham had two late shots blocked, it was a well-beaten Liverpool side that trooped off to the jeers of some of the home supporters.

Liverpool: Lawrence, Lawler, Byrne, Milne, Yeats, Stevenson, Callaghan, Hunt, St John, Graham, Thompson.

United: P. Dunne, Brennan, A. Dunne, Crerand, Foulkes, Stiles, Connelly, Charlton, Herd, Law, Best.

TITLE HEADS TO OLD TRAFFORD

April 24, 1965
First Division
United 3 (Connelly, Law 2), Liverpool 0.

Five League wins in a row had seen United haul themselves above Chelsea and Leeds United in an enthralling race for the title. Having lost just once at home, Matt Busby's side was looking to record the double over their local rivals, whose minds were likely to be pre-occupied with their big day at Wembley where they would face Leeds United in the FA Cup final. It was a chance for Liverpool to win the competition for the first time in their long history.

United attacked from the start and the only shock was how long it took to grab the lead. There were six minutes of the first period remaining when Ron Yeats failed to get sufficient distance on a headed clearance and Denis Law pounced to drive the ball home from ten yards.

The lead was doubled six minutes after the restart when Law met Crerand's cross to hammer home before the United forward crashed into the net. Law might have even grabbed a hat-trick but, after some mesmerising play from George Best, Law was just unable to get on the end of the United winger's cross-cum-shot at the back post.

The game was over as a contest after eighty-eight minutes when John Connelly, Bobby Charlton and Paddy Crerand linked up on the left before Crerand delivered a ball across the box for Connelly to score from close range and allow Matt Busby to dream of a first Division One title since before Munich.

United edged out Leeds on goal difference for the title while Liverpool, who finished seventh after their awful start, also finished with silverware as they lifted the FA Cup. Leeds were the bridesmaids, finishing runners-up in both League and Cup.

United: P. Dunne, Brennan, A. Dunne, Crerand, Foulkes, Stiles, Connelly, Charlton, Cantwell, Law, Best.
Liverpool: Lawrence, Lawler, Byrne, Strong, Yeats, Stevenson, Graham, Hunt, Chisnall, Smith, Thompson.

UNITED TWICE LOSE LEAD

14 August 1965
Charity Shield
United 2 (Best, Herd), Liverpool 2 (Stevenson, Yeats)
(at Old Trafford)

As United held off a strong Leeds United title challenge and Liverpool had beaten Don Revie's side in the FA Cup final the previous season, the sides met in the Charity Shield before the start of the 1965/66 season.

Lacking the cut and thrust of a League or Cup match, it still proved entertaining fare with George Best scoring a thrilling opening goal. He received the ball from Bobby Charlton before cutting inside to beat 'keeper Tommy Lawrence with a rasping drive. The equaliser was just as good, Willie Stevenson cutting though the middle after a solo run before hammering home a drive from twenty-five yards.

David Herd appeared to have won the match when Lawrence misjudged the pace of his shot with eight minutes remaining, but Ron Yeats headed home after eighty-five minutes to see the game end all square as both sides shared the Shield.

United: P. Dunne, Brennan, A. Dunne, Crerand, Cantwell, Stiles, Best (Anderson), Charlton, Herd, Aston.
Liverpool: Lawrence, Lawlor, Byrne, Milne, Yeats, Stevenson, Callaghan, Hunt, St John, Smith, Strong.

UNITED GET BACK ON TRACK

9 October 1965
First Division
United 2 (Best, Law), Liverpool 0.

United made a desperately poor start to their title defence, but showed why they were reigning champions as they recorded a third consecutive League victory over their great rivals with a comfortable win.

They had been in the bottom half of the table, but this victory pushed United up to eleventh place while Liverpool remained in sixth spot.

Denis Law should have given his side an early lead but from almost underneath the posts he somehow conspired to fire over. The Scotsman was then only inches away from getting on the end of George Best's shot before 'keeper Tommy Lawrence pulled off a fine save from a powerful Paddy Crerand drive as United maintained their first-half superiority.

It was no surprise when United took the lead through Best. When he collided with Lawrence, the ball ran free and the Northern Ireland international ignored Liverpool's claims for a free-kick by sweeping home the rebound. Six minutes before the break Manchester United established a commanding lead when Bobby Charlton opened up the Liverpool defence with a beautifully weighted pass that allowed Law to push the ball under the diving Lawrence.

The second half was, with Liverpool offering no serious threat up front, a chance for Matt Busby's side to show off some of their skills with Law, Crerand and Charlton keeping possession and Best constantly picking up any loose balls before beating any defender who attempted to take the ball off him.

United: P. Dunne, Brennan, A. Dunne, Crerand, Foulkes, Stiles, Connelly, Best, Charlton, Law, Aston.
Liverpool: Lawrence, Lawler, Byrne, Strong, Yeats, Stevenson, Callaghan, Hunt, St John, Smith, Thompson.

LIVERPOOL MOUNT TITLE CHARGE

1 January 1966
First Division
Liverpool 2 (Smith, Milne), United 1 (Law).

By the time of the return fixture, both sides had spectacularly moved up the First Division table such that when they ran out at Anfield on New Year's Day it was a case of first versus third, with Burnley in between.

With thousands locked out, the atmosphere inside Anfield was electric. Initially it was the United fans that were in a party mood. There were only two minutes gone when Denis Law, whose upper body strength proved even too much for the muscular Ron Yeats, seized upon Harry Gregg's long clearance and, as Tommy Lawrence raced to block, rounded the 'keeper with a beautiful piece of close control before stroking the ball into the net at the Kop end.

Liverpool poured forward. The ever-alert Ian St John volleyed just over but, just when it seemed United might make it safely through to half-time, Tommy Smith, after beating Best, equalised with a half-hit shot that Gregg should have easily saved. The United 'keeper was to prove far more formidable in the second period, denying in particular St John with a series of great saves. United were fortunate, however, when St John hit the inside of the post with Nobby Stiles hacking clear the loose ball.

Then, with only two minutes remaining, Liverpool struck when Gregg, coming out for a corner, was forced to punch. Gerry Byrne hit the ball back towards the goal and Gordon Milne got the slightest of touches to take it away from the 'keeper and into the net for the winning goal. Liverpool, whose fans were ecstatic, were marching towards their second League title in three seasons while United finished fourth.

Liverpool: Lawrence, Lawler, Byrne, Milne, Yeats, Stevenson, Callaghan, Hunt, St John, Smith, Thompson.
United: Gregg, Dunne, Cantwell, Crerand, Foulkes, Stiles, Best, Law, Charlton, Herd, Connelly.

BATTLE OF THE TOP TWO

10 December 1966
First Division
United 2 (Best 2 (1 pen.), Liverpool 2 (St John 2).

When reigning champions Liverpool travelled to play League leaders United, only two points separated the sides and the large crowd inside Old Trafford was to witness a thrilling match.

The action was only thirteen minutes old when Liverpool took the lead with a marvellous goal. Ian St John was sent clear after a pinpoint pass from Gordon Milne and, as he took the ball away from David Sadler, he advanced to beat Alex Stepney with a cool side-footed finish from ten yards. Milne, a polished wing-half, was to be the outstanding player in this game.

United, unbeaten at home, were soon back on level terms. A misplaced Geoff Strong pass was seized upon by David Herd, who sent George Best away and he finished with a strong, left-foot shot from eighteen yards. The game then moved from end to end, as first one side attacked with pace and then the other. Another goal was a certainty, but who would snatch it?

Paddy Crerand's brilliant ball sent Jimmy Ryan charging into the box and Ron Yeats, attempting to prevent the twenty-one-year-old from shooting, only succeeded in giving away a penalty which Best stroked home. Seconds before half-time, St John scored his second of the match as the United defence hesitated as a Chris Lawler corner bounced around the box.

After four goals and so much excitement in the first period, the second was a more sedate affair. Yeats produced a brilliant last-gasp tackle to deny David Herd a run through on goal. Then, in the last minute, Peter Thompson could have won the match but, after controlling St John's through-ball, the Liverpool winger fluffed his shot and, with the rain lashing down, United survived.

United: Stepney, Brennan, Noble, Crerand, Sadler, Dunne, Best, Ryan, Charlton, Herd, Aston.
Liverpool: Lawrence, Lawler, Milne, Smith, Yeats, Stevenson, Callaghan, Hunt, St John, Strong, Thompson.

UNITED CHAMPIONS AGAIN

25 March 1967
First Division
Liverpool 0, United 0.

It was hardly surprising Anfield was a sell-out as United were unbeaten in ten League games and Liverpool undefeated at home in the League. Fans were hoping for another thrilling occasion as the top two in the League met with ten games of the 1966/67 season remaining. Victory for Liverpool would have taken them level with their opponents but in the event the sides were forced to settle for a point each, a result clearly of greater satisfaction to United.

The game was an uncompromising one, with Ron Yeats and Denis Law constantly at each other's throats, and for a time the action could easily have continued without a ball! Only once in the first half was either 'keeper's goal threatened, when Willie Stevenson drove a free-kick just wide.

The second was little better although Roger Hunt was unfortunate to be denied when Nobby Stiles made a remarkable goal-line clearance and Peter Thompson had a shot that whistled just over.

United remained at the top of the table and, by maintaining their unbeaten run to the end of the season, they were to go on and capture the title for the second time in three seasons. Liverpool were fifth.

Liverpool: Lawrence, Lawler, Hughes, Smith, Yeats, Stevenson, Callaghan, Hunt, St John, Strong, Thompson.

United: Stepney, Dunne, Noble, Crerand, Foulkes, Stiles, Best, Law, Sadler, Charlton, Aston.

GEORGE AT HIS BEST FOR UNITED

11 November 1967
First Division
Liverpool 1 (Hunt), United 2 (Best 2).

First against second and, with Liverpool having previously won all seven home League games, Matt Busby's side knew they would have to play magnificently if they were to return with both points.

As Nobby Stiles was injured, David Sadler was brought into a United side which was also missing the suspended Denis Law. Many of the day's top pundits, including those of the *Liverpool Echo*, felt United, without Law's influence, would struggle to score the goals needed to maintain a title challenge.

George Best took over from Law at inside left with John Fitzpatrick coming in at outside right, and he responded with both goals, securing a massive away win for United. In a season when Law also missed a number of games due to injury, Best was at his goalscoring peak and was to end the season as equal top-scorer – with Southampton's Ron Davies – in the League with 28 goals.

'Liverpool toppled by George,' was the headline in the *Liverpool Sports Echo* after this match on Armistice Day. With Anfield again full to capacity United, playing in blue, won the toss and elected to attack the Kop end in the second half. They were ahead after ten minutes when Best's fine glancing header from a John Aston corner beat Tommy Lawrence. Best was then denied by a fine save from the 'keeper after Bobby Charlton's precision pass had sent him clear. When Liverpool did rally, Tony Hateley headed Peter Thompson's corner wide, Liverpool's only first-half effort.

United took a two-goal lead into the break after Paddy Crerand's long, accurate pass was seized upon by Best, who beat Lawrence from inside the penalty area. Liverpool played a lot better in the second forty-five minutes and Alex Stepney made a great save to deny Tommy Smith, but with Best in outstanding form there was always the constant danger of a third breakaway goal and only two great tackles by Chris Lawler and Emlyn Hughes respectively prevented him from completing his hat-trick.

Liverpool were handed a lifeline five minutes from the end when Roger Hunt took a reverse pass from Ian St John before turning the ball past Stepney. Then, with only seconds to go, St John had the ball in the net only for the effort to be rightly ruled offside as United journeyed home with two valuable points.

Liverpool: Lawrence, Lawler, Byrne, Smith, Yeats, Hughes, Callaghan, Hunt, Hateley, St John, Thompson.

United: Stepney, Dunne, Burns, Crerand, Foulkes, Sadler, Fitzpatrick, Kidd, Charlton, Best.

CHAMPIONS OF EUROPE

6 April 1968
First Division
United 1 (Best), Liverpool 2 (Yeats, Hunt).

Apparently cruising to a second consecutive title with a three-point lead and a game in hand, Matt Busby's side suddenly hit a tricky patch with four defeats in seven League matches. Nevertheless, prior to kick-off they still stood proudly at the top of the League, but all three sides below them – Leeds United, Manchester City and fourth placed Liverpool – were aware they could overtake the leaders if they won their games in hand.

After missing three games due to injury, Tony Hateley returned to the Liverpool side. Meanwhile, United were again without Denis Law and Nobby Stiles but nevertheless took the lead after only two minutes when Ron Yeats' free-kick was hit straight to Bobby Charlton, who took the ball down the right where his fine pass sent Best streaking clear to beat the advancing Lawrence. Things might even have got worse for Bill Shankly's side soon afterwards, but Lawrence kept his side in the game with a great save from Charlton.

It was just the jolt Liverpool needed as they hit back and were 2-1 ahead after seventeen minutes. First Yeats headed an Ian St John free-kick against the upright and, when the ball bounced back along the line, the big central defender turned it into the net. Then Roger Hunt, picking up Paddy Crerand's errant pass, moved the ball on quickly to Hateley, who turned it inside for St John, who pushed it perfectly to one side where Hunt beat Tony Dunne and then had no trouble slotting it beyond Alex Stepney for a great goal.

With Liverpool dominating throughout, only once did United look like they might fashion an undeserved equaliser, Alan Gowling forcing Lawrence into making a fine save. Midway through the second period Hunt had the chance to finish the match off but he shot straight at Stepney. Disappointed by what they were witnessing, many United fans headed home long before the end, fearing the worst in their side's bid to retain the title as Leeds United leapt to the top of the League with Liverpool lurking menacingly two points behind.

Surprisingly, Liverpool were to suffer a poor run of results over the next few matches and, with Leeds United also dropping away, the League title was to end in a battle between the sides from Manchester. Two defeats in the last three League games were to prove crucial for United's bid and, with City winning at St James' Park on the final day of the season, the First Division title went to Maine Road for the second time as Liverpool finished third.

Four days after the final League game, United qualified for the European Cup final by coming from two goals down to draw 3-3 with Real Madrid, progressing 4-3 on aggregate to play Benfica at Wembley. Matt Busby was now only weeks away from conquering Europe, with United set to become the first English side to capture the European Cup.

United: Stepney, Dunne, Burns, Crerand, Sadler, Fitzpatrick, Best, Gowling,
    Charlton, Herd, Aston.
Liverpool: Lawrence, Lawler, Ross, Strong, Yeats, Hughes, Callaghan, Hunt, Hateley
    (Arrowsmith), St John, Thompson.

UNITED EYE WORLD CROWN

12 October 1968
First Division
Liverpool 2 (St John, Evans), United 0.

Having failed to win any of their five away games of the season, this was going to be a difficult test for Matt Busby's side against a Liverpool side unbeaten at home and lying just a point behind Leeds United at the top of the table.

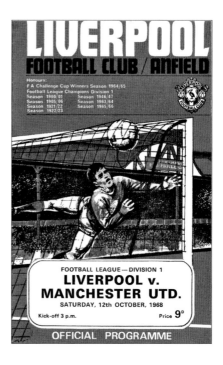

That was especially so because, with Argentinian side Estudiantes due at Old Trafford in midweek for the second leg of the World Club Championship, the United manager decided to rest some of his more experienced players, with Steve James and Carlo Sartori given their debuts and twenty-year-old Frank Kopel making one of his eight League appearances.

It was therefore no great surprise that the home side comfortably took both points. Peter Thompson created the opening goal with a fine run and cross for Ian St John to head home. Alex Stepney kept his side in the game with fine saves from a twenty-yard Tommy Smith drive and a Roger Hunt header. Just before the end, Liverpool's superiority was confirmed through a second goal from Alun Evans after he was set up by Callaghan.

Liverpool: Lawrence, Lawler, Strong, Smith, Yeats, Hughes, Callaghan, Hunt, Evans, St John, Thompson.
United: Stepney, Brennan, Kopel, Crerand, James, Stiles, Ryan, Fitzpatrick, Charlton, Gowling, Sartori.

14 December 1968
First Division
United 1 (Law), Liverpool 0.

Fifteenth place was hardly where you would expect to find the reigning European champions; United were hoping to dent their local rival's dash for the title, which had seen Liverpool establish a four-point lead at the top of the table. It looked a tall order as United had only won twice in eleven games, but they took both points with a brilliant second-half goal from Denis Law.

There was almost a sensational start to the game when, in the first few seconds, Tommy Smith tried to find 'keeper Tommy Lawrence with a back pass on a bone-hard pitch. As the ball bounced David Sadler and Lawrence raced for it and when they both failed to connect, it trickled between them and only just past the post. Lawrence did much better later in the half, going down quickly and bravely at the feet of George Best to prevent the opening goal.

Starting the move deep in the half, Bobby Charlton brought about Law's fifty-second-minute goal. The England man swung a long ball to Best, who took the ball to the edge of the area, where he spotted Law's raised arm on the far side and swung the ball over perfectly for the Scot to race in and head home for a goal worthy of winning any match.

Roger Hunt might have equalised but shot straight at Alex Stepney, but the save of the match came when Charlton hit a powerful drive from fifteen yards which Lawrence did brilliantly to rush out and block with his body.

United: Stepney, Dunne, Burns, Crerand, James, Stiles, Best, Sadler, Charlton, Law, Sartori.

Liverpool: Lawrence, Lawler, Strong, Smith, Yeats, Hughes, Callaghan, Hunt, Evans, St John, Thompson.

WILLIE'S WINNER CAUSES UPSET

13 September 1969
First Division
United 1 (Morgan), Liverpool 0.

Having won only the once that season in the First Division, nineteenth-placed United dented the League leaders' championship charge with a narrow, deserved victory that calmed any premature fears of a relegation struggle under new manager Wilf McGuinness.

Once again it was a match in which George Best sparkled and, although this time he failed to net, he was 'here, there and everywhere', picking up loose balls, beating opponents and at times turning right-back Ian Lawler inside-out.

Roger Hunt, starting for the last time in these fixtures, might have added to his two previous goals only to join Willie Morgan and Best by hitting the woodwork. Best would have an influential part to play in the match-winning goal, however, as he timed his jump to perfection to head the ball onto Alan Gowling, who in turn fed the ball perfectly to Morgan who showed good composure to drive the ball beyond the despairing dive of 'keeper Tommy Lawrence midway through the second half.

Pushing forward in search of an equaliser, Bill Shankly's side found the United defence in determined form, with Tony Dunne doing just enough to keep out Ian Callaghan down the Liverpool right.

United: Stepney, Fitzpatrick, Dunne, Burns, Ure, Sadler, Morgan, Kidd, Charlton, Gowling, Best.

Liverpool: Lawrence, Lawler, Strong, Smith, Yeats, Hughes, Callaghan, Hunt, Graham, St John, Thompson.

CHARLTON GEM SEALS BIG ANFIELD WIN

13 December 1969
First Division
Liverpool 1 (Hughes), United 4 (Yeats (o.g.), Ure, Morgan, Charlton).

Liverpool suffered their biggest home defeat in over five years, one which would not be equalled again until Chelsea arrived at Anfield in October 2005. It followed a tactical re-jig which worked to perfection; with Francis Burns selected to give United's midfield more defensive bite, and with Paddy Crerand selected for the first time since September, they produced a marvellous display.

Under pressure from David Sadler, Ronnie Yeats was unfortunate to put his side behind after twenty minutes through an own goal, only for Emlyn Hughes to quickly draw Liverpool level. Goals either side of the hour mark, however, from Ian Ure and Willie Morgan, both fine efforts, put United in control.

Then, with seven minutes remaining, came a goal of real class as Bobby Charlton played a one-two with Morgan before a slight glance up was followed by a ferocious drive that left Tommy Lawrence helpless. It was vintage Charlton and was so good that it even had Sir Matt Busby jumping to his feet in the directors' box, the ex-manager saying afterwards that he could never recall doing so in the past, even when sitting on the bench directing affairs on the pitch.

Liverpool, now gradually becoming a force under Bill Shankly, finished fifth with United eighth.

Liverpool: Lawrence, Lawler, Wall, Strong, Yeats, Hughes, Callaghan, Ross (Hunt), Thompson, St John, Graham.

United: Stepney, Brennan, Dunne, Burns, Ure, Sadler, Morgan, Best, Charlton, Crerand, Aston (Sartori).

UNITED EASE THEIR TROUBLES

5 September 1970
First Division
Liverpool 1 (A. Evans), United 1 (Kidd).

After a poor start to the season, United arrived at Anfield in need of a good display and, more importantly, points. Wilf McGuinness's side started well enough but, with Peter Thompson and Tommy Smith spurring them on, a young Liverpool side fought like tigers to earn a deserved draw.

Brian Kidd gave United the lead after twenty minutes, heading Nobby Stiles' astute cross beyond Ray Clemence, freshly installed as first-choice 'keeper after learning his trade in the reserves following his arrival from Scunthorpe United for £18,000 in the summer of 1967. Considering the 'keeper was to make 665 first-team appearances for Liverpool and win numerous honours, it is arguably the best money ever invested by Liverpool.

Liverpool were only behind for two minutes, however, as Alun Evans equalised with one of 15 goals scored in what was his most successful season. Manager Bill Shankly had paid Wolves £100,000 for the teenager who, as a sixteen-year-old, had given Ron Yeats a torrid time.

With Clemence between the posts, a Liverpool side slowly being re-fashioned by Shankly fought its way to the FA Cup final at the end of the season but, after taking the lead in extra-time, two late Arsenal goals helped ensure the Gunners did the League and Cup double.

Liverpool: Clemence, Lawler, R. Evans, Smith, Lloyd, Hughes, Callaghan, A. Evans, Graham, McLaughlin, Thompson.
United: Rimmer, Paul Edwards, Dunne, John Fitzpatrick, Ure, Sadler, Stiles, Law, Charlton, Kidd, Best.

LIVERPOOL'S BEST AWAY WIN

19 April 1971
First Division
United 0, Liverpool 2 (Heighway, Edwards (o.g.)).

There might have been only four points between the sides at kick-off, but long before the end United were a well-beaten side against a Liverpool team recording its biggest away victory of the season.

Peter Thompson, making a determined effort to win a place in the FA Cup final starting line-up against Arsenal in a few weeks time, was soon in action and John Toshack should have done better with a headed chance from a fine cross. Ron Yeats, playing only because Emlyn Hughes and Larry Lloyd were absent on England duty, then hit a fine shot that Alex Stepney did well to tip over the bar. Liverpool got their reward for a fine start to the game, Thompson floating over a cross that Toshack headed back across the goal for Steve Heighway to hook home after nineteen minutes.

It took United until after half-time to get in the game and George Best was the man responsible, with a header tipped over the bar by Ray Clemence and a free-kick that flashed narrowly wide. However, on the hour the game as a contest was effectively ended when centre half Paul Edwards, trying desperately to prevent Heighway getting to the ball, got himself in a terrible tangle and headed the ball beyond Stepney and into his own net. Liverpool had only previously scored 7 away League goals in 18 games but still had far too much for a poor United side, for whom Sir Matt Busby had resumed temporary charge of first-team affairs in December when Wilf McGuinness returned to coaching duties.

United: Stepney, Dunne, Burns, Crerand, Edwards, Sadler, Best, Gowling, Charlton, Law, Morgan.
Liverpool: Clemence, Lawler, Yeats, Smith, Ross, McLaughlin, Callaghan, Thompson, Heighway, Toshack, Hall.

UNITED BACK FROM THE DEAD

25 September 1971
First Division
Liverpool 2 (Graham, Hall), United 2 (Law, Charlton).

Power and precision were the trademark feature of many of Bobby Charlton's goals during his distinguished career. So when he received the ball at the angle of the penalty box with eighteen minutes left, Liverpool 'keeper Ray Clemence must have realised what was coming next.

Not that he could do anything about it as the ball rocketed past him to cap a stirring second-half comeback by United. Outplayed in the opening forty-five minutes, in which United were 2-0 behind, they gained a foothold back into the game after fifty-three minutes when George Best's superbly delivered pass gave Denis Law a simple chance.

Although Liverpool had started the match four points behind Frank O'Farrell's side, they were much the quicker into their stride and established a two-goal lead; though both enjoyed a touch of good fortune, they were good value for a 2-0 half-time lead. Bill Shankly's side had gone ahead within eight minutes, Bobby Graham confusing Alex Stepney with the slightest of deflections from Ian Callaghan's shot. If the United 'keeper cursed his bad luck, it was to get a lot worse seventeen minutes later, when he again went the wrong way after a shot from Ian Ross hit Brian Hall on the back before trickling over the line.

With Liverpool noisily backed by their fans on the Kop, they pressed for what would surely have been the killer third goal but, with David Sadler using every ounce of his experience, the United defence ensured they got to half-time still holding on to their 2-0 lead. The fact that at the end of ninety minutes they had surrendered a point was later bemoaned by the Liverpool manager, but with his team in the process of being rebuilt the performance augured well for the future. The result was also a confidence-booster for O'Farrell, who had replaced Sir Matt Busby after the Scotsman had retired permanently in the summer of 1971.

Liverpool: Clemence, Lawler, Lindsay, Ross, Lloyd, Hughes, Keegan, Hall, Heighway, Graham, Callaghan.

United: Stepney, O'Neil, Burns, Gowling, Steve James, Sadler, Morgan, Kidd, Charlton, Law, Best.

LIVERPOOL'S TITLE CHARGE

3 April 1972
First Division
United 0, Liverpool 3 (Lawler, Toshack, Hughes).
Liverpool had claimed nineteen points from a possible twenty from their previous ten matches so this was a game no United fan looked forward to.

Bill Shankly's side was pushing hard in a four-horse race with Derby County, Manchester City and Leeds United for the title. After a promising start to the season, including the earlier draw at Anfield, United had fallen some way behind their opponents. They had, though, won their last three games, taking some of the heat off Frank O'Farrell following a FA Cup quarter-final defeat to Stoke City. Martin Buchan had journeyed south from Aberdeen to shore up a defence that had leaked five goals at Leeds only a few weeks earlier. The Scotsman was to have a fine match but, with few other United players doing so well, his side was to be well beaten.

The first half was a cagey affair. Perhaps Liverpool were just waiting to see if United were as poor as had been reported in the papers or just biding their time? Seeing their side fail to create a serious opportunity was not what the Old Trafford crowd expected and there were murmurings of discontent. When Chris Lawler headed home the first goal on the hour this turned to outright hostility, with the United manager roundly abused from all sides of the ground.

Liverpool won 2-0 on their previous trip to Old Trafford and were now intent on at least equalling that scoreline. John Toshack scored two minutes later and then with five minutes remaining Emlyn Hughes, never the most popular man among the Old Trafford faithful, advanced up the field and with no United midfield player moving to block his run, he whacked a thirty-yard shot past Alex Stepney to give Liverpool their biggest victory at Old Trafford since before the Second World War.

Victory moved Shankly's side to within a point of leaders Derby with five games remaining, but defeat at the Baseball Ground in the penultimate match and only a point from a 0-0 draw at Highbury in their last game meant Derby, under Brian Clough, clinched their first ever League title. United, despite the rumblings of discontent, finished eighth.

United: Stepney, O'Neil, Dunne, Buchan, James, Gowling, Morgan, Best, Charlton, Law, Storey-Moore.

Liverpool: Clemence, Lawler, Lindsay, Smith, Lloyd, Hughes, Keegan, Hall, Heighway, Toshack (P. Thompson), Callaghan.

STROLL IN THE PARK FOR 'POOL

15 August 1972
First Division
Liverpool 2 (Toshack, Heighway), United 0.

As Denis Law was injured, youngster Tony Young was given the toughest test in his short career. Showing some neat touches, he was to do as well as any United player, but that wasn't too hard on a night when Liverpool, 2-0 up after twenty minutes, coasted to an easy victory.

Having held off Steve James to put his side ahead, John Toshack turned provider when, after beating Martin Buchan, he pulled the ball back for Steve Heighway to score an easy goal.

'We're only warming up,' chanted the Kop, and it looked that way as Chris Lawler headed the ball against the post and United narrowly escaped a penalty appeal. Yet with Martin Buchan marshalling the United back four, Liverpool found chances harder to come by the longer the game went on. Not that there was ever a chance of anything other than a home victory as, after the first twenty minutes, Ray Clemence was never called upon to make a serious save. Just two games gone and four points already separated the sides.

Liverpool: Clemence, Lawler, Lindsay, Smith, Lloyd, Hughes, Keegan, Hall,
    Heighway, Toshack, Callaghan.
United: Stepney, O'Neil, Dunne, Young, James, Buchan, Morgan, Kidd, Charlton,
    Best, Storey-Moore.

SHOCK LOSS FOR CHAMPIONS-ELECT

11 November 1972
First Division
United 2 (Davies, McDougall), Liverpool 0.

Top-of-the-table Liverpool were given a rude awakening by Frank O'Farrell's side, which showed, despite a wretched first part to the season, that they still possessed the ability to beat the best on their day. Lying bottom of the League, the two points were vital for the ex-Torquay United manager as he battled to keep his job.

Perhaps not surprisingly it was Liverpool who started the better side, and Peter Cormack was guilty of two poor misses. There was also a moment of high drama when Alex Stepney appeared to clearly bring down Steve Heighway in the penalty area only for Liverpool's penalty demands to be dismissed by the referee.

Ted MacDougall had been on Liverpool's books as a youngster without ever making a first-team appearance. He had recently been signed by United at a cost of £200,000 from Third Division Bournemouth and this was his chance for revenge, which he seized. First he engineered the goal of another new boy, ex-Manchester City man Wyn Davies, before scoring the second early in the second period after a lovely through-ball from Tommy O'Neil.

A substitute the previous weekend, O'Neil had become United's third right-back in as many games, replacing Ian Donald who during his five years at Old Trafford found himself serving under four different managers in Sir Matt Busby (twice), Wilf McGuinness, O'Farrell and later Tommy Docherty. Donald's chance had come after Willie Watson was left out of the side following a 4-0 thrashing at White Hart Lane, but in the event he was to make only four appearances for the club.

'That was a fantastic performance by Manchester United,' conceded Liverpool manager Bill Shankly.

Despite the loss of two points, Liverpool remained at the top of the League and they maintained their position by going ten games unbeaten. Fighting off a challenge from Arsenal, Liverpool won their eighth top-flight championship to draw level with the Gunners in the number of titles captured. To cap things off, the UEFA Cup became the first European trophy won by Liverpool when Shankly's side beat Borussia Mönchengladbach 3-2 over the two legs. Such glories seemed a long way away for Manchester United, who ended the season in eighteenth place.

United: Stepney, O'Neil, Dunne, Morgan, Sadler, Buchan, Best, McDougall,
    Charlton, Davies, Storey-Moore.
Liverpool: Clemence, Lawler, Lindsay, Smith, Lloyd, Hughes, Keegan, Cormack,
    Heighway (Thompson), Toshack, Callaghan.

BIG JIM FRUSTRATES CHAMPIONS

29 September 1973
First Division
United 0, Liverpool 0.

Big central defender Jim Holton was at his very best to help Tommy Docherty's struggling United side battle their way to a deserved point against the League champions and UEFA Cup winners.

Having picked up their first away point of the season the previous weekend at Elland Road, Docherty, who had replaced Frank O'Farrell in December the previous season, had chosen to keep the same defensive shape. Although it worked well enough, it saw his team restricted to a few long-range efforts.

It was, therefore, something of a surprise to see Liverpool fail to take advantage but, after Chris Lawler was unfortunate to see his early header disallowed for offside, Bill Shankly's side rarely threatened Alex Stepney's goal. As a result the large crowd witnessed a drab affair with little goalmouth action.

United: Stepney, Buchan, Young, Greenhoff, Holton, James, Morgan, Anderson, Macari, Kidd, Graham.

Liverpool: Clemence, Lawler, Lindsay, Smith, Lloyd, Hughes, Keegan, Cormack, Heighway, Hall, Callaghan.

HURTLING TOWARDS RELEGATION

22 December 1973
First Division
Liverpool 2 (Keegan (pen.), Heighway), United 0.
It was a dismal Christmas for United fans after a poor performance in which only Martin Buchan and Alex Stepney emerged with any credit.

It was something of a miracle that Tommy Docherty's side was still level after half an hour as Liverpool poured forward at will. Then, after Kevin Keegan headed on, Alan Waddle pushed the ball beyond Stepney only for Tony Young to prevent a goal with the use of his hand and up stepped Keegan to give the scoreline a more honest look.

Unable to hit the proverbial 'barn door', Waddle passed up a series of golden opportunities before nodding on Callaghan's cross for Steve Heighway to double their advantage midway through the second period. The previous season Docherty had engineered end-of-season survival, but after such an awful display it was clear that he now had an even harder task if relegation for the first time since the thirties was to be avoided.

In the event it was something the former Chelsea, Aston Villa, Queens Park Rangers, Rotherham, Porto and Scotland manager was unable to avoid. United had only won once in thirteen games and, though that became two in fifteen shortly afterwards, it was then to be another seven games before another two points was collected. In the penultimate match, Docherty's side were beaten 1-0 by neighbours City and were relegated. And while Liverpool failed to recapture the League title, consolation came in the form of a second ever FA Cup success when Newcastle United were beaten 3-0 at Wembley in the final.

Liverpool: Clemence, Smith, Evans, Thompson, Lloyd, Hughes, Keegan, Cormack, Waddle, Heighway, Callaghan.

United: Stepney, Buchan, Young, Greenhoff, Sidebottom, Griffiths, Morgan, Macari, Kidd, Graham, Best.

6

United Back in the Big Time

With United immediately recapturing their place in the top flight after winning the Second Division title at the first attempt, the two sides met once again in the 1975/76 season. Bob Paisley's first season in charge as manager had been a fine one, with only Derby County obtaining more points as they finished First Division runners-up. The question was could Tommy Docherty's refashioned young side become one of the challengers at the top of the table?

GOALKEEPER GAMBLE BACKFIRES

8 November 1975
First Division
Liverpool 3 (Heighway, Toshack, Keegan), United 1 (Coppell).

It quickly became clear that United, with wins in their first three League matches, could prosper. Indeed, when they travelled to Anfield in early November they were top of the table. Liverpool were back in fifth but, with only two points separating the sides, there was a lot more than pride to play for. The game was certain to be a stiff test for United, who preferred the inexperienced Paddy Roche between the sticks despite Alex Stepney being available after injury.

Fearing trouble, Liverpool had chosen to make the game all-ticket and a steel barrier had been constructed to divide fans in the Anfield Road Stand. On the day it did its job helping 'keep the peace'. Still, over twenty young fans from both sides were ejected and it was an indicator of more violent times ahead.

The atmosphere was electric before kick-off, and it certainly seemed to disturb the United 'keeper, who in the twelfth minute ignored a call from Brian Greenhoff to leave Kevin Keegan's speculative ball into the box. Fumbling the ball, Roche collided with Greenhoff, leaving Steve Heighway with the easiest of opening goals. It proved to be one of a handful of chances in the first forty-five minutes.

Liverpool doubled their lead shortly after the restart when Keegan created a gilt-edged opening for strike partner John Toshack. United hadn't gone to the top of the League by throwing in the towel, though, and Steve Coppell got them back in game with a fine goal soon after. Ray Clemence then ensured Liverpool remained in the lead with a fine save from Sammy McIlroy before Roche remained rooted to his line as the ball flashed across the box to leave Kevin Keegan with the sort of chance he was never going to miss.

Afterwards Tommy Docherty said United had been punished for their mistakes. Perhaps, but there were more than a handful that felt the main mistake had been his in not playing the more experienced of his two 'keepers.

Liverpool: Clemence, Neal, Jones, Thompson, Hall, Hughes, Keegan, Kennedy, Heighway, Toshack, Callaghan.
United: Roche, Nicholl, Houston, Jackson (McCreery), Greenhoff, Buchan, Coppell, McIlroy, Pearson, Macari, Daly.

BATTLE OF THE TOP TWO

18 February 1976
First Division
United 0, Liverpool 0.

Second-placed United sought to become the first side since Ipswich Town in 1962 to win the First Division title after gaining promotion the previous season as they played host to leaders Liverpool.

United were unbeaten in thirteen League and Cup games and Tommy Docherty's side was even in with a chance of the famous double after beating Leicester City 2-1 at Filbert Street in the fifth round of the FA Cup the previous Saturday.

Liverpool had crashed out of the Cup in the fourth round, beaten 1-0 by League Champions Derby County at the Baseball Ground. It was, though, Liverpool's only defeat in thirteen League, Cup and European matches and a tight encounter was assured beforehand. United were defending an unbeaten home record in the League and, while they had little trouble in protecting that proud record, a priceless two points was denied Docherty's side after another night when the defensive qualities that made Liverpool so successful in the seventies and eighties were seen at their very best. United, pressing for much of the game, rarely looked like they would break though, with Emlyn Hughes outstanding at the heart of the Liverpool defence.

It wasn't until midway through the opening period that the first chance arrived, when following fine team play, Lou Macari beat Ray Clemence with a low shot that Stuart Pearson would have done better leaving alone, the United centre forward's intervention sending the ball over the top of the bar as it appeared destined for the back of the net.

Then, after thirty-two minutes, with Ray Kennedy taking too long to clear, Gerry Daly hit a rasping drive that forced a world-class save from Clemence, who showed the sort of form that earned him so many England caps. The Liverpool No. 1 should have been beaten on the stroke of half-time however, Sammy McIlroy wastefully heading Steve Coppell's cross high and wide at the far post. The point maintained Liverpool's place at the top of the table, where they remained until the end of the season when they also added the UEFA Cup to their growing trophy cabinet.

United eventually finished third behind Liverpool and QPR and also missed out on silverware, losing unexpectedly to Second Division Southampton in the final of the FA Cup.

United: Stepney, Forsyth, Houston, Daly, Greenhoff, Buchan, Coppell, McIlroy (McCreery), Pearson, Macari, Hill.
Liverpool: Clemence, Smith, Neal, Thompson, Kennedy, Hughes, Keegan, Case, Heighway, Toshack, Callaghan.

HEIGHWAY HOPPING MAD OVER PENALTY CLAIM

16 February 1977
First Division
United 0, Liverpool 0.

Lying seven points and five places behind League leaders Liverpool, United went into the match knowing victory was vital if they were to give themselves any chance of a first title success in more than a decade. Having looked well out of contention when beaten 3-1 at Ipswich on 3 January, Tommy Docherty's side had hauled themselves up from fourteenth place by winning their next five League games.

Liverpool had crashed 2-1 at Norwich City in their previous away game and were being hotly pursued for the title by Ipswich Town, who were three points behind but with four games in hand. Bob Paisley's side had found goals away from home difficult to come by and had hit only twelve in thirteen away League games.

It proved a dull affair as for the second successive season a packed Old Trafford crowd left having failed to see either team trouble the scoreboard operator. The result left Ipswich, conquerors of local rivals Norwich 5-0, at the top of the table, but it might have been different if referee Pat Partridge had awarded Liverpool a penalty for a seventy-fifth-minute Stewart Houston challenge on Steve Heighway. It led to the Liverpool winger criticising the man in charge after the game, saying, 'It was the most blatant penalty I have had for ages. The referee was right on the spot. They have got to learn the difference between beating a defender with trickery and stumbling past one.'

If any side deserved to win the match it was probably Liverpool, but it was United who had the best chance, Phil Neal reacting quickly to clear Gordon Hill's half-volley off the line.

United: Stepney, Nicholl, B. Greenhoff, Buchan, Houston, Coppell, Macari, McIlroy,
  Hill, J. Greenhoff, Pearson.
Liverpool: Clemence, Neal, Jones, Thompson, Kennedy, Hughes, Keegan, Case,
  Heighway, Toshack, Callaghan.

3 May 1977
First Division
Liverpool 1 (Keegan), United 0.

United started this game knowing that whatever the result, they would end up as
winners!

Were United to lose at Anfield it would almost certainly confirm Liverpool, after
their win against second-placed Ipswich Town at the weekend, as champions. As the
sides were due to meet again in two weeks' time at Wembley in the FA Cup, United
would therefore be guaranteed a place in the now defunct Cup Winners' Cup whatever
the result on the day.

Lacking Martin Buchan and Brian Greenhoff at the back, United were quickly
behind, Kevin Keegan soaring high to head home a David Johnson cross in the
fifteenth minute. Phil Neal should have doubled the lead but blazed high and wide
when left with just Alex Stepney to beat. The United 'keeper then saved smartly from
Terry McDermott as Liverpool played the ball around with ease. Keegan flicked the
ball beyond Stepney but Jimmy Nicholl kept the away side in the match by hacking
clear before a Sammy McIlroy shot finally brought Ray Clemence into action.

The second half was a tedious affair, with United showing little urgency to try and
haul themselves back into the game and Liverpool content to move two points closer
to the title. David Fairclough did rattle the bar but the important statistic was the one
that at full time said Liverpool were four points clear of Manchester City with just four
games left. A few weeks later and Bob Paisley's side were to become the first side to
retain the Division One title since Wolverhampton Wanderers in 1958/59, with United
finishing sixth.

Liverpool: Clemence, Neal, Jones, Smith, Kennedy, Hughes, Keegan, Case, Johnson,
  Fairclough, McDermott.
United: Stepney, Forsyth, Nicholl, Houston, Albiston, Coppell, Macari, McIlroy, Hill,
  Pearson, J Greenhoff (McCreery).

LUCKY SEVEN FOR DOC

21 May 1977
FA Cup Final
Liverpool 1 (Case), United 2 (Pearson, J. Greenhoff).

Lucky sevens – certainly Tommy Docherty was hoping so, as the United manager had failed to win any of the six previous matches against Liverpool, in which his side had only scored once.

Liverpool's consistency made them pre-match favourites in the first of two finals, Borussia Mönchengladbach standing in their way in the European Cup final in Rome just four days later. Victory would enable Liverpool to equal United's success in 1968, when Sir Matt Busby's side had beaten Benfica after extra time at Wembley.

Today the glory of the FA Cup may have long since faded, but in 1977 it remained one of the biggest days in a football calendar, even if you didn't have a ticket or your side wasn't in the final. Competition on the field was mirrored off it with the BBC and ITV competing to attract the largest audience. It meant an early kick-off with 'Auntie' first to the ball with an 11.30 a.m. start, with *World of Sport* coming on stream half an hour later with *Wembley Scene* at noon. Cup final *It's a Knock Out* with compère Arthur Ellis, who in his previous career as a referee took charge of the 1952 final between Arsenal and Newcastle United, was always popular before viewers got the chance to accompany each team on their coach trip to Wembley.

Having already captained Aberdeen to Scottish Cup success in 1970, Martin Buchan was seeking to become the first man to captain successive English and Scottish Cup winners.

The game began with Liverpool pushing forward from the kick-off and Buchan had to be at his very best, making a lunging tackle on Jimmy Case as the Liverpool midfielder looked to get beyond the United back four. With the Merseysiders enjoying the majority of the ball, United were forced to work energetically to prevent an opening. In general they did so, though Liverpool had been finding it difficult to score goals in the previous few weeks, and Wembley was to be no different. Arthur Albiston, the United teenager at full-back, was rarely put under the pressure many thought would be exerted on him in the first half, which ended goalless after Ray Kennedy hit the post with a header just before the break.

United hadn't looked like scoring before Kevin Keegan gave away the ball needlessly early in the second half. For once, Emlyn Hughes then showed poor anticipation by failing to push out to block Jimmy Greenhoff's run and he released Stuart Pearson; he might have expected Ray Clemence to have been more alert as he made it 1-0, sparking pandemonium among the United fans and the watching millions. Could Liverpool respond?

The answer was most definitely yes! Less than a minute later and Jimmy Case had whacked home the equaliser. Silence in the United end and delirium in the Liverpool section of the crowd. Two goals in a minute, and soon it was three in four minutes.

Again it was the result of some uncharacteristic Liverpool defending, when Tommy Smith allowed himself to be pushed out of position by Jimmy Greenhoff. With the ball running free Lou Macari, who had been largely anonymous throughout the game, clearly fancied his chances. It wasn't one of his greatest efforts, the ball flying away from goal until it struck the body of Greenhoff, the ball arcing off him and beyond Clemence and into the net. It was lucky, but it counted.

Could the surprise leaders hang on for a second time? This time the answer was yes. Liverpool had thirty-five minutes to draw level and force the game into extra time. They enjoyed the majority of the ball, but with Buchan and Brian Greenhoff outstanding, United held out more comfortably than might have been expected.

The result meant Liverpool had failed to do the double of League and FA Cup in the same season for the first time in their history. United had lost to Southampton in the previous season's FA Cup final, and victory in 1977 brought their FA Cup successes to four after previous success in 1909, 1948 and 1963.

It was also to be Keegan's last game for Liverpool against United as he joined Hamburger SV shortly after they beat their German rivals Borussia Mönchengladbach in Rome 3-1 to lift the European Cup.

Liverpool: Clemence, Neal, Jones, Smith, Kennedy, Hughes, Keegan, Case, Heighway, Johnson (Callaghan), McDermott.

United: Stepney, Nicholl, Albiston, McIlroy, B. Greenhoff, Buchan, Coppell, J. Greenhoff, Pearson, Macari, Hill (McCreery).

DALGLISH DEBUT FOR LIVERPOOL

13 August 1977
Charity Shield
United 0, Liverpool 0.

United and Liverpool returned to Wembley less than three months after their remarkable FA Cup final.

This time it was in the Charity Shield, the pre-season curtain-raiser to the new campaign, involving the League Champions and FA Cup winners. There was, however, none of the drama of their previous clash at Wembley as it ended goalless with both sides sharing the Shield.

United had a new manager in charge as Dave Sexton had replaced Tommy Docherty, while Liverpool's new record signing Kenny Dalglish, bought from Glasgow Celtic to replace Kevin Keegan, made his debut.

United: Stepney, Nicholl, B. Greenhoff, Buchan, Albiston, McIlroy, Macari, Coppell, J. Greenhoff (McCreery), Pearson, Hill.

Liverpool: Clemence, Neal, Thompson, Hughes, Jones, McDermott, Case, Callaghan, Kennedy, Dalglish, Fairclough.

UNITED TACKLE HOOLIGANS

1 October 1977
First Division
United 2 (Macari, McIlroy), Liverpool 0.

United grabbed the sports headlines with news that they hoped to rid themselves of the hooligan element that had attached itself to the club by refusing tickets for away games. There was relief all round that this match passed off without incident on the terraces. Liverpool arrived at Old Trafford unbeaten in the League, but played poorly and goals from Lou Macari and Sammy McIlroy were deserved rewards for a fine United performance.

A strong wind ensured it was never a great spectacle, and it wasn't until just before the break that anything resembling a scoring opportunity arrived, Jimmy Greenhoff's half-chance being snuffed out quickly.

With the rain lashing down at the break, the soaked Liverpool fans in the Scoreboard end had an ever bigger sinking feeling within a quarter of an hour of the restart when Macari scored easily after Alan Hansen and Ray Clemence failed to clear Gordon Hill's cross. The ball appeared to glance off them both before hitting the upright to leave a joyous Macari to sweep home the rebound. If there was an element of luck about the opening goal there certainly wasn't any with the second after sixty-eight minutes. United's pace and passing dissected the Liverpool defence once again and from a good centre by Macari, McIlroy volleyed an unstoppable shot past Clemence.

It was not until the final moments that Stepney was called into action for the first time when he turned over a twenty-five-yard drive from Terry McDermott, and from the resulting corner Hansen capped a poor day by heading over the bar when left unmarked.

United: Stepney, Nicholl, Albiston, McIlroy, B. Greenhoff, Buchan, McGrath, Coppell, J. Greenhoff, Macari, Hill.
Liverpool: Clemence, Neal, Jones, Smith, Kennedy, Hansen, Dalglish, Case, Fairclough, McDermott, Callaghan.

SOUNESS MIDFIELD MAESTRO

25 February 1978
First Division
Liverpool 3 (Souness, Kennedy, Case), United 1 (McIlroy).

Both sides trailed leaders Nottingham Forest by some distance so the result of this game was probably more important to United, whose supporters had seen their side fail to impress all season. Liverpool, at least, were still in with a chance in two competitions, and were looking forward to playing Forest in the League Cup final and Borussia Mönchengladbach in the European Cup semi-final.

United manager Dave Sexton had opted to play adventurously with a 4-2-4 formation, leaving Sammy McIlroy and Lou Macari to battle it out in midfield against Graeme Souness, Ray Kennedy and Terry McDermott.

It was a big gamble and, not surprisingly, it was a losing one and ensured a tough debut for Gordon McQueen, signed from Leeds in midweek. With Steve Heighway and David Fairclough getting down the United flanks at every opportunity, the only surprise was that it took the home side till the fortieth minute to open their account, Souness doing the damage.

Kennedy struck the second after fifty minutes and, though McIlroy dragged a goal back on the hour, substitute Jimmy Case restored Liverpool's two-goal advantage five minutes from time. The winning margin was the least Bob Paisley's side deserved as they also had two efforts cleared off the line, hit the post and missed a hatful of chances. It had been an all-round team performance, but one man – Souness – stood out, directing play, grabbing a goal and pushing forward at every opportunity.

Liverpool: Clemence, Neal, Smith, Thompson, Kennedy, Hughes, Dalglish, Souness, Heighway, Fairclough (Case), McDermott.
United: Roche, Nicholl, Albiston, McIlroy, McQueen, Houston, Coppell, Jordan, Pearson, Macari, Hill.

WE WERE SECOND-BEST – SEXTON

26 December 1978
First Division
United 0, Liverpool 3 (Kennedy, Case, Fairclough).

United had been hammered 3-0 in the previous game at neighbours Bolton Wanderers so the last thing manager Dave Sexton needed was the arrival of the European champions.

One goal up after only five minutes when the impressive Ray Kennedy headed home, Liverpool doubled their lead through Jimmy Case, who followed up to net after 'keeper Gary Bailey stopped Kenny Dalglish's powerful effort.

It was David Fairclough though who scored the goal of the game. In the side from the start and keen to throw off the 'supersub' tag, he left four defenders trailing his wake to put his side into a 3-0 lead that was never under any threat for the remaining twenty-three minutes of the match.

Sexton was generous in his praise for Liverpool, saying, 'You must fancy them for the title. They're a very impressive team, the best we've played this season. They looked like European champions. Certainly, they were too much for us.'

Liverpool: Clemence, Neal, Hughes, Thompson, R.Kennedy, Hansen, Dalglish, Case, Fairclough, McDermott, Souness.
United: Bailey, B. Greenhoff, Connell, McIlroy, McQueen, Buchan, Coppell, J. Greenhoff, Ritchie, Macari, Thomas.

WHAT DRAMA IN CUP SEMI-FINAL

31 March 1979
FA Cup Semi-Final
Liverpool 2 (Dalglish, Hansen), United 2 (Jordan, Greenhoff).
(at Maine Road)

It was described as one of the most exciting FA Cup semi-final matches ever played, and it was hard to argue after a pulsating match at Maine Road.

Kenny Dalglish had got things up and running in the eighteenth minute, skipping past Martin Buchan and Gordon McQueen before leaving United 'keeper Gary Bailey prostrate as he pushed the ball into the empty net. Within two minutes United were level, Joe Jordan heading home Jimmy Greenhoff's cross with Ray Clemence rooted to his line. It was to mark the start of a period of United dominance and Clemence had to be at his very best to beat away efforts from Mickey Thomas, Steve Coppell and Brian Greenhoff.

Under-pressure Liverpool were given the chance to take the lead after thirty-eight minutes, referee David Richardson pointing to the spot after Buchan had rashly challenged Dalglish. Terry McDermott's shot sent Bailey the wrong way but the ball failed to enter the net after hitting the post.

Eight minutes into the second half, United grabbed the lead when Brian Greenhoff scored. Stung by going behind, Liverpool poured forward, substitute Steve Heighway dragging the United defence inside-out. Buchan looked like he might have saved the day when he twice kicked Graeme Souness shots off the line. But with McQueen and Jimmy Nicholl both injured it was surely only a matter of time before Liverpool got their just desserts and so it proved when after eighty-two minutes Phil Thompson and Alan Hansen combined superbly to carve open the United defence before Hansen neatly tucked the ball past Bailey. After that United were forced to dig deep and were probably the more relieved to hear the final whistle.

Liverpool: Clemence, Neal, Hughes, Thompson, Kennedy, Hansen, Dalglish, Johnson, Case (Heighway), McDermott, Souness.
United: Bailey, Nicholl, Albiston, McIlroy, McQueen, Buchan, Coppell, J. Greenhoff, Jordan, B. Greenhoff, Thomas.

JIMMY CLINCHES CUP FINAL SPOT

4 April 1979
FA Cup Semi-Final Replay
Liverpool 1 (J. Greenhoff), United 0.
(at Goodison Park)

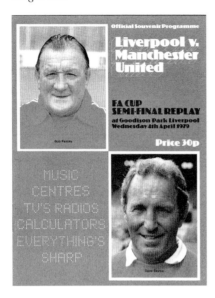

On a night sadly marred by violent scenes in and around Goodison Park, United made it through to their third FA Cup final in four seasons thanks to a late goal from Jimmy Greenhoff. They certainly deserved their success in a game that never touched the heights of the first match, tiredness and weary legs being the major winner over the ninety minutes.

The game might have been over in the first ten minutes if Ray Clemence hadn't exhibited heroics, the England 'keeper denying Lou Macari, Mickey Thomas and Steve Coppell as United ran the Liverpool defence ragged. For United, Gordon McQueen was guilty of a bad miss after eighteen minutes, hammering high and wide from just five yards. Joe Jordan then hit the bar with a header as Macari and Sammy McIlroy pushed and probed, with little the Liverpool midfield could do to prevent the constant pressure on their back four. The Liverpool side of the seventies were masters of absorbing pressure before striking back and after thirty-five minutes only the crossbar prevented Kenny Dalglish from opening the scoring, his header from a Phil Neal cross beating Gary Bailey.

The second half was a much more even affair, and United were grateful when McQueen just managed to get his toe onto a David Johnson pass as Steve Heighway looked to burst through on goal. Steve Coppell then had a penalty claim turned away before United finally struck with twelve minutes left when Greenhoff headed a Thomas cross past Clemence to spark wild scenes of celebration by the United supporters behind the goal. Angered by what they had witnessed, a good number of Liverpool fans headed for the exits to wait outside and subsequently attack the celebrating visitors as they emerged, bringing shame on themselves and the club they claimed to support.

Liverpool: Clemence, Neal, Hughes, Thompson, Kennedy, Hansen, Dalglish, Johnson, Heighway, McDermott (Case), Souness.

United: Bailey, Nicholl, Albiston, McIlroy, McQueen, Buchan, Coppell, J. Greenhoff, Jordan, Macari (Ritchie), Thomas.

14 April 1979
First Division
Liverpool 2 (Dalglish, Neal), United 0.

This was a one-sided game in which Liverpool played majestically to easily beat their FA Cup conquerors. With the final looming, United rested Jimmy Greenhoff, leaving Joe Jordan to partner teenager Andy Ritchie up front.

As United were never in the game, it was a surprise it took Liverpool until the thirty-sixth minute to take the lead, Kenny Dalglish heading home his 22nd goal of the season from a lovely cross as the Scotsman waited until it dropped just beyond Brian Greenhoff before heading inside Gary Bailey's post.

Anyone late back from the half-time break would have missed a marvellous second goal. Man of the Match Ray Kennedy broke up a United attack, hit a forty-yard pass out to Jimmy Case, who immediately put the ball onto the toes of the onrushing Phil Neal, who must have made a dash of seventy yards, and from a narrow angle the Liverpool full-back hit a wonderful shot past the diving Bailey. Maintaining their unbeaten home record, Liverpool were on course for their third title success in four years while United lost to Arsenal in the Cup final and finished ninth in the League.

Liverpool: Clemence, Neal, A. Kennedy, Thompson, R. Kennedy, Hansen, Dalglish,
    Case, Johnson, McDermott, Souness.
United: Bailey, Nicholl, Albiston, McIlroy, Greenhoff, Buchan, Coppell, Ritchie
    (Houston), Jordan, Macari, Thomas.

26 December 1979
First Division
Liverpool 2 (Hansen, Johnson), United 0.

It was the second successive Boxing Day that United had been made to look ordinary by Bob Paisley's Liverpool. With both sides six points clear of third-placed Arsenal before kick-off, Liverpool moved two points clear at the top as they sought to retain the First Division title.

Anfield had been a fortress throughout the seventies and this victory extended their unbeaten home record to a remarkable fifty-two games. They had also lost only thirteen times on home turf throughout the decade of dominance. As Liverpool had suffered only two League defeats in twenty matches, this would be a stiff test for United, who were lying level at the top of the table. Liverpool had doubts beforehand about the fitness of both Kenny Dalglish and Phil Thompson, but in the event both played.

The game was won with goals from Alan Hansen and David Johnson, and Hansen has subsequently described it as the best he scored. Sadly, due to a strike no television cameras were in the ground to record it for him. The Scotsman finished off a fine move after a one-two with Ray Kennedy opened up the United defence after fifteen minutes.

With Liverpool controlling the midfield it was only thanks to some fine saves from Gary Bailey that the score remained at 1-0 at half-time.

There was little to suggest they could get back into the game, though United almost stole an equaliser from an unlikely source when, after seventy-three minutes, Bailey's long clearance was misjudged by Ray Clemence. Thankfully for the England 'keeper, the ball hit the top of the bar before bouncing into the crowd.

Having played so impressively, it was ironic that Liverpool's second owed much to a Bailey mistake as he allowed Johnson's shot to squirm past him with five minutes left.

While both Paisley and Sexton agreed that the result decided nothing, a more balanced assessment came from United midfielder Mickey Thomas who said, 'It's hard to back against Liverpool and they must be a good bet to win it again – but we'll keep trying.'

Liverpool: Clemence, Neal, A. Kennedy, Thompson, R. Kennedy, Hansen, Dalglish, Case, Johnson, McDermott, Souness.

United: Bailey, Nicholl, Buchan, McQueen, Houston, Coppell, McIlroy, Wilkins, Thomas (Grimes) Macari, Jordan.

Liverpool were without question the team of the seventies, as they had an unprecedented haul of silverware – five League titles, two European Cups, two UEFA Cups and one FA Cup. They also finished runners-up in the League a further three times, such was their consistency throughout the decade. 'I don't know who's going to be the team of the eighties. All I know is we've been the team of the seventies,' declared Liverpool manager Bob Paisley.

While Liverpool enjoyed considerable success, the seventies had seen dark days at Old Trafford and relegation six years after becoming the first English team to be crowned champions of Europe. They rebuilt under the charismatic Tommy Docherty, winning the FA Cup in 1977 and finishing runners-up in 1979, by which time Dave Sexton was in charge.

LIVERPOOL GIVEN TITLE FRIGHT

5 April 1980
First Division
United 2 (Greenhoff, Thomas), Liverpool 1 (Dalglish).

If Liverpool thought retaining their First Division title would be a formality, they were in for a rude awakening as United revived their own hopes of becoming champions. Six points behind Liverpool, second-placed United knew they could give themselves an outside chance of nicking the title from the League leaders with victory at Old Trafford.

That looked unlikely when Liverpool swept into a fourteenth minute lead courtesy of a great goal from Kenny Dalglish. For once, Liverpool seemed over-confident and six minutes later confusion in their defence following a Steve Coppell cross allowed Mickey Thomas to grab the equaliser. United secured victory midway through the second period when Jimmy Greenhoff struck the decisive goal to narrow the deficit at the top to four points with six games remaining. It was still the days when two points were awarded for a win.

United further eroded Liverpool's lead, and by the end of the campaign finished only two points behind the Anfield side, who managed to hold on to their crown.

United: Bailey, Nicholl, Albiston, Greenhoff, McQueen, Buchan, Coppell, Wilkins, Jordan, Macari, Thomas.
Liverpool: Clemence, Neal, A. Kennedy (Lee) , Thompson, R. Kennedy, Hansen, Dalglish, Case, Johnson, McDermott, Souness.

BOXING DAY BORE DRAW

26 December 1980
First Division
United 0, Liverpool 0.

The biggest crowd in the Football League so far that campaign – 57,053 – witnessed a largely disappointing goalless draw at Old Trafford on Boxing Day. Despite the heavy pitch causing mistakes from both defences, neither side seriously looked like scoring until the last quarter of an hour.

Liverpool's Ray Kennedy had two clear-cut chances to break the deadlock. First Jimmy Case's long cross was knocked down by Kenny Dalglish and Kennedy produced a superb turn to create space for a drive which struck the upright with 'keeper Gary Bailey beaten. Then, six minutes from time, Kennedy met a cross from Terry McDermott but saw his header easily saved. Liverpool also came within a lick of paint of taking a first-half lead when United left-back Arthur Albiston cleared a shot from Dalglish off the line.

Mid-table United, who were missing Ray Wilkins through a long-term injury, rarely troubled leaders Liverpool. Dave Sexton's side lacked creativity in the absence of Wilkins and only had one clear-cut chance. That came towards the end of the opening period when Mickey Thomas had a close-range shot cleared off the line by Phil Neal.

United: Bailey, Nicholl, Albiston, McIlroy, Jovanovic, Moran, Coppell, Duxbury, Jordan, Macari, Thomas.
Liverpool: Clemence, Neal, A. Kennedy, Irwin, R. Kennedy, Hansen (Money), Dalglish, Lee, Johnson, McDermott, Case.

LIVERPOOL SET TO BE DETHRONED

14 April 1981
First Division
Liverpool 0, United 1 (McQueen).

Soon-to-be-dethroned Champions Liverpool lost a home First Division match for only the second time in more than two years and it was United who inflicted the painful defeat. It had been a disappointing League campaign for Liverpool, whose title was heading towards Aston Villa even before this loss.

After this defeat, however, Liverpool found themselves nine points adrift of Villa with only five games left and ten points still to be contested. Villa were also having a stutter, as on the same night when Liverpool were losing they were also suffering a 2-1 home defeat by Ipswich.

The all-important goal at Anfield came in the seventh minute, following a brief opening burst by Liverpool. Ray Wilkins floated in a corner which was met by centre half Gordon McQueen, who towered above the Liverpool defence to glance a header beyond Ray Clemence. McQueen returned to the back line where, alongside the immaculate Martin Buchan, they managed to keep Liverpool at bay in what was later described as a functional display designed to contain the hosts, achieved with great success.

Though Liverpool finished the season in fifth place – they managed a measly four away League wins from twenty-one attempts – it was by no means a season of failure.

They quickly overcame the disappointment of losing their League title and weeks later were crowned champions of Europe for a third time after defeating Real Madrid in Paris. There was also a further piece of silverware as they captured the League Cup for the first time in their history as they defeated West Ham in the final at Wembley.

Liverpool: Clemence, Neal, Money, Thompson, R. Kennedy, Hansen, Dalglish, Lee, Rush, McDermott, Case.
United: Bailey, Duxbury, Albiston, Moran, McQueen, Buchan, Coppell, Birtles, Jordan, Macari, Wilkins.

BIG RON WEAVES MAGIC WAND

24 October 1981
First Division
Liverpool 1 (McDermott (pen.)), United 2 (Moran, Albiston).

United's fine start to the season under new manager Ron Atkinson continued in this game against a poor Liverpool side, who left the field nine points and eleven places behind the League leaders.

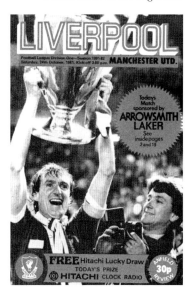

Atkinson, who arrived from West Brom, had remodelled Dave Sexton's side by bringing in three new players. He recruited Frank Stapleton, one of the Arsenal scorers when the Gunners beat United at Wembley in the 1979 FA Cup final, along with Remi Moses and Bryan Robson, who arrived from Atkinson's old club. Robson had only made his debut two weeks earlier but was already showing signs of the great player he was to become over the following years.

It was Stapleton, though, who provided the start the away side needed, his twenty-fifth-minute header carrying such power that Bruce Grobbelaar couldn't keep hold of it and when the ball ran loose, Kevin Moran was on to it in a flash to drive home. Despite going a goal behind, the European Cup winners seemed to lack both the energy and creativity to get back into the game. Graeme Souness hit the post but, with less than twenty minutes remaining, it looked like United were going to see out the match for a comfortable victory.

It was either inspired genius by manager Bob Paisley or just good fortune that got Liverpool back into the game after he replaced striker David Johnson with Ronnie Whelan, who did just enough to convince the referee that Moran had pushed him in the box and Terry McDermott stroked home the resulting penalty. It seemed a harsh decision and one Martin Buchan to this day maintains was the wrong one.

'When the penalty went in, I thought if we just continued to play as we had in the first seventy-five minutes we could win the match,' he recalled.

Yet it wasn't until the last minute that United gained their reward, and it came from an unlikely source, left-back Arthur Albiston. The Scotsman played over 450 games for the Old Trafford club, scoring only 7 times. This was undoubtedly his greatest when, after playing a lovely one-two with Stapleton, he appeared to hesitate before slipping as his shot crept past 'keeper Bruce Grobbelaar to leave the United fans streaming out of Anfield believing the side were genuinely in with a chance of a first title success since 1967.

Liverpool: Grobbelaar, Neal, Lawrenson, Thompson, R. Kennedy, Hansen, Dalglish,
   Lee, Johnson (Whelan), McDermott, Souness.
United: Bailey, Gidman, Albiston, Wilkins, Moran, Buchan, Robson, Birtles,
   Stapleton, Moses, Coppell.

LIVERPOOL COMEBACK KINGS

7 April 1982
First Division
United 0, Liverpool 1 (Johnston).

What a remarkable transformation in the fortunes of both teams since their previous meeting less than six months earlier. Liverpool, seemingly down and out in the Championship race, had reignited their title challenge by collecting a staggering forty-six points from a possible sixty since their meeting at Anfield.

United, by contrast, had failed to consolidate their remarkable start to the season and this defeat effectively ended their title bid. The manner in which the Liverpool players had succumbed to United in the earlier game at Anfield had incurred the wrath of manager Bob Paisley who, after the game, had threatened to make wholesale changes.

The players had evidently heeded his warnings and didn't want to give up appearing for the best side in the land, and by April Liverpool were again in fine form. Where change had taken place was up front. Ian Rush had arrived in 1980 from Chester for a fee of £300,000. Not yet ready for the rigours of either First Division or European football, he had to spend time learning his trade in the reserves before being given a regular chance. Craig Johnston had paid his own fare from Australia to take up the offer of a trial at Middlesbrough, from whom he joined Liverpool for £575,000 at the start of the season.

Johnston made his debut in August as a substitute against Wolves for Ray Kennedy, the player he would replace in the team and who would move to Swansea, where he would play for former Liverpool legend John Toshack. Johnston had scored just the once for Liverpool, but he was to grab the only goal of the game midway through the second half to secure this priceless victory. There was an element of good fortune, however, as a miskick from Rush fell kindly for Johnston to make no mistake.

It was harsh on United, who dominated the game only to find Liverpool 'keeper Bruce Grobbelaar in magnificent form, the Zimbabwean rightly picking up the Man of the Match award at the end. He should have been beaten after only eight minutes when Phil Thompson inexplicably handled a Ray Wilkins free-kick. Frank Stapleton's fierce penalty was pushed out by Grobbelaar and as Scott McGarvey raced in, he struck his shot over the bar. If that was a poor miss the young Scot was unlucky again in the opening period when his shot beat the Liverpool 'keeper before hitting the post.

In the previous season, Liverpool had played much better at Old Trafford without winning. This time they played poorly and left with all three points, proving football can be a funny game. Liverpool moved two points clear at the top of the table and the result effectively ended United's chances of capturing the title for the first time since 1967 by leaving them eight points adrift of their rivals with only ten games of the season remaining. Liverpool went on to win the title, finishing nine points clear of third-placed United. They also retained the League Cup, which was known as the Milk Cup, defeating Tottenham in the Wembley show-piece.

United: Bailey, Duxbury, Albiston, Wilkins, Moran, Buchan, Robson, McGarvey,
  Stapleton, Moses, Coppell.
Liverpool: Grobbelaar, Neal, Lawrenson, A. Kennedy, Whelan, Thompson, Dalglish,
  Lee, Rush, Johnston, Souness (McDermott).

UNITED SHOW CHAMPIONSHIP CLASS

16 October 1982
First Division
Liverpool 0, United 0.
United underlined why they were top of the table after a battling display earned a terrific draw at Anfield. As Liverpool had rattled home sixteen goals in the first five home games of the season, including five in the previous game against Southampton, this was therefore viewed as a useful away point for United. It maintained their narrow lead over their rivals at the top of the First Division at this early stage of the campaign.

However, in terms of entertainment the match was a non-event as a swirling wind proved impossible to cope with for the players on both sides. The conditions resulted in it being an error-strewn game in which Liverpool dominated territorially, but United defended resolutely.

United also had their moments and were aggrieved not to be awarded a first-half penalty when they claimed Ray Wilkins was fouled by Alan Kennedy. Liverpool had the better of the attacking play, with Mark Lawrenson, Sammy Lee, Ian Rush and Ronnie Whelan having chances, though 'keeper Gary Bailey made a couple of decent saves.

When Bailey was beaten, the upright came to his rescue as Kenny Dalglish was denied by a matter of inches. Steve Coppell and Ashley Grimes were a threat for United going forward, though Liverpool's defence held firm.

Liverpool: Grobbelaar, Neal, A. Kennedy, Thompson, Whelan, Hansen, Dalglish,
  Lee, Rush, Lawrenson, Souness.
United: Bailey, Duxbury, Albiston, Wilkins, Moran, McQueen, Robson, Grimes,
  Stapleton, Whiteside, Coppell.

ONE TO REMEMBER

26 February 1983
First Division
United 1 (Muhren), Liverpool 1 (Dalglish).

'The match itself should be packaged and sold as a film to every club in the country for an example of basic skills, individual brilliance, organisation, reorganisation, entertainment and the right spirit', wrote Frank McGee in the *Daily Mirror*. That was an expert's viewpoint after witnessing the thrilling spectacle between runaway League leaders Liverpool and third-placed United.

In the seventeen League games since their earlier meeting, Liverpool had suffered only one defeat. They were looking for a seventh victory in a row as they were fourteen points clear of second-placed Watford. United were one point further behind in third spot. In a captivating contest, United became the first side in 1983 to take a League point off Liverpool, who were in electrifying form. And with the sides set to meet again one month later in the League Cup final at Wembley, this curtain-raiser for the big day certainly whetted the appetite.

With Bryan Robson out injured, his England colleague Ray Wilkins was drafted into the United midfield against a Liverpool side featuring Phil Thompson for the first time in fifteen games as he replaced the injured Alan Hansen. United suffered a big loss when Kevin Moran was injured in a no-nonsense first half, Ron Atkinson reshuffling his defence with Lou Macari coming on as an emergency full-back. Any hopes Liverpool might have had of exploiting the Scotsman's lack of experience in the position proved misplaced and he even had time to get forward to lay on Arnold Muhren's goal.

Macari also had, like every other player in the United side, no chance to prevent the Liverpool equaliser, which was finished off in some style by Kenny Dalglish as both goals came in a three-minute spell late in the opening half.

Liverpool went on to be crowned champions for the fourth time in five seasons while United finished third behind surprise-package Watford.

United: Bailey, Duxbury, Albiston, Moses, Moran (Macari), McQueen, Wilkins, Muhren, Stapleton, Whiteside, Coppell.
Liverpool: Grobbelaar, Neal, A. Kennedy, Thompson, Whelan, Lawrenson, Dalglish, Lee, Rush, Johnston, Souness.

LIVERPOOL'S LEAGUE CUP TREBLE

26 March 1983
Milk Cup Final
Liverpool 2 (Kennedy, Whelan), United 1 (Whiteside) after extra time.

Liverpool completed a hat-trick of League Cup triumphs, but there was still Wembley cheer for the beaten United side. Having won the previous two League Cup competitions, Liverpool were big pre-match favourites to secure the treble. In the end they managed it, but for United fans there was the consolation of having seen their side refuse to submit in the face of some awful bad luck and the promise of greater days to come.

It looked as though United would cause an upset for a lengthy period, as they were ahead for over an hour before Liverpool hit back and sealed victory in extra time. Bob Paisley's side fell behind after twelve minutes. Norman Whiteside's goal was a surprise as United had hardly been beyond the halfway line before he netted.

For once Alan Hansen appeared to allow his opponent too much time on the ball, and slipping away from him, Whiteside hit a shot that just had the legs to beat Grobbelaar.

Ian Rush's record against United had been terrible, and it was to continue in the final as he then passed up two decent goal-scoring opportunities as Ron Atkinson's side somehow made it to half-time still leading by a single goal.

When the scoreline remained unchanged with twenty minutes left, an unlikely first United League Cup success seemed on the cards. Disaster, though, was just around the corner after Kevin Moran, who had played impressively at the heart of the United defence, went off injured. Five minutes after Moran had gone off Alan Kennedy, who scored Liverpool's winner in the 1991 final of the European Cup against Real Madrid in Paris, struck another priceless goal. Kennedy advanced and saw his shot swerve beyond the outstretched arms of Gary Bailey.

Few in the crowd would at that point have wagered much on United's chances of making it to extra time, such was Liverpool's stranglehold on the game. This was especially so when Moran's central defensive partner Gordon McQueen was himself injured. With substitute Lou Macari already on the field, the Scotsman could do little more than move up front and try and make a nuisance of himself. Meanwhile, Frank Stapleton was asked to drop back and play at centre-back, where he did a fine job, but could do little to stop Ronnie Whelan beating 'keeper Gary Bailey as he curled in a delightful shot from outside of the penalty area during the first period of extra-time. It proved to be the match-winning effort, and deservedly so as Liverpool had been the better side.

However, their victory had not come without controversy as in the last minute of ordinary time Bruce Grobbelaar had unceremoniously upended the injured McQueen as the former Leeds man somehow got beyond the Liverpool defence. With referees having earlier in the season been told to act strongly against such challenges, it was a surprise that George Courtney refused to send off the Liverpool 'keeper.

Despite the defeat, it was United's best effort in the thirty years of the League Cup, though that was about to change!

Liverpool: Grobbelaar, Neal, A. Kennedy, Lawrenson, Whelan, Hansen, Dalglish, Lee, Rush, Johnston (Fairclough), Souness.
United: Bailey, Duxbury, Albiston, Moses, Moran (Macari), McQueen, Wilkins, Muhren, Stapleton, Whiteside, Coppell.

ROBBO'S CHARITY CHEER

20 August 1983
FA Charity Shield
United 2 (Robson 2), Liverpool 0.

Often these games are little more than meaningless pre-season kick-abouts, but not this clash which, turned out to be a terrific spectacle.

As David White from the *Oldham Evening Chronicle* observed,

> If England's two finest teams can translate the kind of excitement they produced at Wembley to the intense competitiveness of the First Division title race, then the country's footballing public are in for the most dramatic League campaigns for many years.
>
> There can be no doubting that United have the players to break Liverpool's grip on the domestic game and the curtain-raiser to the new campaign showed they now also have the confidence.

The display from Ron Atkinson's United was a sharp contrast to the way they were hammered into submission by reigning League Champions Liverpool five months earlier in the final of the Milk Cup, and they deserved their victory. It was clear that winning the FA Cup in May had galvanised a belief that had previously been absent from their DNA. The performance of Bryan Robson, who also scored both United goals, also demonstrated just how important he was to their cause as he was again inspirational, along with midfield partners Ray Wilkins and Arnold Muhren.

Liverpool controlled the opening twenty minutes before Robson, Wilkins and Muhren helped wrestle control of the midfield from Mark Lawrenson, Sammy Lee and Graeme Souness. United suddenly gained belief as new boy Arthur Graham began to cause problems on the right wing as Liverpool faded after their bright opening. The one bright spot was the display of Kenny Dalglish, who operated in the hole behind strikers Ian Rush and Michael Robinson, a £200,000 summer signing from Brighton.

Dalglish struck the frame of the United goal before Robson gave United the lead midway through the opening half as he rounded off an intricate passing move by rounding Liverpool 'keeper Bruce Grobbelaar and Alan Kennedy before slotting the ball home. Robson's second goal, shortly after the hour mark, came as Liverpool were in disarray following the double substitutions of David Hodgson and Craig Johnston for Robinson and Phil Thompson. Liverpool failed to clear Kevin Moran's header from Graham's corner as Robson struck again.

United: Bailey, Duxbury, Albiston, Wilkins, Moran, McQueen, Robson, Muhren (Gidman), Stapleton, Whiteside, Graham.
Liverpool: Grobbelaar, Neal, Kennedy, Lawrenson, Thompson (Johnston), Hansen, Dalglish, Lee, Rush, Robinson (Hodgson), Souness.

UNITED'S THREE-IN-A-ROW

24 September 1983
First Division
United 1 (Stapleton), Liverpool 0.

Having already beaten Liverpool in the Charity Shield opener to the season, not to mention a thrilling 4-3 win in Belfast in outgoing Irish FA secretary Harry Drennan's testimonial two weeks previously, this was United's third victory in little more than two months against their rivals.

For once Liverpool were outplayed in midfield where Bryan Robson, scorer of both goals in the Charity Shield at Wembley, Ray Wilkins and Arnold Muhren were in sparkling form and only some fine defensive play from a formidable Liverpool back four of Phil Neal, Alan Kennedy, Mark Lawrenson and Alan Hansen kept their side level at half-time.

As the masters of soaking up pressure before snatching a lead, there must have been a good number of United fans who feared the worst at the start of the second period, but after fifty-two minutes came the breakthrough they so desperately craved. Arthur Graham had cost only £45,000 when transferred from Leeds at the start of the season and he showed Hansen a clean pair of legs as he delivered a beautiful cross which Frank Stapleton memorably half-volleyed beyond Bruce Grobbelaar to leave the Merseysiders' new manager Joe Fagan impressed enough to concede afterwards that it was 'a magnificent goal'. It was a game in which the surprise was that there was only one goal, and that was due to the brilliance of 'keepers Bruce Grobbelaar and Gary Bailey, who were both at their best.

Now it was up to United, who moved into second spot, to build on their victory and push for their first title in seventeen years. The match was also described as a glowing spectacle which restored faith in the game following England's home defeat by Denmark days earlier. There was entertainment, excitement, incident and class from the country's two premier teams which had been missing at Wembley.

Yet some of the problems affecting the national team today were in evidence back in the early eighties. Of the twenty-three players who appeared at Old Trafford, only eight were eligible to play for England though, in those days, they were squeezed out more by British players than foreign talent.

United: Bailey, Albiston, Duxbury, Graham, McQueen, Moran, Robson, Muhren, Stapleton, Whiteside, Wilkins.
Liverpool: Grobbelaar, Neal (Nicol), A. Kennedy, Lawrenson, Johnston, Hansen, Dalglish, Lee, Rush, Robinson, Souness.

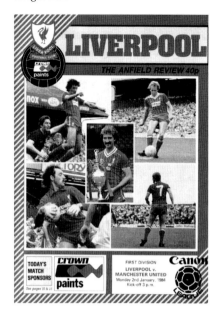

BIG GUNS IN SHOOT-OUT

2 January 1984
First Division
Liverpool 1 (Johnston), United 1 (Whiteside).

Norman Whiteside's last-gasp equaliser kept Manchester United only three points behind Liverpool at the top of the First Division.

It was a draw United scarcely deserved so it was no wonder United manager Ron Atkinson was elated. 'It was a very useful point for us. The result keeps the title race alive and it is a great lift for us,' he explained.

United would probably have not grabbed a share of the spoils had the inspirational Kenny Dalglish not been forced to leave the field early in the second half when poleaxed by a hefty Kevin Moran challenge shortly after half-time. It left the Scotsman with a fractured cheekbone and divided opinion as to whether the United defender had deliberately set out to injure him. 'It was a nasty one which will keep him out for several weeks. It is a big loss for us, but we will have to carry on and sort something out,' explained Liverpool manager Joe Fagan.

At that point Liverpool were leading courtesy of a thirty-second-minute Craig Johnston goal, stabbed home after a Graeme Souness effort had been blocked on the line by Arthur Albiston. It could have been more but, despite opening up the United defence on a number of occasions, Liverpool failed to put United 'keeper Gary Bailey under any serious pressure.

It didn't seem as though this would matter until the final minute, when the previously anonymous Whiteside unexpectedly popped up in the penalty area to latch on to a flick from substitute Garth Crooks and fire a shot past the despairing dive of Bruce Grobbelaar.

Fagan's first season as manager was a dream as he won the three pieces of silverware: the League, Liverpool's third in a row and fifth in six seasons, the European Cup, and the Milk Cup as United, who finished fourth, ended up empty-handed.

United: Bailey, Albiston, Duxbury, Graham, McQueen, Moran (Crooks), Moses, Muhren, Stapleton, Whiteside, Wilkins.
Liverpool: Grobbelaar, Neal, A. Kennedy, Lawrenson, Nicol, Hansen, Dalglish (Hodgson), Lee, Rush, Johnston, Souness.

SPURS EARLY-SEASON PACESETTERS

22 September 1984
First Division
United 1 (Strachan (pen.)), Liverpool 1 (Walsh).

The draw kept both teams just behind early-season League leaders Tottenham, though it was by no means one of the greatest games between these sides. Only the goals from Gordon Strachan and Paul Walsh and a magnificent Bruce Grobbelaar save from Bryan Robson stood out.

First Strachan drew Alan Kennedy into a rash challenge midway through the opening half and then whacked home the resulting penalty to give United the lead. With half-time approaching, Robson was already celebrating a trademark thunderbolt that a stationary Liverpool 'keeper really had no right to even try to save. Grobbelaar, though, always had the knack of doing the unexpected, and this was certainly one of those occasions, hurtling across the goal to palm the ball away to safety. Later it was even rumoured that some United supporters had applauded, so good was the save.

It proved just the tonic for Joe Fagan's side, which after winning the European Cup at the end of the previous season and not forgetting the League title again, were once more everyone's favourites to win everything in sight. John Wark, who had been signed in March, was the sort of player every side needs, wholehearted, enthusiastic and a lovely passer of the ball, and he began to wrestle from United the midfield authority they had enjoyed in the first period.

At first it didn't seem to matter as Liverpool couldn't break down the United back four. However, just as it seemed the home side might hold on to grab all three points, the equaliser came with seventeen minutes left. Steve Nicol curled an inch-perfect cross onto the head of Walsh, who finished in style. Undeserved, probably; lucky, certainly not.

United: Bailey, Duxbury, Albiston, Moses, Moran (Muhren), Hogg, Robson, Strachan, Hughes, Whiteside, Olsen.

Liverpool: Grobbelaar, Neal, A. Kennedy, Lawrenson, Whelan, Hansen, Dalglish, Lee, Walsh, Wark, Nicol.

UNITED TITLE DREAM STILL ALIVE

31 March 1985
First Division
Liverpool 0, United 1 (Stapleton).

Victory for Ron Atkinson's side kept them in with an outside chance of the First Division title, but for reigning champions Liverpool the result meant that they were now twelve points behind leaders Everton with less than a quarter of the season left.

With millions watching on television, Frank Stapleton grabbed the only goal when he rose to majestically head home a seventy-fourth-minute Norman Whiteside cross.

It was reward for an attacking performance, and came after United had withstood strong second-half pressure during which Liverpool had two strong penalty appeals waved away.

Referee Joe Worrall waved away appeals for a foul on Steve Nichol by Arthur Albiston and then a handball when Kenny Dalglish's shot appeared to strike the arm of Paul McGrath.

It was described, however, as a spectacle which failed to live up to expectations, with both sides lacking imagination. With the sides set to meet again the following weekend at Goodison Park in the FA Cup semi-final, Stapleton's classic goal was a big boost to United's confidence and kept alive their outside chance of doing 'the double', last recorded by Arsenal in 1971. It was a second successive home defeat for Liverpool following their loss against Spurs and left the title race appearing a three-way race between Everton, United and Tottenham, all of whom had triumphed at Anfield.

A late surge, though, saw Liverpool finish as runners-up to the neighbours as Manchester United slipped to fourth spot. There was also defeat for Fagan in the final of the European Cup to Juventus, though that result paled into insignificance in the wake of the Heysel disaster that night in Brussels, where thirty-nine fans lost their lives. And there were ramifications, as English clubs were banned from European football and Liverpool were unable to compete for the next six years.

Liverpool: Grobbelaar, Neal, A. Kennedy (Walsh) Lawrenson, Nicol, Hansen, Dalglish, Whelan, Rush, MacDonald, Wark.
United: Bailey, Gidman, Albiston, Whiteside, McGrath, Hogg, Robson, Strachan, Hughes, Stapleton, Olsen.

SUPER-SUB WALSH PREVENTS CUP EXIT

13 April 1985
FA Cup semi-final
United 2 (Robson, Hughes), Liverpool 2 (Whelan, Walsh) after extra time.
(at Goodison Park)

Substitute Paul Walsh's last-gasp extra-time header kept the dream of a first ever Merseyside FA Cup final alive after Everton beat Luton Town in the other semi-final. Liverpool, in fact, hauled themselves back into the game twice, having looked set to bow out of the Cup at the end of normal and extra time.

United manager Ron Atkinson said,

> You have to be disappointed when you have not won a game you deserved to. We gave a tremendous performance, though the rub of the green may have gone against us in that Liverpool's second equalising goal came after a linesman had signalled a decision for us. The referee was looking at the players and Liverpool went on to score. I have no complaints about the referee (George Courtney) was superb.

Ex-Luton man Walsh might have grabbed the goal but it was Kenny Dalglish who deserved the plaudits, robbing Gordon Strachan before dashing down the left to deliver a wonderful cross for Ian Rush to head powerfully towards goal. United 'keeper Gary Bailey made a good save but was unable to hold the ball as Walsh was given an easy chance to draw the sides level. The fact that Dalglish was even on the field was remarkable as at half-time he required an ice-pack on his swollen ankle to help get his boot back on.

United had been the better side, with strikers Mark Hughes and Frank Stapleton constantly troubling Liverpool defenders Alan Hansen and Mark Lawrenson. They took the lead after sixty-nine minutes when Bryan Robson, in his only serious contribution to the game, broke the deadlock with a shot that was deflected over the line by Mark Hughes, though it was credited to Robson.

With time running out and many of the United faithful set to celebrate their second Goodison Park semi-final success against Liverpool in seven seasons, Ronnie Whelan struck with a sweet edge-of-the-box curler with just three minutes of ordinary time remaining.

Yet if United were downhearted by being denied so late on, they failed to show it and were soon back in the lead in the first period of extra-time when Stapleton's strike took a slight deflection to leave Bruce Grobbelaar stranded and United rightly back in front. Stapleton had a chance to kill off Liverpool following a poor clearance from Grobbelaar, who redeemed himself by beating away the striker's goal-bound shot.

Liverpool hung on and their sheer resilience was rewarded in the 119th minute when Walsh had the final word, with his goal forcing a replay at Maine Road four days later.

United: Bailey, Gidman, Albiston, Whiteside, McGrath, Hogg, Robson, Strachan, Hughes, Stapleton, Olsen.

Liverpool: Grobbelaar, Neal, Beglin, Lawrenson, Lee, Hansen, Dalglish, Whelan, Rush, MacDonald, Wark (Walsh).

UNITED BOOK WEMBLEY PLACE

17 April 1985.
FA Cup Semi-Final Replay
United 2 (Robson, Hughes), Liverpool 1 (McGrath (o.g.))
(at Maine Road)

United produced a performance full of character to reach their third final of the FA Cup in six years. There were many who thought United had blown their chances by failing to win at the first attempt at Goodison Park, where Liverpool managed to escape from jail.

Liverpool played better in the second meeting, but United performed with the same confidence and flair which most clubs can only dream about when playing the Merseysiders.

There was disappointment for Liverpool fans before kick-off when Ian Rush was declared unfit to play. True, the Welshman had failed to score in his ten games against United, but his absence was a big blow for Joe Fagan's side. Paul Walsh, who deputised for Rush, failed to repeat the success he enjoyed after coming on as a substitute and scoring the late goal which forced the replay.

Liverpool might have, probably justifiably, claimed that Mark Hughes' winner was offside but there was no question that the better side triumphed to go through to Wembley and play Everton in May. United also had to come from a goal down, Paul McGrath scoring past his own 'keeper in the thirty-ninth minute as he nudged Steve Nicol's cross past Gary Bailey as John Wark put the young Irish defender under pressure.

United were level within two minutes of the restart and the goal from Bryan Robson was one of the greatest ever seen in an FA Cup semi-final. Picking the ball up a good fifty yards from the Liverpool goal, the United skipper tore down the field, left Mark Lawrenson for dead and smashed a glorious shot past 'keeper Bruce Grobbelaar. Hughes' goal on the hour wasn't as good as that, but it was still a cracker. Dashing onto a Gordon Strachan through-ball, he finished powerfully as the Liverpool defence appealed for offside.

Stung by falling behind, the Merseysiders played their best football of the two games, with Kenny Dalglish missing narrowly and Kevin MacDonald almost catching out Bailey.

United manager Ron Atkinson had little sympathy for Liverpool's claims for offside, saying, 'When you play the offside trap, that's the risk you take. We were worth our win.' The result meant that with Everton odds-on to win the League title, Liverpool fans were left with a choice of wanting United to win the FA Cup or Everton to complete the double.

Liverpool, at least, had the consolation of knowing they had the European Cup final to look forward to after winning the first leg of the semi-final 4-0 at home to Greek side Panathinaikos.

The after-match scenes around Maine Road sadly tarnished football's image as celebrating United fans retaliated after being attacked as they left the ground. Over twenty people were arrested as houses and cars were damaged on another sad night for English football. Things were, of course, to get a lot worse over the next few weeks with deaths at St Andrews, Ayresome Park and Heysel, not forgetting the tragedy at Valley Parade.

United: Bailey, Gidman, Albiston, Whiteside, McGrath, Hogg, Robson, Strachan, Hughes, Stapleton, Olsen.
Liverpool: Grobbelaar, Neal, Beglin, Lawrenson, Nicol, Hansen, Dalglish (Gillespie), Whelan, Walsh, MacDonald, Wark.

QUICK OUT OF THE BLOCKS

19 October 1985
First Division
United 1 (McGrath), Liverpool 1 (Johnston).

This was United's chance to show who were the new kings of English football after a remarkable start to their First Division campaign. They went into the game having collected thirty-four points from a possible thirty-six, Luton Town the only team to hold them to a draw.

Their exploits had completely overshadowed Liverpool, who themselves had made a decent start having collected twenty-four points from their first twelve League matches. In the wake of English clubs being banned from European football following the Heysel tragedy, the League campaign became even more important. And with a further win for United, already ten points clear of Liverpool by mid-October, surely not even Liverpool would be able to catch their arch-rivals.

It was hardly surprising, therefore, that United fans were buoyant before kick-off at Old Trafford, though Bryan Robson was out with a torn hamstring and Gordon Strachan was still to recover from a dislocated collarbone. There was considerable pressure on Norman Whiteside and Remi Moses to deliver in midfield. Manager Ron Atkinson had chosen to partner them with Paul McGrath.

Though Liverpool were marginally the better side in the opening period, United's defence comfortably dealt with their opponents and Gary Bailey's goal was rarely in danger. The tempo of the game changed following the restart when, within seconds,

Craig Johnston scored for Liverpool. He applied the neatest of touches to head beyond the United 'keeper and threaten to end the home side's unbeaten start to the season.

The fact they didn't was largely down to McGrath, who, timing his run to perfection, met Albiston's cross midway through the second period to equalise. With United now scenting a winner, Liverpool were forced to defend deeply and could consider themselves fortunate when in the last few seconds of the game Alan Hansen diverted a cross against his own bar.

If that had gone in would Liverpool have been out of the title race, even at this early stage of the season?

United: Bailey, Duxbury, Albiston, Whiteside, Moran, Hogg, McGrath, Moses
    (Barnes) Hughes, Stapleton, Olsen.
Liverpool: Grobbelaar, Nicol, Beglin, Lawrenson, Whelan, Hansen, Wark
    (MacDonald) Johnston, Rush, Molby, McMahon.

LIVERPOOL PENALTY CONTROVERSY

26 November 1985
Milk Cup, Round Four
Liverpool 2 (Molby 2 (1 pen.)), United 1 (McGrath).

There was controversy surrounding the penalty which earned Liverpool victory in their Milk Cup fourth round tie against United at Anfield.

The differing post-match views as to what happened from offender Kevin Moran and Liverpool's Ian Rush only served to complicate matters further and leave the issue far from resolved. Moran insisted he was outside the penalty area when he accidentally handled a bobbling ball, but Rush maintained he was stood on the eighteen-yard line with the defender behind him. The fifty-sixth-minute penalty from Jan Molby, barely one minute after he had scored a spectacular solo effort, transformed the match after United had threatened to end Liverpool's unbeaten ten-match run.

The Kop had been silenced in the second minute when Paul McGrath rounded off a brilliant move involving John Gidman and Norman Whiteside to put United ahead with a spectacular strike past 'keeper Bruce Grobbelaar. Throughout the opening half United, who were without six injured first-team players, nullified the Liverpool machine without too much difficulty, making a mockery of their recent results.

Gordon Strachan and McGrath might have added a second goal early in the second half before Liverpool staged their great fightback. The turning point came in the fifty-fifth minute when Molby, who had abandoned his defensive role, made a terrific solo run before firing an unstoppable shot past 'keeper Gary Bailey. Liverpool struck again barely one minute later when Molby was spot-on from twelve yards. Once ahead, Liverpool were rarely troubled, though United were denied an equaliser in the dying minutes when Alan Brazil's shot was headed off the line by Molby.

United manager Ron Atkinson said, 'For all their pressure, we had the better chances. When we were one up, we had a couple of chances to wrap up the game.'

Moran was angry at the decision to award a penalty against him, saying, 'It was a joke. I was at least a yard, possibly two, outside the area when Rush jumped and backed into me. I don't dispute I handled the ball, but no way was it a penalty.'

Liverpool: Grobbelaar, Nicol, Beglin, Lawrenson, Whelan, Hansen, Walsh, Johnston, Rush, Molby, McMahon.

United: Bailey, Gidman, Blackmore, Whiteside, Moran, Hogg, McGrath, Strachan, Stapleton, Brazil, Olsen.

UNITED'S TITLE COLLAPSE

2 February 1986
First Division
Liverpool 1 (Wark), United 1 (Gibson).

When the sides had last met in October, United had left the field with a ten-point lead at the top of the First Division. However, with just twenty points from the next fourteen games, Ron Atkinson's side found itself in second spot for the return at Anfield.

Previous season's League Champions Everton had squeezed to the top in what was now the tightest League in seasons with Liverpool, Chelsea and West Ham all in the mix for the title. With four defeats away from home in their last six, this was going to be a stiff test for United, especially as Liverpool were unbeaten at Anfield in fourteen League games and had won eleven of them. There was therefore plenty to look forward to before kick-off.

Sadly, though, a more than decent game was to be overshadowed by events off the pitch prior to kick-off when stones and a brick were hurled at the United team-coach as it pulled into the Anfield car-park. Then, as the shaken players disembarked, they were sprayed by a so-called Liverpool fan, leaving them and nearby fans with their eyes streaming. Reserve Clayton Blackmore was the player worst affected in an incident that left twenty fans, many of them children, needing treatment. Coming less than a year after the Heysel tragedy, it was another indicator that all was still not well with English football.

Chris Turner, in the United goal, was the star of the match. Signed from Sunderland at the start of the season, he had been reserve to Gary Bailey for much of it, but was drafted in at the last minute. Turner performed heroically, particularly during the second half when Liverpool piled on the pressure. 'He was superb,' said Ron Atkinson afterwards. The 'keeper's best save was a great diving save to deny Ian Rush, and he was to be beaten only once when John Wark drilled home a shot after thirty-eight minutes. The Scot's effort brought the scores level, Colin Gibson having stroked home a penalty after fourteen minutes.

The result maintained United's fine record at Anfield over recent years, with 1979 being the last time they had lost there. Liverpool lost to neighbours Everton in their next game before beginning a magnificent run which saw them collect thirty-four points from their last twelve League matches to be crowned champions. United, who were ten points clear of Liverpool in October having picked up thirty-four points from their first twelve League matches, didn't even finish in the first three, with Everton and West Ham United coming second and third.

There was now real pressure on Atkinson to deliver at the start of the following season, while for Liverpool the defeat of Everton in the FA Cup final at Wembley at the season's end meant they had finally entered the record books alongside Preston North End, Aston Villa, Tottenham and Arsenal as League and Cup 'double' winners.

Liverpool: Grobbelaar, Lee, Beglin, Lawrenson, Whelan, Hansen, Walsh (Wark)
    Johnston, Rush, Molby, Gillespie.
United: Turner, Gidman, Albiston, Whiteside, McGrath, Moran, Sivebæk, T. Gibson,
    Hughes, C. Gibson, Olsen (Stapleton).

FERGIE'S FIRST ANFIELD VISIT

26 December 1986
First Division
Liverpool 0, United 1 (Whiteside).

Both clubs were determined to ensure there was no repeat of the ugly scenes prior to the previous season's game at Anfield and it was decided that legendary former manager Bob Paisley would travel to the ground on the United team bus. Accompanying him was the new man in charge at Old Trafford, Alex Ferguson. The Scot had arrived with an impressive record during his time in charge at Aberdeen, even managing to break the hold of Celtic and Rangers on the vast majority of trophies north of the border.

In November he had replaced Ron Atkinson after he had started his sixth season in charge of United poorly. United arrived on Boxing Day just two points outside the relegation zone. Liverpool had brushed aside Chelsea 3-0 in the previous game and the Kop were set to celebrate a first League home victory against United in the League since 1979.

Player-manager Kenny Dalglish had selected himself to play for the first time since October, but in the event he had a poor game. Worse still, he messed around with the general formation of his side, preferring to play Jan Molby as a sweeper with Mark Lawrenson in midfield. It was enough to see the always honest Scot admit afterwards, 'We were totally disjointed, which is my fault.'

Ferguson had altered his line-up, with Bryan Robson moved into the back four and Norman Whiteside playing in midfield. The changes paid off in the seventy-eighth minute when Whiteside grabbed the winner with a powerful twenty-yard drive that Grobbelaar had no chance of saving. The defeat meant Liverpool had won only two of their last seven League games and speculation continued to mount that they were about to make a move for Oxford United's John Aldridge as a long-term replacement for Ian Rush.

Liverpool: Grobbelaar, Gillespie, Beglin, Lawrenson, Whelan, Hansen, Dalglish, Venison, Rush, Molby, McMahon.
United: Walsh, Sivebæk, Gibson, Whiteside, Moran, Duxbury, Robson, Strachan, Stapleton, Davenport, Olsen.

UNITED DOUBLE WRECKS TITLE HOPES

20 April 1987
First Division
United 1 (Davenport), Liverpool 0.

Three points adrift of League leaders Everton, Liverpool were aware this was a game they had to win to maintain any chance of catching their near neighbours. Knowing that the Goodison side were three Wayne Clarke goals up at home against Newcastle United, Kenny Dalglish's side had no option but to seek a winner in the final ten minutes.

It was a gamble that backfired badly when Peter Davenport belted home a shot from just outside the box for the winner with two minutes remaining. Liverpool's misery was made even worse by the news that 'keeper Bruce Grobbelaar had fractured an elbow and would be out for the rest of the season.

Liverpool, for whom Ian Rush again failed to score against United in what was his fifteenth match, knew that only a win at Goodison Park the following Saturday would be good enough to hold onto any chances of retaining the League. For United the pleasure of beating the near neighbours was tempered by the knowledge that they were

closer to the relegation zone than the top, and at the season's end they would finish a disappointing eleventh out of twenty-two.

Liverpool: Grobbelaar, Gillespie, Venison, Spackman, Whelan, Hansen, Walsh Johnston, Rush, Ablett, McMahon.

United: Walsh, Sivebæk, Albiston (Stapleton), Moses, McGrath, Moran, Duxbury, Strachan, Davenport, Whiteside, C. Gibson.

LIVERPOOL'S ELECTRIFYING START

15 November 1987
First Division
United 1 (Whiteside), Liverpool 1 (Aldridge).

Liverpool had made a magnificent start to the season, in which they had won nine and drawn one of the first ten League games.

They were on track to continue that remarkable run until Norman Whiteside scrambled home a hotly disputed forty-ninth-minute equaliser, with Bruce Grobbelaar after the game declaring that 'it was a nice pass with [Kevin] Moran's hand that led to their goal. I reckon United must be picking up tips from their basketball team these days.'

Liverpool had taken the lead after twenty minutes when John Aldridge soared to score with a header. For a while the goal seemed to knock the confidence out of a United side that had started the game in attacking fashion. By half-time, however, United were again pushing back Liverpool and it was no great surprise when they forced the equaliser soon after the restart.

Getting a winner proved much more difficult, as was the case for all but two teams in the League that season – Everton and Nottingham Forest, both away – being good enough to beat Liverpool. In the circumstances it wasn't a bad point for United.

United: Walsh, Anderson, C. Gibson, Duxbury, Blackmore, Moran (Davenport), Robson, Strachan, McClair, Whiteside, Olsen.
Liverpool: Grobbelaar, Gillespie, Lawrenson, Nicol, Whelan, Hansen, Beardsley, Aldridge, Johnston, Barnes, McMahon.

TEN-MAN UNITED PULL BACK TWO-GOAL DEFICIT

4 April 1988
First Division
Liverpool 3 (Beardsley, Gillespie, McMahon), United 3 (Robson 2, Strachan).

Though this was a clash of the heavyweights, it was of no great significance as Liverpool had all but wrapped up the League title.

True, United were second behind Liverpool, but it was a very long way behind – ten points in fact, and they'd played two games more and only had six more to play before the season's end. The title was as good as dusted and the only question now was whether Liverpool would go on to beat Nottingham Forest in the following weekend's FA Cup semi-final, moving forward to record their second double in two seasons.

United were 3-1 down with half an hour left and the game seemed over for Alex Ferguson's side, especially when Colin Gibson was dismissed after a second yellow card following a foul on Steve McMahon.

They refused to lie down and five minutes later were back in the game when Bryan Robson's shot took a deflection off Gary Gillespie, and with the United fans in the ground urging their side forward it was after seventy-eight minutes when Gordon Strachan struck.

Ferguson's side had started the game in dramatic fashion when Robson scored after two minutes, but were stung either side of half-time when Gary Gillespie and two from Steve McMahon established what appeared an impregnable lead. Not so, but even though his side had come back to grab an unlikely point, Ferguson was incandescent with rage at the end and launched a verbal attack on what he felt was the intimidation of referees at Anfield.

He blazed, 'I can now understand why clubs come away from here choking on their own vomit and biting their own tongues knowing they've been done by the referee. You need a miracle to win here. When you lose it sounds like sour grapes. That's why no-one complains. But we got a result and I am saying it. Referees are under provocation and intimidation here.'

If the Glaswegian thought he'd get away with such an attack he was mistaken. Liverpool manager Kenny Dalglish, walking past with his daughter, responded with a few verbals of his own, stating, 'You might as well talk to my daughter. You will get more sense out of her.'

It was a sad end to a magnificent game, and afterwards the Football Association investigated the comments of both managers.

Liverpool: Grobbelaar, Gillespie, Ablett, Nicol, Spackman, Hansen, Beardsley, Aldridge (Johnston), Houghton, Barnes, McMahon.

United: Turner, Anderson, Blackmore (Whiteside), Bruce, McGrath, Duxbury (Olsen), Strachan, Robson, McClair, Davenport, C. Gibson.

PUTTING THE RECORD STRAIGHT

3 September 1988
First Division
Liverpool 1 (Molby (pen.)), United 0.

Having won impressively at Charlton Athletic in the first game of the season, courtesy of a John Aldridge hat-trick, Liverpool were buoyant as they prepared to entertain their rivals.

Liverpool had failed to beat the visitors at home in the League since 1979 so it was viewed as time to put the record straight. Both teams had seen the return of old favourites, Ian Rush to Liverpool while Mark Hughes was back at Old Trafford as neither had performed with distinction on their respective European duties. Rush had failed to settle in Italy at Juventus and, in Hughes' case, at Barcelona and Bayern Munich. Rush was on the bench and witnessed his Welsh team-mate struggle to make an impact on the game.

In fact, only one of the United team emerged with honour at the end, Jim Leighton in goal performing heroically and only beaten by a Jan Molby penalty after thirty-eight minutes.

If it looked a harsh decision, John Barnes going down far too easily when challenged by Steve Bruce, the overall result was not and United's performance showed they were in for a difficult season.

Liverpool: Grobbelaar, Gillespie, Venison, Nicol, Whelan, Molby, Beardsley, Aldridge (Rush), Houghton, Barnes, McMahon (Spackman).

United: Leighton, Anderson, Blackmore, Bruce, McGrath (Garton), Duxbury, Robson, Strachan (Davenport), McClair, Hughes, Olsen.

LIVERPOOL'S LATE COLLAPSE

1 January 1989
First Division
United 3 (McClair, Hughes, Beardsmore), Liverpool 1 (Barnes).

When John Barnes raced onto Peter Beardsley's through-ball to put Liverpool into the lead with twenty minutes remaining, few of those watching inside Old Trafford and on the television could possibly have predicted what would happen next. Yet within seven minutes United had raced into a two-goal lead, sending the Old Trafford faithful into a frenzy.

Brian McClair started things off with a spectacular overhead free-kick that gave Liverpool 'keeper Mike Hooper no chance. Three minutes later Mark Hughes hit a trademark drive from a narrow angle to give United the lead. Within sixty seconds it was 3-1, Russell Beardsmore leaving Hooper helpless and sending Liverpool back along the M62 defeated.

For Alex Ferguson it was a welcome win. His team was lying ninth in the table and he was under pressure from a restless home crowd and newspaper rumours were that he was set to be sacked. The manager's happy New Year was made even brighter by Paul McGrath's return midway through the second half following a knee operation.

After a nervous start, the Irishman showed just how good a player he could be, making some crucial interventions as Liverpool pushed to get back into the game in the final fifteen minutes.

Liverpool finished runners-up to Arsenal, but finished with silverware after beating Everton in the second all-Merseyside final in three years. United ended the campaign a disappointing eleventh.

United: Leighton, Martin (McGrath), Sharpe, Bruce, Beardsmore, Robson, Strachan (Robins), McClair, Hughes, Milne.
Liverpool: Hooper, Ablett, Staunton (Molby), Nicol, Whelan, Burrows, Beardsley, Aldridge, Houghton, Barnes, McMahon.

UNITED RAISE THEIR GAME

23 December 1989
First Division
Liverpool 0, United 0.

There was still a wide gulf between the two teams when they met at Anfield two days before Christmas as Liverpool were second while United were in the bottom half, lying in thirteenth place.

Yet there was a surprise in terms of their relative League standings as United came away with a point following a goalless encounter. And it was once again a case of the results of these matches failing to follow the form book.

Liverpool may have enjoyed unprecedented success in the eighties yet United lost only once in ten League visits to Anfield during the decade. United, by all accounts, were unlucky not to come away with all three points after producing a display which belied their lowly League standing. Liverpool may have won numerous footballing honours but they failed once more to show consistency against their rivals from Old Trafford.

Had the out-of-sorts strike duo of Mark Hughes and Brian McClair not squandered six chances between them, then surely United would have emerged victors. Liverpool 'keeper Bruce Grobbelaar pulled off a couple of decent saves, but overall the standard of United's finishing left much to be desired.

United certainly raised their game, hustling Liverpool out of their usual rhythm and restricting them to only two chances, a rarity for a team visiting Anfield. Both fell to Steve McMahon, who was unable to find a way past 'keeper Jim Leighton.

Liverpool: Grobbelaar, Hysen, Venison, Ablett, Whelan, Hansen, Beardsley, Houghton, Rush, Molby (Nicol), McMahon.
United: Leighton, Blackmore, Martin, Bruce, Phelan, Pallister, Robson, Ince, McClair, Hughes, Wallace (Sharpe).

7

Manchester Monopoly

The nineties began with Liverpool still asserting their dominance of the previous decade as they lifted the First Division trophy for what was then a record-breaking eighteenth time.

Little did they realise at the time that it would be their last success, as there would be a dramatic shift in the power balance, with United emerging from a period in which they could only look with envy at the successes achieved by their Merseyside rivals, both in domestic and European competitions.

Yet the nineties began with Liverpool still holding on to their power base, with little inkling as to the way in which the fortunes of the respective clubs would dramatically change.

UNITED IN RELEGATION BATTLE

18 March 1990
First Division
United 1 (Whelan (o.g.)), Liverpool 2 (Barnes 2 (1 pen.)).
United were experiencing a harrowing time when they played host to Liverpool as they were only two points and two places clear of the First Division relegation places.

Two goals from John Barnes earned Liverpool only their second League win in a decade at Old Trafford to pile on the misery.

These were certainly challenging times for United, who would finish sixteenth, and by all accounts it was only their FA Cup win in May that saved Alex Ferguson from the sack. Liverpool, by contrast, would go on to secure their eighteenth League title.

United had in recent years always raised their game against Liverpool. But this was one of the occasions in which they failed to do so as Barnes, with his jinking runs and trickery, ripped their defence to shreds. They were well beaten and the scoreline does not do justice to the all-round superiority of the visitors, who were in a different class as they moved to within two points of leaders Aston Villa with a game in hand.

Liverpool opened the scoring after quarter of an hour when Ray Houghton and Peter Beardsley set up Barnes, who was left unmarked on the left to sprint clear to score.

United were caught cold eight minutes into the second half when Barnes struck again, this time from the penalty spot after Viv Anderson had brought down Ian Rush.

Barnes was denied a hat-trick by a brave save from Jim Leighton which would have spared an anxious last ten minutes.

Grobbelaar pulled off a superb save to keep out Brian McClair's spectacular overhead kick. Then moments later Grobbelaar was finally beaten, but not by a United player, as Ronnie Whelan's errant back pass from twenty-five yards sailed over his head.

United: Leighton, Anderson (Duxbury), Martin, Bruce, Phelan, Pallister, Blackmore, Ince, McClair, Hughes, Wallace (Beardsmore).
Liverpool: Grobbelaar, Hysen, Venison, Nicol, Whelan, Hansen, Beardsley, Burrows (Houghton), Rush, Barnes, McMahon.

SHIELD SHARED SIX MONTHS APIECE

18 August 1990
FA Charity Shield
Liverpool 1 (Barnes (pen.)), United 1 (Blackmore).

United returned to Wembley three months after their FA Cup triumph and this time they were again unbeaten as they held First Division champions Liverpool in the Tennents FA Charity Shield, the curtain-raiser to the new campaign.

It was a case of Alex Ferguson trying something innovative as he introduced a defensive sweeper system which certainly worked against Liverpool. Having seen

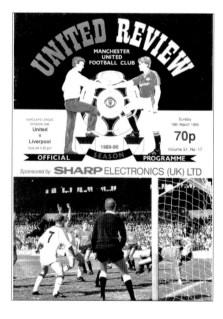

Bobby Robson use the system in that summer's World Cup, Ferguson played Steve Bruce, Mal Donaghy and Gary Pallister as three central defenders with Denis Irwin and Clayton Blackmore urged to bomb forward as wing backs. The formation may only have been in its infancy, but Ferguson was delighted at how it worked, saying he hoped it would help them in their bid to land that elusive First Division title.

United, who had been by far the busier and more effective team in the opening period, took the lead in the dying seconds of the opening half. Mike Phelan crossed the ball from the byline and Blackmore was on hand to convert from inside the six-yard box.

The lead did not last long as Liverpool equalised four minutes into the second half when Pallister was harshly judged by referee George Courtney to have brought down Barnes in the penalty area when he looked to have played the ball first.

Barnes picked himself up to score from the spot. The equaliser fired up United and only three superb saves from Grobbelaar ensured Liverpool remained on level terms as he twice denied Blackmore as well as McClair and the two clubs each shared the Shield for six months.

Liverpool: Grobbelaar, Hysen, Burrows, Venison, Whelan, Ablett, Beardsley (Rosenthal), Houghton, Rush, Barnes, McMahon.
United: Sealey, Irwin, Donaghy, Bruce, Phelan, Pallister, Blackmore, Ince, McClair, Hughes, Wallace (Robins).

UNITED'S HEAVIEST LOSS FOR SIXTY-FOUR YEARS

16 September 1990
First Division
Liverpool 4 (Beardsley 3, Barnes), United 0.

One month after holding Liverpool in the FA Charity Shield at Wembley, United suffered humiliation at Anfield, where they were dealt a 4-0 defeat. Peter Beardsley scored a hat-trick for Liverpool but it was John Barnes, who also found the net, who inflicted torture as United went down to their heaviest defeat against their rivals in sixty-four years.

Champions Liverpool were unstoppable as they made it five successive wins at the start of the season to open up a four-point lead at the top of the table.

Alex Ferguson was not too displeased with United's performance, saying their general play was good and that they created chances. They had started the day in third place after a much-improved start to the season, having narrowly avoided relegation in the previous campaign. 'We didn't handle John Barnes, however, and his vision was magnificent and his passing unbelievable. He's a superb player who is really on song,' he explained.

Even Liverpool were said to be slightly embarrassed by their margin of victory, which was only their third in seventeen League meetings against United.

LIVERPOOL

● CHAMPIONS OF THE FOOTBALL LEAGU

Here's your new-look, all-colour Anfield Review
... and still only £1

CLUB SPONSORS

Candy ❋ ◻ ⊡

SEE PAGE 21

★ SEE ALSO BACK COVER FOR DETAILS OF A GREAT NEW PRIZE COMPETITION!

BARCLAYS LEAGUE DIVISION 1
LIVERPOOL
versus
MANCHESTER UNITED
Sunday, 16th September, 1990
Kick-off 3 p.m.

MATCH SPONSORS

EN-5 E
Sportswear

SEE PAGE 31

Beardsley was the difference between the two teams as he responded in the most positive way imaginable to being dropped by both club and country in the previous week, scoring the first hat-trick of his Liverpool career. Beardsley opened the scoring in the eleventh minute with a simple tap-in, but United were unlucky not to equalise moments later when Neil Webb headed against the crossbar. The live-wire Beardsley struck again on the half-hour and Barnes headed Liverpool's third goal shortly before the break.

United produced a spirited second-half display, but there was never any way they were going to wipe out a three-goal deficit. Beardsley, fittingly, had the final word when he completed his hat-trick with eight minutes left, a clever lob from a quickly taken free-kick.

Liverpool: Grobbelaar, Hysen, Burrows, Nicol, Whelan, Gillespie, Beardsley, Houghton, Rush, Barnes, McMahon.
United: Sealey, Irwin, Blackmore, Bruce, Phelan, Pallister (Donaghy), Webb, Ince (Beardsmore), McClair, Hughes, Robins.

CUP WIN ERASES EARLIER HORROR

31 October 1990
Rumbelows League Cup, Third Round
United 3 (Bruce (pen.), Hughes, Sharpe), Liverpool 1 (Houghton).

Victory is always sweet for United against arch-rivals Liverpool, but none more so than their Rumbelows League Cup triumph at Old Trafford. It was a win to savour, coming a matter of six weeks after United suffered their humiliating 4-0 defeat in the League at Anfield. It was the first loss Liverpool had suffered in thirteen League and Cup games this season and a first defeat in twenty-one matches in total.

Alex Ferguson had always maintained that the early-season loss was a 'freak' result and so it was proved as United outplayed Liverpool from start to finish. Perhaps it might have been a different story had Liverpool's mercurial John Barnes not been an absentee through injury as he had tortured and tormented United in recent matches.

The defeat also prompted harsh criticism of his players from Liverpool manager Kenny Dalglish, who said, 'At Liverpool we set higher standards than that, and our house is not in order at the moment.'

There were early warning signs for Liverpool as they were indebted to goalkeeper Bruce Grobbelaar, who pulled off fine early saves to deny Clayton Blackmore and Steve Bruce. The only surprise was that it took United thirty-six minutes to make the breakthrough, which eventually came when Steve Nicol handled a Denis Irwin cross and Bruce scored from the spot. Only seventeen seconds after Liverpool kicked off again, Grobbelaar was picking the ball out of the net for a second time when Mark Hughes found the net with a brilliant dipping shot from twenty-five yards.

Peter Beardsley and Ian Rush, who had failed to score against United in twenty-one games, squandered second-half chances which could have given Liverpool a foothold back into the game. United sealed victory through an eighty-first-minute goal from Lee Sharpe after Liverpool failed to clear a corner. Ray Houghton scored a consolation goal for Liverpool, following a wicked deflection off Gary Pallister, but it was nothing more than that.

United: Sealey, Irwin, Blackmore, Bruce, Phelan (Donaghy), Pallister, Webb, Ince, McClair, Hughes (Wallace), Sharpe.
Liverpool: Grobbelaar, Hysen, Burrows (Rosenthal), Nicol, Staunton, Gillespie, Beardsley, Houghton, Rush, Molby, McMahon.

LIVERPOOL STILL IN TITLE HUNT

3 February 1991
First Division
United 1 (Bruce), Liverpool 1 (Speedie).
Liverpool manager Kenny Dalglish viewed it as a better point for his team than United

following their 1-1 draw at Old Trafford. It strengthened Liverpool's hand as they moved behind leaders Arsenal on goal difference having played one less match, though they would finish the season runners-up to the Gunners.

As for United, they were fifth with Alex Ferguson refusing to concede defeat in their title challenge, though they would ultimately finish sixth.

United and Liverpool both had their chances to earn maximum points but, on reflection, a draw was probably the fairest result. In comparison to the usual titanic clashes between these two teams, this latest meeting proved a disappointing affair.

In a game of few chances, Steve McMahon went as close as anyone as he struck the crossbar in the opening minute.

United took the lead midway through the opening half when Liverpool defender Glenn Hysen inexplicably handled in the penalty area, enabling Steve Bruce to coolly slot home his eighth spot-kick of the season. They would have doubled their advantage late in the opening half but for a brilliant reflex save from Bruce Grobbelaar to keep out a point-blank header from Bryan Robson. Had that gone in, it would have been hard for Liverpool to recover and it proved to be the defining moment of the match as seconds later they equalised.

Inevitably it was John Barnes, who revelled in these Merseyside/Manchester clashes, who was the provider as he beat three men on the left before setting up David Speedie, Liverpool's new £750,000 capture from Coventry, who marked his debut by crashing a shot into the roof of the net.

United: Sealey, Irwin, Blackmore, Bruce, Phelan (Martin), Pallister, Robson, Webb (Wallace), McClair, Hughes, Sharp.
Liverpool: Grobbelaar, Hysen, Burrows, Nicol, Stainton, Gillespie, Speedie, Staunton, Rush, Barnes (Molby), McMahon.

SHIFT IN POWER

6 October 1991
First Division
United 0, Liverpool 0.

The shift in power from Merseyside to Manchester began to gather pace in 1991/92, when United would have won their first championship for twenty-five years but for an end-of-season capitulation.

They had looked odds-on to win the title after losing only once in the first half of the season. However, they were unable to replicate that, winning only three of their last eleven matches as they allowed Leeds to be crowned champions. Liverpool finished the season sixth, their lowest League finish since 1964/65, and a massive eighteen points behind Leeds as they were about to experience an almighty fall from grace compared to the successes of the previous two decades.

Liverpool visited Old Trafford for the eleventh game of the season with United top of the table and still unbeaten .Yet Liverpool joined Everton in becoming the only two teams up to that time to have taken points off United, with both involved in goalless draws. United regarded the result as a case of two points lost while Liverpool, who were in ninth place at that stage, viewed it as one gained.

It was another match which scored extremely low on the entertainment scale and it proved to be an ill-tempered affair, with Mark Hughes and Gary Ablett sent off and too many fouls and explosions of bad temper. Ablett was dismissed for collecting two bookings while Hughes saw red following an off-the-ball clash with David Burrows.

The only chance in the dour opening half came when Bryan Robson's effort was well kept out by Liverpool 'keeper Mike Hooper. Andrei Kanchelskis, Hughes and Brian McClair on two occasions had chances in the second half, but none of the players were able to convert them as the match ended in stalemate.

United: Schmeichel, Phelan (Kanchelskis), Irwin, Bruce, Blackmore, Pallister,
    Robson, Ince (Donaghy), McClair, Hughes, Giggs.
Liverpool: Hooper, Ablett, Burrows, Nicol, Jones (Marsh), Tanner, Saunders
    (McManaman), Houghton, Rush, Walters, McMahon.

DAY THE DREAM DIED

26 April 1992
First Division
Liverpool 2 (Rush, Walters), United 0.

United visited Liverpool for the penultimate match of the season, still clinging to the hope of that elusive first title since 1967.

It was a tall order to say the least, because United had to win at Anfield and then rely on leaders Leeds losing at Sheffield United simply to take the Championship race to the final day. It was destined not to be as Liverpool beat United 2-0 while Leeds triumphed 3-2 at Bramall Lane to be crowned champions, a remarkable achievement bearing in mind they had only been promoted from the Second Division two years earlier.

Liverpool had nothing at stake with their UEFA Cup place assured, though the pain of a disappointing season was eased with victory over their arch rivals. It was as though this was Liverpool's cup final, with one local radio commentator saying he had never seen them so fired up. And the fans were also pumped up, with Anfield described as a cauldron in which United's Championship challenge melted.

It was not for the want of trying, as United attacked for most of the match but just couldn't conjure a goal as they were three times denied by the woodwork as Paul Ince, Brian McClair and Andrei Kanchelskis all rattled the frame of the goal.

Liverpool had taken an eleventh-minute lead through Ian Rush which, incredibly, was the striker's first ever goal against United in any competition. And they sealed victory with three minutes left when Ray Houghton's shot struck the crossbar and

Mark Walters, anonymous until that moment, slotted home the rebound.

Perhaps the most poignant sight at the final whistle was that of Bryan Robson, who had been a colossus despite not being fully fit, dejectedly leaving the pitch. Robson was thirty-five years of age and it was remarked that could this possibly be his last chance of a Championship medal given he was in the twilight of his playing days. This was the second time he had finished a runner-up.

Fortunately Robson was not to miss out on the big prize as there would be further twists in the latter stages of his illustrious career.

Liverpool: Hooper, Jones, Burrows, Tanner (Venison), Molby, Wright, Saunders, Houghton, Rush (McMahon), Barnes, Thomas.
United: Schmeichel, Irwin, Donaghy, Bruce, Kanchelskis, Pallister (Phelan), Robson, Ince, McClair, Hughes, Giggs.

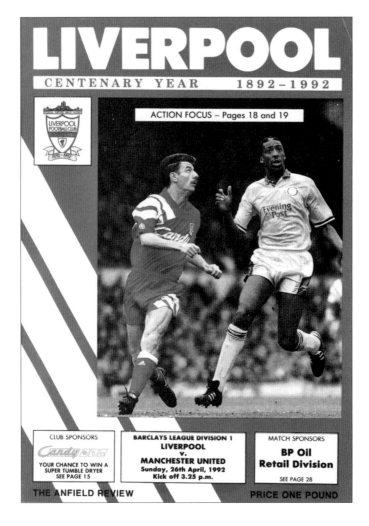

HUGHES SPARKS FIGHTBACK

18 October 1992
Premiership
United 2 (Hughes 2), Liverpool 2 (Hutchison, Rush).

Mark Hughes came to United's rescue, scoring twice in the final twelve minutes to rescue a point from the jaws of defeat.

Liverpool went into the game in a scarcely believable fifteenth place in the table, yet they belied their lowly League standing by opening a 2-0 half-time lead through goals from Don Hutchison and Ian Rush. Hutchison's long-range effort and Rush's clinical finish from eight yards in the dying seconds of the opening period put Liverpool in a commanding position.

The goal from Rush was memorable in that it took him past Roger Hunt's club-record haul of 286 for the Anfield club. Incredibly, it was also his first ever goal at Old Trafford in his long and illustrious career.

United were devoid of ideas in the second half as Liverpool's control of the match was never in question until the final twelve minutes. It needed a spark of genius to change that and Hughes provided that in the seventy-eighth minute when he ran onto a through-ball from substitute Clayton Blackmore and chipped the ball over the head of 'keeper Bruce Grobbelaar as he sprinted from his line.

Liverpool, who had made a massively disappointing start to the season, were beginning to rock and it was no surprise when Hughes equalised with a brilliant diving header from a cross by teenage winger Ryan Giggs.

Hughes later admitted that United did not deserve to take anything from the game. He said, 'My first goal came out of the blue and gave us impetus to get back into the game. Overall, we did not deserve anything, but we got a point because we kept at it.'

United: Schmeichel, Parker, Irwin, Bruce, Ferguson, Pallister, Kanchelskis
    (Blackmore), Ince, McClair, Hughes, Giggs.
Liverpool: Grobbelaar, Marsh, Burrows, Nicol, Piechnik, Hutchison, McManaman,
    Redknapp (Thomas), Rush, Molby (Tanner), Rosenthal.

UNITED ON CUSP OF TITLE GLORY

6 March 1993
Premiership
Liverpool 1 (Rush), United 2 (Hughes, McClair).

The disappointment of the previous year appeared to have galvanised United, who were determined not to lose out this time round in the inaugural Premier League campaign.

Once again they visited Liverpool during the title run-in and triumphed 2-1, their first victory at Anfield since 1986. It was a match described as one of the trickiest hurdles left in what most pundits were saying was United's Championship run-in.

It was a point acknowledged by Alex Ferguson after seeing goals by Mark Hughes and Brian McClair take his team back to the top of the table as they capitalised on Aston Villa's Cup-enforced lay off. He said, 'We have got to come to places like Anfield and win if we are to become champions. There is still a long way to go [eleven matches] and we must not get carried away. The result will mean nothing if we lose at Oldham.'

United did lose at Oldham in their next match and experienced a wobble as they endured a four-match run without a win. However, they snapped out of their malaise and finished the season with seven straight League victories to finish ten points clear of Aston Villa. Ironically it was Oldham's win at Villa on the penultimate weekend which handed the title to United, who had beaten Blackburn the previous day.

Ferguson had sensed his side was on the cusp of glory after the win at Anfield as he remarked, 'There is a mood and determination to succeed, and that showed. We have had the odd little stumble, but in the main have been consistent. Since December we have been playing well, and our good form has come at the right time. I cannot hide my pleasure at this result. It was a difficult game, particularly in view of the history and rivalry between the clubs. This was Liverpool's cup final.'

Liverpool, despite being once again out of the running for honours, were still more than a match for United in a match described as fast, frenetic and a credit to football.

Before the match kicked off there was a sombre moment as one minute's silence was observed in memory of Tony Bland, who the previous week had become the ninety-sixth victim of the Hillsborough disaster.

United had to survive an early onslaught as Paul Parker sliced a clearance against his own crossbar and Peter Schmeichel made a top-drawer save to deny Don Hutchison.

Once United survived that fraught opening, you had a feeling it was destined to be their day, and so it proved.

United made the vital breakthrough shortly before half-time through a Hughes header, only for Liverpool substitute Ian Rush to equalise early in the second period. Rush had replaced the injured Paul Stewart one minute before the break. Rush, who had failed to score for nearly a decade against United, had now netted three goals in as many games.

Liverpool's joy was short-lived as McClair regained the lead in the fifty-fifth minute as he glanced a header wide of 'keeper David James. That was by no means the end of the drama, as late in the game Schmeichel pulled off a brilliant stop to deny Rush, while United would have sealed victory had Hughes not missed a sitter and Andrei Kanchelskis struck the inside of the upright.

Liverpool: James, Redknapp, Jones, Nicol, Wright, Bjørnebye, McManaman,
    Hutchison, Walters (Burrows), Barnes, Stewart (Rush).
United: Schmeichel, Parker, Irwin, Bruce, Sharpe, Pallister, Kanchelskis, Ince,
    McClair, Hughes, Giggs.

LIVERPOOL BACK FROM THE DEAD

4 January 1994
Premiership
Liverpool 3 (Clough 2, Ruddock), United 3 (Bruce, Giggs, Irwin).

United must be wondering how they came to pick up only a point following an epic match at Anfield in which they held a commanding 3-0 lead midway through the opening period.

Liverpool came back from the dead in an extraordinary match which was a reversal of those epic meetings of the eighties. Then Liverpool were England's top team, but United always seemed to summon that extra resolve to provide an upset.

Now United were undoubtedly the best team in the land and it was Liverpool's turn to overturn the form book as they did on this occasion. United, reigning League Champions and current leaders, had an air of invincibility about them as they opened a 3-0 lead after twenty-three minutes to leave seventh-placed Liverpool on their knees, as one observer pointed out. Liverpool somehow pulled it back to 3-2 at the break and then salvaged a point with an equalising goal eleven minutes from time.

Alex Ferguson was left disappointed as he conceded that this was the first time in his long managerial career that he had seen one of his teams squander a three-goal lead. But he and Liverpool counterpart Graeme Souness concurred it was a great game of football with Souness arguing that it would have been unjust had either team lost. He remarked, 'United are deservedly top of the Premiership because they perform to a high degree consistently. We can perform to that level, but we have to find that consistency.'

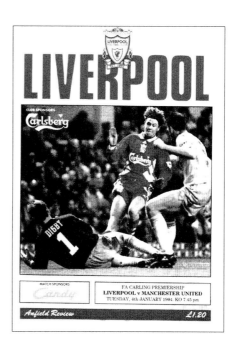

United scored from their first attack after eight minutes when Eric Cantona provided an inch-perfect cross for Steve Bruce to head home. It got even better when Ryan Giggs found the net with an audacious chip over 'keeper Bruce Grobbelaar and that was quickly followed by an equally stunning twenty-five-yard free-kick from Denis Irwin.

Liverpool gained a foothold back into the match when Nigel Clough drilled home a shot from twenty-five yards and then he struck again in the thirty-eighth minute with another strike from outside the penalty area.

The action did not wane after the break, though the goals failed to rain as they did in the opening period. Grobbelaar made a stunning save to deny Giggs while United 'keeper Peter Schmeichel did equally well to thwart Jamie Redknapp. Liverpool eventually conjured an equaliser in the seventy-ninth minute when substitute Stig Inge Bjørnebye delivered a perfect cross for central-defender Neil Ruddock to power home a header from six yards for the final twist in an extraordinary match.

Liverpool: Grobbelaar, Jones, Dicks, Redknapp, Wright, Ruddock, Clough, McManaman (Bjørnebye), Rush, Barnes, Fowler.
United: Schmeichel, Parker, Irwin, Bruce, Kanchelskis, Pallister, Cantona, Ince, McClair, Keane, Giggs.

CHAMPIONS LIVE DANGEROUSLY

30 March 1994
Premiership
United 1 (Ince), Liverpool 0.

One of the characteristics of a champion is to win while not playing well, something which was very much the case when United scraped a 1-0 victory against Liverpool. Yet it was a win which was massively important to United as they opened a six-point lead at the top as the business end of the season unfolded.

United had created a hatful of chances in the 3-3 draw at Anfield three months earlier, yet in their latest clash managed only one effort on target. That chance, however, was enough to earn United victory as Paul Ince was left unmarked in the thirty-seventh minute to head home Lee Sharpe's in-swinging corner.

The match will largely be remembered for the penalty that never was after referee Keith Hackett pointed to the spot after Michael Thomas went down following a challenge by Andrei Kanchelskis. Bryan Lowe was flagging furiously, and after Hackett consulted his linesman he overturned his decision and gave a free-kick to United.

'The linesman said the Liverpool player had committed the offence earlier by holding the United player,' explained Hackett. It was difficult to judge from television evidence who was fouling who. What was certain, however, was that United lived dangerously for long periods of the game.

United would go on to retain their League title while Liverpool finished eighth after another disappointing campaign.

United: Schmeichel, Parker, Irwin, Bruce, Sharpe (Giggs), Pallister, Cantona (Robson), Ince, Keane, Hughes, Kanchelskis.
Liverpool: James, Jones, Dicks, Redknapp, Wright, Ruddock, Thomas (Fowler), Whelan, Rush, Barnes, McManaman.

TALE OF THE SUBSTITUTES

17 September 1994
Premiership
United 2 (Kanchelskis, McClair), Liverpool 0.

United inflicted a first League defeat of the season on Liverpool in what turned out to be a tale of two substitutes.

Liverpool were bewildered to leave Old Trafford empty-handed after being in complete command for the opening hour. Two substitutions altered the course of the match as United brought on Brian McClair for the unfit Mark Hughes while Liverpool lost influential midfield playmaker Jan Molby, who was replaced by Phil Babb as that switch signalled the visitors' acceptance of a point. The departure of Molby was highly significant as, within three minutes of his exit, United scored twice to seal an unlikely victory.

Liverpool defender John Scales handed United their opening goal with an awful back-header to David James that was intercepted by Andrei Kanchelskis, who lobbed the 'keeper. The second goal, barely one minute later, was classic United as McClair exchanged passes with Eric Cantona before firing home a low shot from ten yards.

The change in fortune for United was a sharp contrast to the opening hour, in which Liverpool dominated.

Alex Ferguson admitted Liverpool were on top for the opening hour of the match and that bringing on McClair for Hughes changed the course of the match. Liverpool manager Roy Evans agreed, declaring, 'With hindsight, Alex made the right decision about his substitution, and I did not over mine. Babb came on at a difficult time, but the fact we conceded the goals had nothing to do with him.'

United had 'keeper Peter Schmeichel to thank for keeping them in the game in the opening hour as he produced a string of super saves to deny Neil Ruddock, Steve McManaman, Robbie Fowler and Jamie Redknapp, who also saw an effort clip the crossbar.

United: Schmeichel, May, Irwin, Bruce, Sharpe, Pallister, Kanchelskis, Ince, Cantona, Hughes (McClair), Giggs.
Liverpool: James, Jones, Bjørnebye, Scales, Molby (Babb), Ruddock, McManaman, Redknapp, Rush, Barnes, Fowler.

UNITED TITLE HOPES FADING

19 March 1995
Premiership
Liverpool 2 (Bruce (o.g.), Redknapp), United o.

Alex Ferguson conceded that United's hopes of landing a hat-trick of Premiership League titles was slipping away following their defeat at Anfield, coupled with a failure to beat Tottenham at home the previous Wednesday.

Those results left United six points behind Blackburn, though the significance of those slips only became clear on the last day of the season. United would have retained their League crown had they won at West Ham, where they were held to a 1-1 draw.

There were no complaints from Ferguson following the defeat to Liverpool, who were fourth, the position in which they would end the season. 'I didn't think we deserved anything more. Liverpool weren't particularly good, but we didn't play anywhere near the form we are capable of,' explained the United manager.

It turned out to be a stirring match with Liverpool, beaten at home by Tottenham and Coventry in their previous two matches, fired up. It was as though their entire season hinged on this result. The battle was won in midfield, where Jamie Redknapp eclipsed United's Paul Ince while John Barnes gave another accomplished display and Steve McManaman was also a constant source of danger.

Fittingly, it was Redknapp who put Liverpool ahead after twenty-four minutes with an excellent finish, having been set up by Barnes and Ian Rush. It might have been even worse but for Peter Schmeichel, who pulled off a great save to keep out a strike by Robbie Fowler.

United's best spell came early in the second half when they briefly threatened a comeback, Mark Hughes being brilliantly denied by David James. Liverpool had to wait until five minutes from time before sealing victory through a Steve Bruce own goal as he deflected McManaman's shot past Schmeichel.

Liverpool: James, Wright, Bjørnebye, Scales, Babb, Ruddock, McManaman, Redknapp, Rush (Walters), Barnes (Thomas), Fowler.
United: Schmeichel, Irwin, Sharpe (Cole), Bruce, Keane (Butt), Pallister, Kanchelskis, Ince, McClair, Hughes, Giggs.

KING ERIC RETURNS

1 October 1995
Premiership
United 2 (Butt, Cantona (pen.)), Liverpool 2 (Fowler 2).

This was the day Eric Cantona made his much-acclaimed return for United, having served a nine-month ban for attacking a spectator at Crystal Palace.

It was as though the flamboyant Frenchman had never been away as he found the net, albeit from a penalty, and also set up a goal for Nicky Butt as well as providing his usual feints, flicks and subtle contributions. Yet Cantona was eclipsed by young Liverpool striker Robbie Fowler, who scored both his side's goals in a memorable match. It was all about Cantona, however, as the theme tune from the film *The Magnificent Seven* – Cantona, of course, wears the number seven – was just part of the welcome reserved for the return of Old Trafford's prodigal son.

There was controversy but, happily, none of it surrounded Cantona. Liverpool felt more sinned against than sinning as they had two shouts for penalties turned down by referee David Elleray. They were also unhappy when United were awarded a penalty as Liverpool manager Roy Evans claimed Jamie Redknapp had won the ball legitimately from Ryan Giggs. Looking back, it was a point won by United as opposed to the loss of two.

United went ahead after only sixty-seven seconds when Cantona's cross fell to Butt, who jabbed the ball past 'keeper David James from six yards.

After a dream start, United lost their way for an hour in which Fowler scored twice with two excellent pieces of finishing, putting Liverpool ahead. But fittingly it was Cantona who had the final word as he made it 2-2 from the penalty spot as he wrong-footed James. United's king went to his subjects to celebrate and they paid him due homage.

United: Schmeichel, G. Neville, P. Neville (Scholes), Bruce, Sharpe, Pallister, Cantona, Keane, Cole, Butt (Beckham), Giggs.
Liverpool: James, Scales, Harkness, Babb, Wright, Ruddock, McManaman, Redknapp, Rush, Thomas, Fowler.

ROBBIE AT THE DOUBLE

17 December 1995
Premiership
Liverpool 2 (Fowler 2), United 0.

By the return at Anfield in mid-December, it looked as though United's championship challenge was crumbling. They looked anything but title material as their form continued to falter, even though they remained in second place. They had collected only three points from a possible twelve to slip seven points adrift of runaway leaders Newcastle.

And they were lucky to escape with a 2-0 defeat at Anfield following a below-par performance. Fowler put a sizeable dent in their challenge, scoring both goals in what was described as a supercharged clash. Had Liverpool's finishing been more clinical, it was observed they could well have inflicted one of the heaviest defeats on United in recent years.

Stan Collymore, Britain's costliest player at £8.5 million, had no fewer than thirteen goal attempts during the ninety minutes. Ten were on target, but a combination of fine goalkeeping by Peter Schmeichel and wayward finishing meant Collymore failed to find the net.

Ferguson made no excuses for a lacklustre display, declaring,

> We were dreadful in the first half, and in second improved only slightly. It was one of our worst performances for a long time. It was the most lifeless performance for years, and surprising bearing in mind it was at this place. We did not show the passion and fight you would expect in games between the two clubs.

Fowler curled a delightful free-kick from twenty-five yards round the defensive wall to put Liverpool, who were without the injured Ian Rush, Jamie Redknapp, Neil Ruddock and Phil Babb, ahead in the final minute of the opening half. Schmeichel was left rooted to the spot. It remained one-way traffic in the second half but Liverpool only sealed victory with four minutes left with another sublime finish from Fowler. His finishing was clinical and it was observed that it was just as well for United that Collymore's thirteen goal attempts had not fallen to him.

However, by the end of the campaign, United seized on Newcastle's dramatic collapse and were crowned champions for a third time in four seasons as they were attempting to become the first club to achieve the domestic double on two occasions, while Liverpool clinched a top-three spot for the first time in five years.

Liverpool: James, McAteer, Jones, Scales, Wright, Harkness, McManaman, Thomas, Collymore, Barnes, Fowler.
United: Schmeichel, G. Neville, Irwin, Bruce, Sharpe, May, Cantona, McClair, Cole (Scholes), Beckham, Giggs.

DOUBLE DOUBLE FOR UNITED

11 May 1996
FA Cup Final
Liverpool 0, United 1 (Cantona).

As United created a piece of footballing history by becoming the first team to twice land the domestic double of League and FA Cup, the irony was that it was secured against their arch-rivals.

Liverpool, their Cup final opponents, stood between them and glory but were unable to prevent their 1-0 victory at Wembley courtesy of a late goal from Eric Cantona. Though it was another momentous day in United's illustrious history, manager Alex Ferguson had his thoughts elsewhere – conquering Europe.

He said, 'We desperately want to do better in the Champions League after our performances in the last two or three years. We are capable, but tactically need to improve. We haven't done well in that competition and hopefully we can do better next season.'

Ferguson admitted he was surprised to land the title because they had been written off after their defeat at Aston Villa on the opening day of the season. That was when television pundit Alan Hansen boldly declared to the nation that you don't win anything with kids. Ferguson, who had lost a number of senior players and introduced youngsters David Beckham, Ryan Giggs, Paul Scholes, Nicky Butt and the Neville brothers in that campaign, said, 'We have reached a pinnacle this year with a young side. It is the first time a double double has been achieved and it is fantastic for our supporters. It is beyond our expectations. I felt we had a chance with the League, but I did not think we would last the pace.'

The achievement far outweighed the Wembley final, which proved to be a disappointing affair which was settled by Cantona's goal five minutes from the end.

And it was a moment to cherish for the Frenchman, who had emerged from a dark period in his career when his kung fu-style kick at a Crystal Palace fan in response to being taunted had earned him a nine-month ban. Cantona repaid Manchester United for loyally standing by him, scoring 19 goals in 38 League and Cup appearances during the double-winning campaign.

United: Schmeichel, Irwin, P. Neville, May, Keane, Pallister, Cantona, Beckham (G. Neville), Cole (Scholes), Butt, Giggs.

Liverpool: James, McAteer, Jones (Thomas), Scales, Wright, Babb, McManaman, Redknapp, Collymore (Rush), Barnes, Fowler.

BECKHAM MAKES HIS MARK

12 October 1996
Premiership
United 1 (Beckham), Liverpool 0.
Liverpool's unbeaten start to their Premiership campaign came to an end at Old Trafford where David Beckham was United's match-winner. The twenty-one-year-old Beckham, described as the sunshine boy of English football, struck the decisive blow as United inflicted a first League defeat on Liverpool, who had been unbeaten in their opening eight League fixtures.

Beckham also helped extend United's unbeaten start, though four draws from their first nine League matches were responsible for them lying in fourth place, one spot behind Liverpool, as Newcastle and Arsenal were ahead of them in the top-two spots.

The match-winning strike came midway through the opening half as Gary Neville and Ole Gunnar Solskjær set up Beckham, who scored with a sweetly struck shot from outside the penalty area which went in off the upright. Apart from another Beckham effort, which was superbly saved by David James, that was about the sum effort of United's attacking play.

Indeed, Liverpool could count themselves unlucky to leave Manchester empty handed as they definitely shaded the contest. United were indebted to 'keeper Peter Schmeichel, who pulled off a series of stunning saves to deny Stan Collymore, John Scales and Patrik Berger while Steve McManaman had two astonishing misses which also played their part in United's victory.

It was a measure of what a good side United had become that they were able to grind out a victory when playing so badly, something which must have struck a psychological blow to their Championship rivals.

United: Schmeichel, G. Neville, Irwin, May, Poborský (Scholes), Johnsen, Cantona, Butt, Solskjær (Giggs), Beckham, Cruyff.
Liverpool: James, McAteer, Bjørnebye, Matteo, Scales (Redknapp), Babb, McManaman, Collymore, Berger, Barnes, Thomas.

UNITED CLOSE IN ON TITLE

19 April 1997
Premiership
Liverpool 1 (Barnes), United 3 (Pallister 2, Cole).

United's end-of-campaign victory at Liverpool left them within touching distance of a fourth Premiership title in five seasons. The win helped United open a five-point lead at the top of the table with only four games remaining.

It turned out to be a comprehensive victory which also effectively ended the title hopes of Liverpool who, along with second-placed Arsenal, were on the same points total with only three matches to play.

Alex Ferguson, while warning his players there was still work to be done, was delighted with United's display as they completed a League double over their arch-rivals. 'It is a massive step for us. You have to earn the right to be champions, and we have done that here,' he declared.

United were aided by a nightmare display by Liverpool goalkeeper David James, who gifted them two of their goals. James was not at fault, however, for United's thirteenth-minute opener as Gary Pallister headed home a David Beckham corner. Liverpool responded and quickly equalised through a header from John Barnes following a Jason McAteer cross.

There was a twenty-minute spell when Liverpool were in the ascendancy, though that was ended three minutes before half-time when Beckham's corner tempted James from his line. The 'keeper failed to cut out the dead ball, allowing Pallister to head into the empty net. United sealed victory in the second half when James misjudged a Gary Neville cross as a grateful Andy Cole scored with a free header.

United duly went on to be crowned champions yet again while Liverpool finished a disappointing fourth as their own challenge petered out.

Liverpool: James, McAteer (Collymore), Bjørnebye, Kvarme, Wright, Harkness, McManaman, Redknapp, Fowler, Barnes (Berger), Thomas.

United: Schmeichel, G. Neville, P. Neville, Johnsen, Keane, Pallister, Cantona, Butt, Cole, Beckham, Scholes (McClair).

UNITED HEAP PRESSURE ON EVANS

6 December 1997
Premiership
Liverpool 1 (Fowler (pen.)), United 3 (Cole 2, Beckham).

League leaders United piled on the agony for Liverpool, inflicting a painful defeat at Anfield where they triumphed by a 3-1 scoreline for the second time in less than eight months.

The manner of United's emphatic victory sent shock-waves not only throughout the Premiership but also Europe as they had a Champions League group game against Italian giants Juventus days later, though they were already assured of a quarter-final place.

As for Liverpool, who were eighth in the table, they were again plagued by inconsistency as the pressure mounted on manager Roy Evans. In the previous fortnight, they had suffered a surprising defeat by Barnsley yet recorded a win against Arsenal, who would go on to be crowned champions. It was a case of wondering which Liverpool turned up and against United it was the side which invariably frustrated and under-achieved.

As for Alex Ferguson, he was keen to play down his side's excellent start to the campaign, saying, 'We've got big games coming up – Juventus on Wednesday, Aston Villa the following Monday, then Newcastle and Leeds. December is always a big month, and we have to keep our feet on the ground.'

After a goalless opening period, the match ignited after the restart and it was Andy Cole who broke the deadlock, punishing Bjørn Tore Kvarme for his hesitancy.

Robbie Fowler equalised on the hour from the penalty spot after Michael Owen had been fouled by Nicky Butt. David Beckham stepped up to regain the lead for United with a breathtaking free-kick, with Cole sealing victory with the third goal.

There was no stopping Cole, who was in a rich vein of form as his double made it 15 goals in his last 8 games, a remarkable run.

Liverpool: James, McAteer, Bjørnebye (Riedle), Kvarme (Berger), Matteo, Leonhardsen, McManaman, Carragher, Fowler, Owen, Redknapp.

United: Schmeichel, G. Neville, Johnsen, Berg, Butt, Pallister, Beckham, P. Neville, Cole, Sheringham, Giggs.

UNITED'S COSTLY SLIP

10 April 1998
Premiership
United 1 (Johnsen), Liverpool 1 (Owen).

Leaders United were left with egg on their faces following an Easter slip-up against Liverpool in their Good Friday clash at Old Trafford. They had only themselves to blame for failing to maintain the pressure on Arsenal, their closest title rivals.

They proved two costly points to drop, especially as they were subsequently to miss out on the title to the Gunners by a margin of one point. Though United remained top, they only held a precarious one-point advantage over Arsenal, who had played two less matches.

It was frustrating for United as they had taken the lead after twelve minutes when Norwegian central defender Ronny Johnsen headed home David Beckham's corner. That goal was cancelled out by a goal by Michael Owen, who punished Gary Pallister for a moment's hesitation as the pair chased on to Danny Murphy's forward pass.

Pallister, who had an eight-yard advantage, dithered as he was caught by Owen, who chipped the ball over 'keeper Peter Schmeichel from the edge of the penalty area.

It was disappointing for United, as was their failure to capitalise on Liverpool having to play more than half the match with ten men. Owen was sent off five minutes before the interval for a second bookable offence as he hacked down Johnsen, who left the field on a stretcher having damaged ankle ligaments. Without leading marksman Owen, Liverpool pushed midfield-man Murphy into a more advanced role as an emergency striker as the visitors mounted a superb rearguard action to keep United at bay.

For all their pressure, United could not find a way through as frustration gave way to despair. Paul Scholes was the biggest culprit in front of goal in a game of missed chances.

To add to their misery, Arsenal piled on the agony with Easter wins against Newcastle and Blackburn to strengthen their title challenge. Indeed, it would take an almighty slip to deprive the Gunners of the title, which they duly wrapped up in the final month of what turned out to be a double-winning campaign for the Londoners.

United: Schmeichel, G. Neville, Irwin, Johnsen (May), Butt, Pallister, Beckham, P. Neville, Cole (McClair), Scholes, Giggs (Thornley).
Liverpool: Friedel, Jones, Harkness, Babb, Matteo, Leonhardsen, McManaman, Ince, Owen, Murphy (Berger), Redknapp.

UNITED SHOW SPIRIT OF CHAMPIONS

24 September 1999
Premiership
United 2 (Irwin (pen.), Scholes), Liverpool 0.

Liverpool could only watch in envy as United created footballing history by capturing the historic treble of Champions League, Premier League and FA Cup.

It was something Liverpool had never achieved, but would have done so in 1977 had United not beaten them in the final of the FA Cup. To make matters worse for the Merseysiders in the 1998/99 campaign, they had endured another disappointing campaign, finishing seventh in the League. They didn't even have success in the Cup competitions to soften the blow of seeing their rivals conquer all before them.

The first of three meetings this season – they also clashed in the FA Cup – took place in the fourth week of September. It came four days after United had suffered their first League defeat, a thumping 3-0 loss at Arsenal. But they displayed character to overcome Liverpool, who arrived at Old Trafford unbeaten in their first five League matches.

David White wrote in the *Oldham Evening Chronicle*,

> The wind of change, which blew icy blasts of recrimination through Old Trafford after Sunday's debacle at Arsenal, switched direction to a balmy satisfaction of victory over bitter rivals Liverpool. Reports of Manchester United's demise as one of England's footballing giants had proved greatly exaggerated. United's performance at home to Liverpool showed it to be a complete fallacy.

In a game of eight bookings – four for each side – controversy surrounded many of the decisions made. Liverpool joint-managers Gérard Houllier and Roy Evans were aggrieved when United were awarded a nineteenth-minute penalty after Jason McAteer was adjudged to have handled. Denis Irwin scored from the spot.

Both teams had further penalty appeals turned down and United had to wait until eleven minutes remained, when Paul Scholes sealed victory with a spectacular strike.

United: Schmeichel, P. Neville, Irwin, G. Neville, Keane, Stam, Beckham, Solskjær (Cole), Yorke, Scholes (Butt), Giggs.
Liverpool: Friedel, McAteer, Bjørnebye, Redknapp, Carragher, Babb, McManaman, Ince, Riedle (Fowler), Owen, Berger.

INJURY-TIME DRAMA

24 January 1999
FA Cup, Fourth Round
United 2 (Yorke, Solskjær), Liverpool 1 (Owen).

The second meeting of the campaign took place in January in the fourth round of the FA Cup, which proved as dramatic a match as any between the two teams.

Liverpool took a third-minute lead through Michael Owen and held on to it until the dying seconds of the game, when United snatched victory from the jaws of defeat.

Last-gasp goals from Dwight Yorke and substitute Ole Gunnar Solskjær, who struck deep into stoppage time, gave United victory. It was something they would also repeat at the end of the season when capturing the Champions League in an equally dramatic way.

There was a certain irony that Solskjær, labelled the baby-faced assassin because of his goalscoring exploits, should apply the killer blow as he was a Liverpool fan growing up in Norway. In hindsight, perhaps Liverpool's goal came too early to justify a siege mentality as eighty-seven minutes is a long time to have to survive against a team of United's ability on a stage such as Old Trafford. Yet, incredibly, they almost achieved it.

United were caught cold at the start as the diminutive Owen somehow managed to get in between Jaap Stam and Henning Berg to head home an excellent cross from Vegard Heggem from six yards. Liverpool were then able to frustrate United while still posing problems up front through the pace of Owen and Robbie Fowler. United's only notable chance in the opening half came when Roy Keane's header struck an upright.

You sensed the second half would bring death or glory for United, and so it turned out. United's attacks became more frequent and ferocious and Keane was denied by the frame of the goal for a second time.

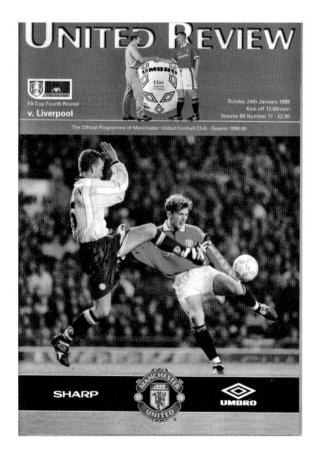

Alex Ferguson brought on Paul Scholes, Solskjær and Ronny Johnsen as United went for broke. It was the last throw of the dice. They were to prove inspired substitutions as the replacements were pivotal figures in the mother of all comebacks.

Johnsen was brought down by Jamie Redknapp thirty yards from goal in the eighty-eighth minute. Andy Cole headed down David Beckham's free kick into the path of Yorke, who scored from close range.

You could sense there was a further and final twist, and so it proved as Solskjær struck the match-winning goal in the second minute of injury time, something he would repeat four months later in the final of the Champions League when United scored twice in stoppage time to come from behind to beat a stunned Bayern Munich.

This time Liverpool were rocked to the core as they had looked set to take United to a replay at Anfield. Scholes set up fellow substitute Solskjær, who showed some neat footwork before driving the ball home from eight yards.

Liverpool were stunned as four minutes earlier they were ahead and seemingly set for a place in the fifth round.

United: Schmeichel, G. Neville, Irwin (Solskjær), Berg (Johnsen), Keane, Stam, Beckham, Butt (Scholes), Cole, Yorke, Giggs.
Liverpool: James, Heggem, Bjørnebye, Matteo, Carragher, Harkness, Redknapp, Ince (McAteer), Fowler, Owen, Berger.

INCE DENTS TREBLE DREAM

5 May 1999
Premiership
Liverpool 2 (Redknapp, Ince), United 2 (Yorke, Irwin).

United old boy Paul Ince put a dent in their bid for the first part of the historic treble, scoring a late leveller for Liverpool. It looked as though United, 2-0 ahead at one stage, would turn the heat on Arsenal who extended their lead at the top to three points following their derby win at Tottenham.

Though United had three matches left to Arsenal's two, the bookmakers had the Gunners as favourites for the title. It was a sweet moment for Ince – who had previously been described as a 'big time Charlie' by Alex Ferguson, who well and truly had those words rammed back down his throat – having been forced to endure the taunts of opposing fans for a number of years.

Ince was naturally jubilant, declaring,

> I'm not bothered if my goal costs United the title. They have won it so many times that it would be nice to see other clubs in there challenging. It was a special moment for the side as well as for me. I've taken a lot of stick over the last two years from these United lads so it's nice to get one back. It's always nice if you score against United.

Ince admitted he thought Liverpool were beaten when they were 2-0 down as United rarely slip up in such circumstances, but praised his side's spirit, maintaining that they deserved the reward they gained.

Ferguson was furious with referee David Elleray for sending off Denis Irwin for kicking the ball away after it had run out of play, something the match official deemed deliberate to the astonishment of most observers. It was a decision which left United with ten men and also ruled Irwin out of the FA Cup final. 'The referee handed it to them. It doesn't do our game any good to see things like that,' he declared.

United seemingly had victory in the bag as Dwight Yorke's header and a penalty from Irwin put them 2-0 ahead after fifty-four minutes. Liverpool were handed a lifeline when they were also awarded a spot kick following a foul by Jesper Blomqvist on Øyvind Leonhardsen, before Ince had the final word with the equalising goal two minutes from time.

Ferguson admitted his side should not have been held having been 2-0 ahead, saying, 'At that stage you should be able to cut things off. It means the title race is going right down to the wire. I suppose Liverpool deserved something for their passion. It was a fantastic game, but we should not have let it slip.'

Luckily for United the slip wasn't costly. They went on to pip Arsenal for the Premiership title, defeat Newcastle in the final of the FA Cup and then complete the treble with their Champions League triumph against Bayern Munich. Liverpool finished a disappointing seventh.

Liverpool: Friedel, Song (Berger), Matteo, Babb, Carragher, Staunton (Thompson), McManaman, Ince, Riedle, Leonhardsen, Redknapp.
United: Schmeichel, G. Neville, Irwin, Johnsen, Keane, Stam, Beckham, Scholes, Cole (Butt), Yorke, Blomqvist (P. Neville).

JAMIE'S OWN-GOAL NIGHTMARE

11 September 1999
Premiership
Liverpool 2 (Hyypiä, Berger), United 3 (Carragher 2 (o.gs), Cole).

United received a helping hand in their early-season victory at Anfield from two first-half own goals by Liverpool defender Jamie Carragher.

The win extended United's unbeaten run in the League to twenty-seven games as they showed no adverse reaction to the previous season's exploits. Indeed, United had made one of their best ever starts to a campaign as they had amassed nineteen points from their first seven League matches.

That had established a six-point lead at the top, though second-placed Chelsea had played two less matches. Liverpool, by contrast, had made a wretched opening, collecting only nine points from their first six League matches to lie twelfth in the table.

England Under-21 defender Carragher unwittingly gave United a fourth-minute lead when he turned a cross by Ryan Giggs into his own net. Liverpool's woes continued when United doubled their lead after eighteen minutes when Andy Cole continued his excellent goalscoring burst, rising to head David Beckham's free-kick past Dutch 'keeper Sander Westerveld.

Liverpool halved the deficit midway through the half when Jamie Redknapp's free-kick was headed home by Finnish defender Sami Hyypiä, his first goal for the club.

Hyypiä's job was made easier when United's Italian 'keeper Massimo Taibi, who was handed his debut following a British record £4.5 million move from Venezia, failed to gather the dead ball. Taibi would later redeem himself, however, with splendid saves to deny Patrik Berger and Vladimir Šmicer. United restored their two-goal advantage in the final minute of the opening half when the unlucky Carragher, under pressure from Henning Berg, guided Giggs' corner past Westerveld.

Liverpool manager Gérard Houllier replaced Titi Camara with youngster Michael Owen midway through the second half. His introduction had an immediate effect as Liverpool reduced the deficit to 3-2, Dominic Matteo setting up Berger, who scored.

Liverpool's renewed vigour and self-belief was reinforced by Cole's late sending-off for kicking out at Liverpool defender Rigobert Song. In a frantic final ten minutes, United pulled players behind the ball and battled bravely to preserve their advantage as the victory enabled them to move six points clear at the top.

Liverpool: Westerveld, Song, Matteo, Redknapp, Carragher, Hyypiä, Gerrard (Heggem), Thompson (Šmicer), Fowler, Camara (Owen), Berger.

United: Taibi, P. Neville, Silvestre, Berg, Scholes, Stam, Beckham (Sheringham), Butt (Wallwork), Cole, Yorke, Giggs.

8
The New Millennium

The new millennium kicked off as the old one ended, with United still the dominant team in English football.

United secured their sixth League title since the Premiership was formed in 1992 as only Blackburn and Arsenal had managed to muscle in with Championship successes.

And the noughties, as they were to become known, would see United remain at the forefront of the English game with Liverpool unable to re-establish their supremacy of the seventies and eighties, despite briefly threatening to do so under Gérard Houllier's tutelage when they won three pieces of silverware in 2000/01 and the Champions League in 2005.

UNITED SUFFER WOBBLE

4 March 2000
Premiership
United 1 (Solskjær), Liverpool 1 (Berger)

Liverpool provided evidence to suggest United should not regard winning the Premiership title as a foregone conclusion. After being held at Wimbledon in their previous League match, United surrendered two more points. The slips provided a ray of hope for second-placed Leeds, whose victory against Coventry reduced United's lead at the top to four points with eleven League games remaining.

'Even if we had won – and we could have done so – I still believe United will win the League,' explained Liverpool manager Gérard Houllier. Had Liverpool pulled off their first League win at Old Trafford since the 1989/90 season, it would have given further belief to the rest that United were not invincible.

United's defence was far from as robust as usual and Liverpool could have sealed victory in the opening half. While Liverpool edged the first forty-five minutes it was the opposite after the restart, when United took charge as the visitors lived dangerously, Jamie Carragher coming to the rescue three times with vital goal-line clearances.

What a change in his fortunes – in their early-season meeting he had twice put it into his own goal for Liverpool.

Sir Alex Ferguson said, 'We created a lot of chances and were unlucky not to win. When you are continually pressing you do get caught on the counter attack and Vladimir Šmicer and Michael Owen could have won it for Liverpool.'

Ferguson fielded a new strike-force of Dwight Yorke and Ole Gunnar Solskjær, who replaced Andy Cole and Teddy Sheringham from their previous match.

Liverpool took a twenty-seventh-minute lead through a superbly taken free kick from Patrik Berger which was measured at 32.8 metres according to television's latest hi-tech gadgetry. It might have been worse for United as Berger and Titi Camara both had great chances to extend the lead.

United equalised in first-half stoppage time when Liverpool were temporarily down to ten, when Sami Hyypiä went off to have a gashed ankle patched up. It was Solskjær, who caught Hyypiä – he did not reappear for the second half – who equalised, though with an element of luck. Ryan Giggs provided the cross from the left and Solskjær turned on a sixpence to shoot through the legs of Dominic Matteo and beyond 'keeper Sander Westerveld.

Carragher was the star of the second half for Liverpool with goal-line clearances to deny Solskjær, Giggs and Sheringham, the latter's coming in stoppage time when United so nearly snatched victory.

United overcame their wobble and regained their composure to win the title by a whopping eighteen-point margin over second-placed Arsenal. Liverpool were one point further adrift in third spot.

United: van der Gouw, G. Neville, Irwin, Silvestre, Keane, Stam, Beckham, Butt, Solskjær (Cole), Yorke (Sheringham), Giggs.
Liverpool: Westerveld, Heggem (Song), Matteo, Hamann, Henchoz, Hyypiä (Murphy), Carragher, Šmicer, Camara (Owen), Meijer, Berger.

HOULLIER A WINNING CENTURION

17 December 2000
Premiership
United 0, Liverpool 1 (Murphy).

Gérard Houllier celebrated his 100th match as manager of Liverpool with a memorable victory at runaway League leaders United. It was a notable way to reach the landmark as Liverpool won at Old Trafford for the first time since 1990.

Houllier was naturally jubilant, declaring,

> I am proud and pleased. Winning here is special because of their record at Old Trafford. We are proud and happy because we have beaten one of the best teams in Europe. Maybe they had a bad day, but they are still a great side and we are not at their level yet. We are just starting out and it might be two or three years before we can match United.

The scale of Liverpool's achievement was that this was United's first home defeat for two years, a sequence stretching to thirty-six matches. Liverpool's match-winner was Danny Murphy as the midfield man kicked off a remarkable scoring sequence against United.

They would go on to win three times in the space of four seasons at Old Trafford, with Murphy netting the decisive goal each time in a 1-0 triumph.

United were suffering a mini-mid-season wobble as the previous week they had drawn 3-3 at Charlton, so picking up only one point from a possible six. Until that point, they had opened an eight-point lead at the top of the table and the only question seemed to be by what margin they would win the League. Suddenly a seventh Premiership title in nine seasons did not seem the foregone conclusion it once did.

The performance against Liverpool was one of those rare off days as Liverpool revived their faltering campaign. They were in fifth place. Liverpool defended so well that 'keeper Sander Westerveld hardly had a save to make, though the absence of the injured Teddy Sheringham and Andy Cole and the suspended Dwight Yorke left them lightweight up front.

Sir Alex Ferguson initially pushed up Paul Scholes alongside Ole Gunnar Solskjær while later Ryan Giggs switched to a central striking spot. The United manager had no complaints, saying, 'It might not have made any difference who we played up front because the quality of our passing was disappointing. It was a disappointing performance and nowhere near the level of quality you normally expect.'

Murphy had a couple of decent attempts at goal while Emile Heskey's effort was headed off the line by Scholes before Liverpool made the breakthrough two minutes before the break. Gary Neville inexplicably handled a couple of yards outside the penalty area and Murphy bent a delightful free kick over the defensive wall and beyond the grasp of 'keeper Fabien Barthez.

Michael Owen should have doubled Liverpool's lead before the break and then shortly after the restart he saw a shot strike the crossbar. Westerveld's only serious save was to keep out an effort from Solskjær, while a miserable afternoon for United ended with substitute Luke Chadwick sent off as referee Mike Riley deemed his challenge on Vladimir Šmicer as preventing a clear goalscoring opportunity.

United: Barthez, G. Neville, Irwin, Brown, Stam, Silvestre, Beckham (Chadwick), Butt (Greening), Solskjær, Scholes, Giggs.
Liverpool: Westerveld, Carragher, Biščan, Babbel, Henchoz, Hyypiä, Gerrard, Barmby, Heskey, Owen (Šmicer), Murphy (McAllister).

LEAGUE DOUBLE FOR LIVERPOOL

31 March 2001
Premiership
Liverpool 2 (Gerrard, Fowler), United 0.

United's relentless charge towards a seventh Premiership title in nine seasons continued, but they were unable to prevent Liverpool from securing a notable League double. The leaders suffered a 2-0 defeat at Anfield, where Steven Gerrard and Robbie Fowler gave the Liverpool fans something to ease the pain and anguish of seeing United claim yet another Championship.

There was plenty to cheer for Liverpool, however, as they won three pieces of silverware that season as manager Gérard Houiller guided them to success in the FA Cup, Worthington Cup and UEFA Cup as well as third place in the League.

It was one of those rare occurrences when Sir Alex Ferguson found defeat against their arch-rivals a little easier to swallow than previous ones. The reason was that United had a healthy advantage in the top spot which enabled Ferguson to rest Jaap Stam, Andy Cole and Ole Gunnar Solskjær for the Champions League quarter-final against Bayern Munich three days later, while Paul Scholes and Mikaël Silvestre only made the bench.

Ferguson explained his strategy:

> Tuesday's game is a more important one for us as that's when our season really starts. We've had one or two injuries over the last couple of weeks and, in our position, we could afford to do what we did. If we had come here chasing the League, we would have played a different side. We still wanted to win and we showed a determination to keep going.

United still fielded eleven full internationals in their starting line up but Liverpool were again the stronger, as they were at Old Trafford three months earlier. Gerrard gave Liverpool the lead after sixteen minutes with a spectacular drive from thirty-plus yards into the top corner. Liverpool landed the killer blow five minutes before the break when Gary Neville failed to cut out a Gerrard cross which was fatal, with Fowler ready to pounce as he did.

United exerted more control in the second half when they were even unable to capitalise on Danny Murphy being sent off for two bookable offences. Dwight Yorke also had a goal ruled out for offside, further evidence that it was destined not to be United's day.

Ferguson's decision to play a weakened team against Liverpool failed to improve their prospects against Bayern Munich, who triumphed at Old Trafford and also won in Germany to book their semi-final spot. United, who had been top of the table since early October, finished ten points clear of second-placed Arsenal. Liverpool were third, one point behind the Gunners.

Liverpool: Westerveld, Babbel, Carragher, Hamann, Henchoz, Hyypiä, Gerrard (Owen), Murphy, Heskey, Fowler (McAllister), Berger (Barmby).
United: Barthez, P. Neville, Irwin (Chadwick), Brown, Stam, G. Neville, Beckham, Butt (Scholes), Yorke, Sheringham (Silvestre), Giggs.

NOTHING TO WORRY ABOUT

12 August 2001
FA Charity Shield
United 1 (van Nistelrooy), Liverpool 2 (McAllister (pen.), Owen).

United were losers on their first visit to Cardiff's Millennium Stadium as Liverpool scored a pre-season victory in the One2One FA Charity Shield.

Sir Alex Ferguson wouldn't have lost any sleep, however, as it was hardly a pointer as to their prospects for the forthcoming campaign. If history repeated itself United, beaten in this curtain-raiser for each of the previous three seasons, would be crowned Premiership Champions for a record-breaking fourth successive year.

Ferguson, as usual, looked at the wider picture after their final warm-up match, saying the pace and intensity probably wouldn't be surpassed in the League as neither team took any prisoners. 'It was pulsating, end-to-end and having to chase the game is exactly what we needed pre-season,' he said.

Though the FA Charity Shield was little more than a pre-season friendly, this match again demonstrated there is never any such match between these two fierce rivals.

Ferguson conceded Liverpool were far sharper as they established a 2-0 lead after sixteen minutes. He was pleased with the desire his side displayed in the second half, when they were decidedly unlucky not to draw level. This was underlined when Liverpool goalkeeper Sander Westerveld was named Man of the Match.

The problem of starting at a snail's pace was clearly something which needed addressing by Ferguson. They were two down earlier against Celtic in four minutes and trailed by the same margin after sixteen minutes in Cardiff. Only forty-four seconds had elapsed when Liverpool, who were without Steven Gerrard and Robbie Fowler, won a penalty after Roy Keane tripped Danny Murphy. Gary McAllister sent 'keeper Fabien Barthez the wrong way from the spot. It got even better for Liverpool when they doubled their advantage, having caught out United with a long punt forward. Jaap Stam slipped, then Gary Neville was left standing by a sharp turn by Michael Owen, who slotted the ball past Barthez.

United set about clawing their way back into the game as Roy Keane had a header brilliantly saved by Westerveld and also struck the crossbar with a thunderous drive, while there was also a shout for a penalty as Stéphane Henchoz clearly looked to have handled. Ruud van Nistelrooy halved the deficit early in the second half, showing nimble footwork to round Westerveld and score from six yards. Suddenly it was game on. Westerveld did well to keep out efforts from Paul Scholes and Keane before they had another penalty appeal rejected by referee Andy D'Urso as it was destined not to be their day.

United: Barthez, Irwin, Silvestre, G. Neville, Keane, Stam, Beckham, Butt (Yorke),
    Van Nistelrooy, Scholes, Giggs.
Liverpool: Westerveld, Babbel, Riise (Carragher), Hamann, Henchoz, Hyypiä,
    Murphy (Berger), McAllister, Heskey, Owen, Barmby (Bišćan).

FERGIE QUESTIONS PLAYERS' HUNGER

4 November 2001
Premiership
Liverpool 3 (Owen 2, Riise), United 1 (Beckham).

Liverpool caretaker manager Phil Thompson described his players as 'absolutely superb' while Sir Alex Ferguson questioned the appetite of his footballers. Ferguson admitted he had grave reservations about his side's ability to deliver a fourth successive Premiership title following their defeat at Anfield.

He explained,

> Individual errors continue to haunt us, but they are not so much of a concern to us as the fact that Liverpool worked much harder than we did. They were like we were four years ago. Maybe the players have been here too long and success is being taken for granted.

Liverpool displayed the hunger United lacked as they recorded a fourth successive victory over United's side, which had already lost three League matches and were lying sixth. And if Liverpool were to win their game in hand, they would establish a seven-point lead over United. 'You can have all the skill in the world but, if you don't work your socks off, you won't get anything against Manchester United,' declared Thompson.

United had problems even before the game had kicked off as they were without defenders Laurent Blanc, David May and Ronny Johnsen while Ryan Giggs and Roy Keane were also absentees. Liverpool took the lead in the thirty-second minute following a complete miskick from Wes Brown which let in Michael Owen, who scored with an exquisite finish. They doubled their advantage seven minutes later with a spectacular long-range missile from John Arne Riise as his free kick was measured at 65 mph. Brown had again been at fault, conceding the free kick following a foul on Owen.

Thompson's half-time message centred on United's 5-3 win at Tottenham where they trailed 3-0 at the interval. And he admitted to fearing the worst when David Beckham halved the deficit five minutes after the restart as United's stand-in captain scored with his left foot after Riise's attempted clearance fell invitingly to him.

Liverpool restored their two-goal advantage within one minute when 'keeper Fabien Barthez was beaten in the air by Riise's long throw; Emile Heskey flicked the ball on and Owen out-jumped Mikaël Silvestre to head home.

It was a win savoured by the Liverpool fans as they ridiculed United, chanting for Jaap Stam and even taunting them about being City in disguise. Ferguson must have hoped the defeat had hurt sufficiently to provide the jolt which was clearly needed if they were to hold on to their Premiership crown.

Liverpool: Dudek, Carragher, Riise, Hamann, Henchoz, Hyypiä, Gerrard, Šmicer (Berger), Heskey, Owen (Fowler), Murphy.

United: Barthez, G. Neville, Irwin (O'Shea), Brown, Butt, Silvestre, Beckham (Scholes), Solskjær (Yorke), van Nistelrooy, Verón, Fortune.

LIVERPOOL'S TREBLE JOY

22 January 2002
Premiership
United 0, Liverpool 1 (Murphy).

Liverpool had the last laugh after United fans taunted the visitors with a giant banner which proclaimed their three trophies last season represented a 'Mickey Mouse Treble'. Yet it was Liverpool who completed a different kind of treble at Old Trafford, where they won to make it three wins out of three against United this season.

Liverpool completed a League double as well as having beaten their great rivals in the Charity Shield. It was also the second successive season in which they had beaten United home and away in the League.

Liverpool's win prevented United from making it nine Premiership victories in a row as their season had well and truly lifted off after an indifferent start. The victory also catapulted Liverpool back into the title race and, with only four points separating the top five teams, Ferguson predicted the chase for glory would be 'the mother of all title races', as it subsequently proved, with Arsenal crowned champions, Liverpool runners-up and United third.

Ferguson criticised Liverpool for their defensive tactics at Old Trafford, where their back line was so solid that 'keeper Jerzy Dudek hardly had a save to make as the visitors snatched victory through a late goal from Danny Murphy.

It was the second successive season in which Murphy had been the match-winner in a 1-0 League victory at Old Trafford. 'It was just the same as last year when they kicked the ball forward and hoped for a break. They came looking for a 1-0 win and got it,' explained Ferguson. The United manager was overall satisfied with his side's display, saying all they lacked was a little more subtlety in the final third of the pitch.

As Ole Gunnar Solskjær was on the bench because he was not fully fit, Ferguson used Ryan Giggs as a central striker, meaning they lacked the width he normally provided. United had eight goal attempts in the opening half, but never troubled Dudek and, as the match progressed, you had the feeling it would be a goalless draw.

There were raised eyebrows when Michael Owen was replaced by Nicolas Anelka with thirteen minutes left, especially as the out-of-form Emile Heskey was again toiling.

It proved to be an inspired substitution as Anelka, with his first touch, forced 'keeper Fabien Barthez to make a splendid save. And from the resulting corner, Barthez came to his side's rescue again with another super stop to deny John Arne Riise.

As the clock counted down, Liverpool grabbed the winning goal when Steven Gerrard played a delightful through-ball for Murphy to hook a first-time shot over the head of Barthez. It was a move executed with deadly precision to leave the United fans stunned.

United: Barthez, P. Neville, Silvestre, G. Neville, Keane, Blanc, Beckham (Solskjær), Verón, van Nistelrooy, Scholes, Giggs.
Liverpool: Dudek, Wright, Carragher, Hamann, Henchoz, Hyypiä, Gerrard, Murphy (Berger), Heskey, Owen (Anelka), Riise.

TALE OF TWO 'KEEPERS

1 December 2002
Premiership
Liverpool 1 (Hyypiä), United 2 (Forlán 2)

The fortunes of 'keepers Jerzy Dudek and Fabien Barthez could not have been further removed as United's victory at Anfield propelled them back into the title race. While Dudek was haunted by the howler which handed United the initiative for only their second League away win, Barthez played a blinder. In the dying minutes, Barthez pulled off a breathtaking stop to deny Dietmar Hamann and also ensure United ended a miserable run of five successive defeats against Liverpool.

Sir Alex Ferguson admitted Dudek's blunder midway through the second half was the game's defining moment. Until then it looked as though the game would end in a goalless stalemate, with Arsenal the main beneficiary as their title rivals slipped further adrift.

He said, 'It seems the breaks are starting to turn our way. That was without question the defining moment of the match which turned the game for us.' Ferguson thought his side was finally achieving the consistency they had lacked in the early part of the season. 'You are going to be under pressure because Liverpool don't lie down and are a team of great courage. It was an emotional and passionate game. You need your goalkeeper to perform at the highest level, and we saw that with Fabien.'

Not so Dudek. There was seemingly no danger when Jamie Carragher made a routine headed back-pass to his 'keeper midway through the second half. The under-fire Pole, who had made several costly mistakes in recent matches, inexplicably allowed the ball to slip through his hands and legs, leaving Diego Forlán with the simplest of tap-ins. Less than three minutes later and live-wire Uruguayan Forlán found a way past the hapless Dudek for a second time. Paul Scholes and Ryan Giggs unlocked the Liverpool defence with some neat and incisive approach play, enabling Forlán to cut in from the right before rifling home his second goal by beating Dudek at his near post.

Liverpool may have been down, but they were certainly not out as they came back strongly, the introduction of John Arne Riise signalling an upturn in their fortunes.

United encountered difficulty dealing with Riise's long throws, which he propelled into the penalty area. And it was United's failure to clear one which enabled Sami Hyypiä to half the deficit with eight minutes left.

Liverpool, whose build-up play was described as predictable and disjointed until that point, suddenly found a purpose they had previously lacked. United, who had hardly been troubled, found themselves in retreat and desperately defending their lead. And but for Barthez's brilliant late save to deny Hamann, Liverpool would have snatched the unlikeliest of points.

Liverpool: Dudek, Carragher, Traoré (Riise), Hamann, Henchoz, Hyypiä, Gerrard, Šmicer (Diouf), Baroš (Heskey), Owen, Murphy.
United: Barthez, O'Shea, Silvestre, Brown, Fortune (P. Neville), G. Neville, Solskjær, Scholes, van Nistelrooy (May), Forlán (Stewart), Giggs.

DUDEK DAZZLES IN CUP WIN

2 March 2003
Worthington Cup, Final
Liverpool 2 (Owen, Gerrard), United 0.

Goalkeeper Jerzy Dudek was again the pivotal figure as Liverpool defeated United to lift the Worthington Cup at Cardiff's Millennium Stadium.

It was the seventh time Liverpool had won the League Cup in its various guises, but only thanks to the heroics of Pole Dudek, who had won an unexpected recall for the final. It was a remarkable turnaround in the fortunes of Dudek, who had been axed from the side three months earlier after his terrible gaffe in the League match at Anfield when he allowed Diego Forlán's shot to slip through his hands.

Dudek, who had been ridiculed for that blunder, was summoned after Chris Kirkland was ruled out through injury. In a typical *Roy of the Rovers* storyline, it was Dudek who emerged the villain-turned-hero as he was named Man of the Match, with a string of important saves keeping United at bay.

And in a turnaround from their earlier League meeting, too many United players were off-colour while Liverpool produced their best display for some time. Gérard Houllier's side proved stubborn opponents and the Frenchman outmanoeuvred Sir Alex Ferguson tactically. United were frustrated as Liverpool lined up with their midfield four operating just in front of the defence. And those two walls of four prevented United from being able to produce their usual slick passing routines.

Instead they were forced to resort to the long ball in a desperate attempt to find a route to goal, something which simply played into their opponents' hands.

The game exploded to life six minutes before the break when Liverpool stole ahead with a goal out of nothing. Steven Gerrard's speculative strike from thirty yards took a deflection off David Beckham and looped over the head of 'keeper Fabien Barthez.

The goal belatedly brought United to life as a drive from Juan Sebastián Verón was well saved by Dudek while a follow-up shot from Paul Scholes was kicked off the goal-line by Stéphane Henchoz.

United had enough chances in the second half to get back into the game as Dudek denied Ruud van Nistelrooy three times and also Scholes, with United beginning to wonder if it was destined not to be their day. And that was confirmed when Liverpool sealed victory with four minutes left, United again caught on the counter as Dietmar Hamann broke and released Michael Owen, who shot low past Barthez.

Liverpool: Dudek, Carragher, Riise, Hamann, Henchoz, Hyypiä, Gerrard, Diouf (Bišćan), Heskey (Baroš)(Šmicer), Owen, Murphy.
United: Barthez, G. Neville, Silvestre, Brown (Solskjær), Keane, Ferdinand, Beckham, Verón, van Nistelrooy, Scholes, Giggs.

THE PERFECT RIPOSTE

5 April 2003
Premiership
United 4 (van Nistelrooy (2 pens), Giggs, Solskjær), Liverpool 0

United brushed aside the disappointment of their Worthington Cup final defeat by Liverpool barely one month earlier to record their biggest win over their rivals for fifty years. 'Four-nil is an unbelievable result for us,' remarked Ruud van Nistelrooy, who scored two penalties in the rout to make it thirty-four goals for the season.

It was also the perfect start to a crucial six-match spell which would determine whether they would win any silverware. After an indifferent start to the campaign, United extended their unbeaten run to twelve Premiership matches, which yielded thirty-two points from a possible thirty-six. They were coming good at precisely the right time, just as Arsenal had lost their momentum in recent weeks.

Sir Alex Ferguson also put the importance of the win into perspective, saying:

> If you said at the start of the season would you prefer two League victories or the League Cup, what would the answer have been? It is always a disappointment losing to Liverpool at any time and they will say the same with us, but a double in the League satisfies us.

While United could only have dreamed of such an emphatic margin of victory, there were mitigating circumstances for Liverpool, who had Sami Hyypiä sent off after only four minutes while Michael Owen's absence also influenced events. It was still an afternoon to savour for United, especially as Liverpool had won six of the previous seven meetings.

The match was effectively settled in the fourth minute when van Nistelrooy was hauled back by Hyypiä as he burst through on goal, referee Mike Riley brandishing the red card as he deemed the striker was in a goalscoring position. Dutchman van Nistelrooy scored from the resulting penalty as Liverpool were forced to substitute Milan Baroš. But with no defender on the bench, midfield man Igor Bišćan had to slot into the back line.

As so often happens against ten men, United struggled and didn't break through again until midway through the second half. Again it was from the penalty spot, following Bišćan's clumsy challenge on Paul Scholes, and van Nistelrooy was again on target from twelve yards.

Liverpool heads visibly dropped and substitute David Beckham whipped in a cross after seventy-nine minutes for Ryan Giggs to fire into the roof of the net. There was still more to come as Ole Gunnar Solskjær rounded off the scoring when he cut in a fired a shot through the legs of Djimi Traoré which left unsighted 'keeper Jerzy Dudek rooted to the spot.

United went on to regain their championship crown, having had an incredible finish to the season. They were unbeaten in their last eighteen Premiership games, winning fifteen of them. Liverpool finished fifth.

United: Barthez, G. Neville, Silvestre (O'Shea), Brown, Keane, Ferdinand, Solskjær, P. Neville (Beckham), van Nistelrooy, Scholes (Butt), Giggs.
Liverpool: Dudek, Carragher, Riise, Hamann, Traoré, Hyypiä, Murphy (Cheyrou), Gerrard, Heskey, Baroš (Bišćan), Diouf (Šmicer).

LIVERPOOL HIT BY G-FORCE

9 November 2003
Premiership
Liverpool 1, United 2 (Giggs 2).

It was no wonder Liverpool manager Gérard Houllier spoke about the fine line separating success and failure after United's somewhat fortuitous victory. On another day Liverpool may well have enjoyed the breaks which went the way of the visitors, who won at Anfield for the second successive season in the Premiership.

United had to withstand a late Liverpool onslaught to register an important success in their bid to defend their League title. While Ryan Giggs' two goals earned him the Man of the Match award, it was United's defence which had to stand firm in a frantic finale as Liverpool pressed for an equaliser. 'We were more than hanging on, and it was a nerve-biting finish,' confessed Sir Alex Ferguson.

Liverpool certainly contributed to an enthralling second half which developed into a superb spectacle, and they were desperately unlucky to finish empty handed. Ferguson said: 'It was a fantastic, incredible game and you have to give full marks to every player on the pitch. They gave everything and made it such an exciting match and a pleasure to be involved in.'

When Giggs scored his second goal to put United 2-0 ahead with twenty minutes left, they looked home and dry. Harry Kewell quickly halved the deficit and, in a dramatic finish, Liverpool had a penalty appeal rejected which television replays showed was a spot-kick. Then in stoppage time, Emile Heskey wasted a clear-cut chance to make it 2-2 and complete a remarkable recovery.

That excitement was a stark contrast to the sterile opening half, in which both sides lacked a cutting edge, with Liverpool badly missing the injured Michael Owen.

Liverpool goalkeeper Jerzy Dudek, haunted by the blunder which presented Diego Forlán with the first of his two goals in United's 2-1 win at Anfield last season, had another match to forget. Giggs' fifty-ninth-minute opener was scored direct from a free kick with his rapier-like left foot. Admittedly Dudek had to cover the near post in case Ruud van Nistelrooy made contact with the cross, which eluded everyone as it flew into the far corner. It got even worse for the second goal as Dudek could only parry Giggs' near-post shot into the roof of the net.

Liverpool's change of fortune coincided with the introduction of Florent Sinama Pongolle, as the teenage French striker was the catalyst for all Liverpool's attacking play. And it was the lively Sinama Pongolle who wriggled free on the right to provide the cross for Kewell to volley home his sixth goal for Liverpool. Sinama Pongolle's electrifying pace also led to the penalty appeal as Rio Ferdinand clearly caught the player before making contact with the ball.

Then deep into injury time came arguably the biggest let-off as Heskey was put clean through by Murphy's brilliant ball. As the England striker prepared to shoot, he slipped in a way reminiscent of David Beckham's penalty miss for England in Turkey as his scuffed shot flew harmlessly wide.

Liverpool: Dudek, Finnan, Traoré, Gerrard, Bišćan, Hyypiä, Diouf (Le Tallec) ,
    Murphy, Heskey, Šmicer (Sinama Pongolle) Kewell.
United: Howard, G. Neville, O'Shea, Ferdinand, Keane, Silvestre, Giggs, P. Neville,
    van Nistelrooy, Forlán, Fortune (Fletcher).

MURPHY'S RULE OF LAW

24 April 2004
Premiership
United 0, Liverpool 1 (Murphy (pen.)).

It was very much a case of Murphy's Law as Liverpool won at Old Trafford for the third time in four seasons. Danny Murphy completed a remarkable hat-trick as in each of those three victories the midfield man had scored the match-winning goal.

This was United's third home defeat of the season and dented their hopes of finishing runners-up to Champions-elect Chelsea. United had been only one point adrift of Chelsea until this defeat as they eventually finished third. The win was welcomed by Liverpool as they chased the fourth Champions League place, which Gérard Houllier's side would later secure.

Murphy struck the decisive goal midway through the second half after Gary Neville scythed down Steven Gerrard as he burst into the penalty area. Right-back Neville, who had scored twice in the previous three matches, suddenly turned villain as referee

Mike Riley pointed to the spot. Murphy stepped forward as he had taken over duties from Michael Owen after his recent string of misses from twelve yards.

Murphy blazed high into the roof of the net past 'keeper Tim Howard as he became the first visiting player to score a penalty in the Premiership at Old Trafford for over ten years. Norwich's Ruel Fox had last achieved the feat in December 1993, since when three visiting teams had been awarded spot kicks, but all had missed. It was just as well there was Murphy's penalty to discuss because the remainder of the match was as dull as dishwater.

Sir Alex Ferguson pointed out United had five decent chances to win the game, but groaned that they failed to work 'keeper Jerzy Dudek. He mentioned two which fell to Louis Saha, and another to Ole Gunnar Solskjær while Ryan Giggs struck both uprights with the same shot. Despite those chances, Dudek was a near spectator as United clearly missed the injured Ruud van Nistelrooy and suspended Paul Scholes.

Liverpool were equally feeble in front of goal as they humped long balls to Owen and Harry Kewell while their biggest striker, Emile Heskey, was sat on the substitutes' bench. Murphy's penalty provided a wake-up call for United, who until then had only the odd flash of brilliance from Cristiano Ronaldo. United's end-of-match formation was very much like yesteryear with an adventurous 2-3-5 line up.

Though they had three excellent chances in the last ten minutes, they could not find a way through Liverpool's well-marshalled back line. It turned out to be one of the less memorable clashes between the two teams, a contrast to some of the classics of recent seasons.

United: Howard, G. Neville, O'Shea (Solskjær), Brown, Butt, Silvestre, Fletcher, P.
    Neville (Bellion), Giggs, Saha, Ronaldo.
Liverpool: Dudek, Finnan (Šmicer), Carragher, Hamann, Henchoz, Hyypiä, Murphy,
    Gerrard, Kewell (Cheyrou), Owen (Heskey), Riise.

RIO UPSTAGED ON RETURN

20 September 2004
Premiership
United 2 (Silvestre 2), Liverpool 1 (O'Shea (o.g.)).

This Monday night match marked the return of United's Rio Ferdinand after his eight-month ban, punishment for the infamous missed drugs test.

While the eyes of everyone were on Ferdinand, it was his central defence partner Mikaël Silvestre who was United's unlikely hero as they inflicted a first derby defeat on new Liverpool manager Rafael Benítez, who had succeeded Gérard Houllier. The Frenchman, hardly renowned for his goalscoring exploits, scored two headers to hoist United up to eighth place and erase some of the disappointment of their worst start to a season for fifteen years. They had won only one of their first five League matches.

Despite his double strike, Silvestre was never going to knock Ferdinand off the back pages. It was a calculated gamble by Ferguson to throw Ferdinand – whose suspension ended the previous midnight – straight into the fray for arguably their biggest game of the season without any competitive match practice. Ferdinand, however, looked as though he had never been away with a near foot-perfect display. Sir Alex Ferguson was hoping Ferdinand's return would tighten the team defensively and eradicate the mistakes which had been glaring in his absence.

Ferdinand said, 'It was brilliant to be back. It was nice to get out there and forget about what had gone on in the past. It was never going to be easy, both physically and mentally. It was all new again after being out for so long.'

After an indifferent start to the campaign, United at last produced a performance that had their fans smiling again. They defeated Liverpool far more comprehensively than the scoreline suggested and, while Ferdinand won the Man of the Match award, there could easily have been a number of other recipients.

Ronaldo produced some sublime touches while Roy Keane controlled the centre of the five-man midfield.

United's task was obviously made easier when Steven Gerrard limped off shortly before half-time with a suspected broken metatarsal bone in his foot. The only criticism of United's first-half display was that they only had Silvestre's twentieth-minute goal to show for their efforts.

Ronaldo struck an upright with a long-range drive and saw another effort fly just wide while Gabriel Heinze, Ruud van Nistelrooy and John O'Shea also went close.

Silvestre scored with a header from a free kick by Ryan Giggs, who was making his 600th first-team appearance, only the third United player to reach that milestone.

Those missed chances looked as though they might prove costly when Liverpool equalised early in the second half. Xabi Alonso's free kick was headed towards goal by Steve Finnan and O'Shea inadvertently turned it past 'keeper Roy Carroll.

United regained the lead midway through the second period when Giggs again provided the assist as Silvestre stole in unmarked to head his corner into the roof of the net. Silvestre had, incredibly, doubled his goal tally for United within the space of an hour.

As is usually the case in these matches, there is often a twist and Liverpool were far from beaten as Alonso, with an effort from the half-way line, and a Dietmar Hamman free-kick could have snatched a point for the visitors in the latter stages.

United: Carroll, Brown, Heinze, Ferdinand, Keane, Silvestre, Ronaldo, O'Shea, van Nistelrooy, Scholes (Smith), Giggs.
Liverpool: Dudek, Josemi, Riise, Gerrard (Hamann), Carragher, Hyypiä, Finnan, Alonso, García, Cissé (Baroš), Kewell.

ROONEY'S HAPPY RETURN

15 January 2005
Premiership
Liverpool 0, United 1 (Rooney).

There was further pain as United completed a League double and secured a Premiership win at Anfield for the third successive season.

To add insult to injury for Liverpool and to provide a bizarre twist, United's match-winning goal came from former Evertonian Wayne Rooney. The teenage Rooney was making his first return to Merseyside since his big-money summer move to United and it appeared destiny that he should score.

The defining moment came midway through the opening half when Liverpool 'keeper Jerzy Dudek was again cursed in these derby battles. The Pole, who had made a number of high profile and costly gaffes against United, did it yet again. This time Dudek allowed Rooney's twenty-five-yard shot to slip through his grasp when he appeared to have it covered. Rooney had a mobile telephone hurled at him as he celebrated in front of the Kop, an incident which resulted in the Football Association seeking a police report into the flashpoint.

What made the victory even more commendable was that they had to play the final twenty-five minutes with ten men after Wes Brown's sending off for a second booking. United, thanks to the efforts of Mikaël Silvestre and John O'Shea, who replaced Brown in the centre of defence after his dismissal, stood up to what was thrown at them. Liverpool failed to take advantage with only Jamie Carragher and Igor Biščan having lukewarm attempts on goal.

Earlier United had limited Fernando Morientes, Liverpool's new £6.3 million striker, to three half-chances on his debut as they comfortably kept a seventh successive clean sheet, equalling a club record.

It was a measure of Chelsea's dominance that United's win briefly reduced the deficit between the two clubs to eight points. Chelsea would go on to claim their first title for fifty years while Arsenal edged out United for second spot and Liverpool's first season under Rafael Benítez saw them finish fifth.

Liverpool would still controversially qualify for the Champions League, however, by virtue of winning the competition. The disappointment at their fifth-place finish was more than compensated for, however, on that magical night in Istanbul at the end of the season when they defeated AC Milan after a dramatic final to lift the Champions League for a fifth time, though four of those triumphs were in the days when it was known as the European Cup.

It was a rare moment when Liverpool upstaged United, who had been dominant since the beginning of the nineties when it had come to winning silverware. Liverpool fans in forthcoming years would be keen to remind United they were still kings of Europe with five triumphs in the top competition compared to United's two at that time.

Liverpool: Dudek, Carragher, Traoré, Hamann (Bišćan), Pellegrino, Hyypiä, García, Gerrard, Baroš, Morientes (Nunez), Riise (Sinama Pongolle).
United: Carroll, P. Neville, Heinze, Brown, Keane, Silvestre, Fletcher, Scholes, Saha (Fortune), Rooney (Bellion), Ronaldo (O'Shea).

DERBY LACKS SPARK

18 September 2005
Premiership
Liverpool 0, United 0.

As Liverpool/United games go, this was described as one of the less memorable ones, a dull, goalless draw in which neither side seriously looked like breaking the deadlock.

It certainly did not live up to the pre-match hype as United supporters had arrived at Anfield fearing noses would be rubbed in it following Liverpool's fifth European Cup triumph less than four months earlier. That never materialised, with the atmosphere in the stands as flat as play on the pitch.

The rivalry between the two teams remained as intense as ever – there was some ferocious tackling and occasional flare ups, which was always on the cards when England's two most successful clubs went head to head. It had to be remembered, though, that there had been a shift in the power base as Chelsea had suddenly emerged as the power-brokers in English football, with Arsenal also dominant. That effectively left United and Liverpool scrapping for third and fourth places in the previous two seasons.

Liverpool went into the derby having won only three Premiership matches, a legacy of having to pre-qualify for the Champions League. United, meanwhile, had started the campaign with five straight wins in League and European matches. They went to Anfield on the back of two draws as they had lost their 100 per cent League record the previous weekend in the Manchester derby, and four days earlier had been involved in a goalless draw at Villarreal in the Champions League.

They headed for Merseyside buoyed by the fact that they had won on their previous three visits and triumphed seven times at Anfield since the Premiership was formed in 1992.

There was disappointment for United, however, as the two points dropped saw them slip further behind Chelsea, who were looking ominous as they were bidding to remain champions.

It was also a measure of how times had changed that drawing at Anfield was deemed an unsatisfactory result. To make matters worse for United, it was later revealed that Roy Keane had broken a metatarsal in his left foot.

Florent Sinama Pongolle had Liverpool's one chance of the opening half as they launched long balls up to Peter Crouch, prompting chants of 'Wimbledon' from the United fans. Ruud van Nistelrooy had two chances for United, but neither troubled Pepe Reina, who had still to let in a League goal for Liverpool following his summer move from Villarreal.

The second half was hardly much better, though Steven Gerrard forced Edwin van der Sar to make a super save to keep out his long-range drive. Luis García went close for Liverpool with a header late on, but the game fizzled out to the goalless draw that had looked likely throughout.

Liverpool: Reina, Finnan, Warnock (Traoré), Alonso, Carragher, Hyypiä, García, Gerrard, Crouch, Sinama Pongolle (Sissoko), Riise.
United: van der Sar, O'Shea, Richardson, Keane (Giggs), Ferdinand, Silvestre, Smith, Scholes, van Nistelrooy, Rooney (Fletcher), Ronaldo (Park).

BATTLE FOR SECOND SPOT HOTS UP

22 January 2006
Premiership
United 1 (Ferdinand), Liverpool 0.

It was unlucky thirteen for Liverpool, whose three-month unbeaten run in the Premiership was ended by a last-gasp goal by Rio Ferdinand as the battle for second spot hotted up.
Liverpool suffered their first League defeat for thirteen games in a match United could not afford to lose, as a win for Rafael Benítez's side would have given them a two-point lead with two games in hand.
Though United's victory cut Chelsea's lead, it hardly made any inroads as they held what would prove an unassailable fourteen-point lead. Ferdinand certainly erased the pain of United's defeat in the Manchester derby one week earlier as his goal brought unbridled joy, given the opponents.
The emotions at Old Trafford could not have been further removed from those of eight days earlier when they lost to their neighbours. The healing process was swift as United savoured a victory that was even sweeter as it ended Liverpool's long unbeaten run in the League. Not only that but it also silenced the Liverpool fans who came to Old Trafford brandishing '5' banners and with inflatable European Cups.
You only had to look at Gary Neville's celebrations in front of the Liverpool fans – it got him into hot water with the FA – to see what it meant.
The match had been heading towards a goalless draw when Ferdinand struck with an injury-time goal which could be worth millions of pounds for United if it eventually guaranteed automatic qualification to the Champions League. Liverpool manager Rafael Benítez had said beforehand that the winner would be favourite to claim second spot in the League, which was possibly why the game was so tight until Ferdinand's intervention at the death.
New boy Patrice Evra was hauled back by Steve Finnan as he made one last forward burst. Ryan Giggs delivered an inch-perfect free kick from the left and Ferdinand soared to head home from twelve yards, with Liverpool 'keeper Pepe Reina only

helping to divert the ball into the roof of the net. It was an unlikely finish as the match had appeared to be heading for a dour and uninspiring goalless draw, despite the efforts of both managers to win the game.

Benítez brought on Fernando Morientes and Florent Sinama Pongolle, while United switched to three players up front. And the winner came from an unlikely source as the odds on Ferdinand getting the winner in a 1-0 scoreline were 150/1. Equally as important as Ferdinand's goal, however, was his desperate goal-line clearance, which had earlier prevented Liverpool from taking the lead. Mohamed Sissoko played the ball into the penalty area and it took a deflection off Ferdinand and looped over the head of 'keeper Edwin van der Sar. Ferdinand displayed great athleticism to get back to hook the ball off the line.

'The clearance was probably as important as the goal as, had it gone in, it would have been a different game altogether,' explained Ferdinand.

In the awful opening half, the only decent chance fell to Peter Crouch, whose angled shot was well blocked by Wes Brown. Liverpool were left bewildered by their failure to score midway through the second period when, after Ferdinand's goal-line clearance, John Arne Riise's drive was parried by van der Sar only as far as Djibril Cissé, who missed an open goal from six yards. It was a pivotal moment in the match and the element of good fortune which proved the turning point as United rode their luck before snatching victory in the dying seconds.

United would finish the campaign runners-up to Chelsea, with Liverpool third.

United: van der Sar, G. Neville, Evra, Brown, Ferdinand, O'Shea (Saha), Giggs, Fletcher, van Nistelrooy, Rooney, Richardson.
Liverpool: Reina, Finnan, Riise, Alonso, Carragher, Hyypiä, Sissoko (Kronkamp), Gerrard, Crouch (Morientes), Cissé (Sinama Pongolle), Kewell.

LONG AWAITED CUP WIN

18 February 2006
FA Cup, Fifth Round
Liverpool 1 (Crouch), United 0.

Liverpool recorded a long overdue FA Cup victory against United, their first in the competition for eighty-five years. Peter Crouch was Liverpool's match-winner with a nineteenth-minute header, one of the bright spots of an eminently forgettable cup clash which was marred by a serious injury sustained by Alan Smith.

Goalkeeper Edwin van der Sar produced a fine fingertip save to keep out Harry Kewell's header. From the resulting short corner, however, Steve Finnan crossed for Crouch to head home his eighth of the season.

The defeat was disappointing for United and meant that after the end of February, when they beat Wigan Athletic in the Carling Cup final, their season was effectively over. They had been knocked out of the Champions League and FA Cup while Chelsea were racing certainties to defend their League crown. The defeat graphically illustrated why United were no longer the major force, though they finished runners-up to Chelsea while Liverpool were third.

The battle at Anfield was won in midfield, where United were out-muscled, out-thought and out-played. They had a central pairing of Ryan Giggs and Kieran Richardson, neither central players, while Cristiano Ronaldo and Darren Fletcher were on the flanks. They were second-best to German World Cup player Dietmar Hamann and African Momo Sissoko, while Steven Gerrard and Kewell provided the width. They were Liverpool's 'Fab Four', proving too strong for United.

United, starved of possession, provided little ammunition for Ruud van Nistelrooy and Wayne Rooney, who cut isolated figures up front, a damning indictment of the lack of service they received.

Sadly, the eagerly awaited glamour tie of the last sixteen proved something of a damp squib following the pre-match hype. It certainly did not live up to its star billing.

Indeed, all three of this season's clashes had disappointed and failed to replicate some memorable of previous years.

United's Gary Neville had a torrid afternoon as he was jeered every time he touched the ball; it was pay-back time from Liverpool fans after his celebrations in front of them in the previous month's United League victory at Old Trafford.

Liverpool: Reina, Finnan, Riise, Hamann, Carragher, Hyypiä, Sissoko, Gerrard, Crouch (Cissé), Morientes (García), Kewell (Kronkamp).
United: van der Sar, G. Neville, Silvestre (Saha), Fletcher (Smith) (Park), Brown, Vidić, Ronaldo, Richardson, van Nistelrooy, Rooney, Giggs.

SCHOLES CELEBRATES MILESTONE

22 October 2006
Premiership
United 2 (Scholes, Ferdinand), Liverpool 0.

Paul Scholes celebrated his 500th appearance for United in style, with a goal and Man of the Match display. Rio Ferdinand also found the net as United regained the top spot they had temporarily lost the previous day to Chelsea.

It was a big win and the manner of the victory provided a growing belief that they might prevent Chelsea from claiming a hat-trick of League titles. Suddenly there was an eleven-point gap between United and Liverpool, who continued to toil on their travels, which is why they were languishing mid-table. They had picked up only one point from a possible fifteen away from Anfield.

Sir Alex Ferguson admitted it was a massive victory, bearing in mind United had failed to deliver at home to Arsenal, another of the perceived 'big four', the previous month. United also proved there was life without Ruud van Nistelrooy as they had been expected to struggle to find the net after his summer move to Real Madrid.

Ferdinand became the tenth different goalscorer in the opening two months of the season as they had spread the load in the absence of the influential Dutchman. Indeed, with nineteen goals in nine League matches, they were the Premiership's leading scorers.

Scholes said, 'That is the way it used to be with players scoring from all positions. It's great when you don't have to rely on Louis Saha and Wayne Rooney every game. It also takes the pressure off them when others are scoring goals.'

Liverpool strung five players across midfield, ensuring the area was gridlocked, and there was little to inspire until Scholes broke the deadlock in the thirty-ninth minute when he ghosted in to meet a cross from Ryan Giggs. Keeper Pepe Reina blocked the initial effort but it looped into the air and Scholes made no mistake the second time despite a desperate attempt by Sami Hyypiä to clear. It was his 132nd goal for United. And but for a fabulous save from Reina to keep out a twenty-five-yard drive from Saha shortly before half-time, United would have finished the opening half 2-0 ahead.

Giggs provided the assist for Ferdinand's clinching goal midway through the second half with his pinpoint cross which Carragher could only clear as far as Ferdinand, who cut back inside John Arne Riise before smashing an angled shot from six yards high into the roof of the net. This was Ferdinand's fourth goal for United, and two of them had come against Liverpool.

United's victory was more comfortable than the scoreline suggested as 'keeper Edwin van der Sar didn't have a serious shot to save. It extended United's impressive run against their rivals as they had now lost only one of their last nine League meetings and also demonstrated the enormous amount of work Rafael Benítez had to do to revive Liverpool's ailing fortunes.

United: van der Sar, G. Neville (O'Shea), Evra (Brown), Carrick, Ferdinand, Vidić, Fletcher, Scholes, Saha, Rooney, Giggs.
Liverpool: Reina, Finnan, Riise, Alonso (Crouch), Carragher, Hyypiä, Gerrard, Sissoko, García, Kuyt, González (Pennant).

UNITED SHATTER RECORD

3 March 2007
Premiership
Liverpool 0, United 1 (O'Shea).

They say records are there to be broken and how United savoured ending Liverpool's impressive thirty-match unbeaten home run in the Premiership. United's last-gasp victory at Anfield provided compelling evidence that they appeared destined to recapture the League title they last won four years ago.

Substitute John O'Shea's dramatic injury-time winner saw United maintain their nine-point lead over Chelsea, who were bidding to complete a hat-trick of championships.

Sir Alex Ferguson admitted fortune was smiling kindly on his side after fortuitous back-to-back wins against Fulham and Liverpool. He said,

> You need that bit of luck to win the title, and I think we have had that in the last two weeks. This was a massive result. We broke away and scored in the last couple of minutes at Fulham, and we did it again. It happens in championship races. We had a lot of narrow escapes and Liverpool upset our rhythm. They will feel very unlucky, and they deserve to.

United's lucky break came in the opening period, when Craig Bellamy had a goal wrongly ruled out for offside when replays revealed he was clearly onside.

Even Liverpool manager Rafael Benítez believed this would be the season in which United regained their championship crown. Benítez explained,

> I couldn't explain how we lost that game in Spanish, let alone English. We were in control and had plenty of attacks. When you have so much of the play and make chances without

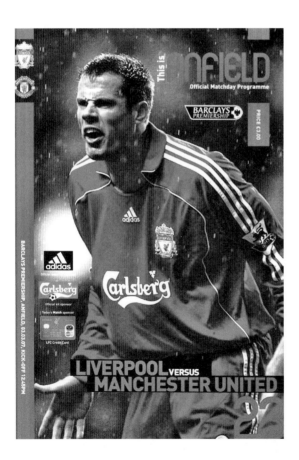

scoring, you must be careful against a team as good as United. They have a great defence and fine goalkeeper [Edwin van der Sar] who stopped one from Peter Crouch at the end that everyone felt was going in.

Crouch chested the ball down and fired in an angled shot from six yards which had goal written all over it until the Dutchman, diving low to his left, somehow managed to turn it to safety. To compound Liverpool's misery, United almost immediately broke up-field to score the match-winning goal. Ryan Giggs, who was making his 700th first-team appearance for United, was pulled back by Steve Finnan on the left edge of the penalty area. Giggs fired in a low free kick which 'keeper Pepe Reina could only parry and O'Shea was on hand to rifle the rebound into the roof of the net from six yards.

The goal ended Liverpool's remarkable home run in which they had kept nine successive clean sheets at home in the League, a club record, and it was the first they had conceded in over fifteen and a half hours or 934 minutes to be precise. It was a magical moment for O'Shea, who had replaced Wayne Rooney, who was taken off with a gash to his thigh which required eight stitches after he had been caught by Jamie Carragher.

O'Shea described the last-minute goal, which was scored in front of the Kop, as the most important of his career. 'I will have to get a picture of it and get it framed. It is one to cherish and a few pints will be sunk over that,' he reflected.

The one sour note for United was Paul Scholes' needless sending off after eighty-six minutes for aiming a punch at Xabi Alonso after a challenge. It failed to land, but referee Martin Atkinson deemed intent and he was dismissed for violent conduct.

United went on to regain the title, finishing six points clear of runners-up Chelsea while Liverpool recovered from their poor start to finish third, though they were a massive twenty-one adrift of the champions.

Liverpool: Reina, Finnan, Riise, Alonso, Carragher, Agger, Gerrard, Sissoko (Crouch), Bellamy (Pennant), Kuyt, González (Aurélio).

United: van der Sar, G. Neville, Evra (Silvestre), Carrick, Ferdinand, Vidić, Ronaldo, Scholes, Larsson (Saha), Rooney (O'Shea), Giggs.

UNITED'S KING CARLOS

16 December 2007
Premier League
Liverpool 0, United 1 (Tévez).

It was described as smash-and-grab as United's win at Liverpool proved pivotal in their bid to retain their Premier League title. Though not pretty to watch, as Sir Alex Ferguson admitted, it was a massive win which came courtesy of a lucky deflection which set up the match-winning goal for Carlos Tévez.

It was the sort of break teams need if they are to be crowned champions on the day described by Sky Sports as 'Grand Slam Sunday'; Arsenal entertained Chelsea as the big four went head to head. While Sir Alex Ferguson had plenty to celebrate, it was an afternoon when Liverpool all but blew their title hopes even at this midway point of the season. They were nine points behind United, yet would have cut the deficit to three had they triumphed with a game in hand, further evidence of what a big win it was for the visitors and crushing blow for Liverpool.

Ferguson, who had won on five of his last six visits to Anfield, said, 'It was a typical United/Liverpool game and fluency was not an issue. It was about winning. The games between the top sides are going to be important this year, and this was an important win for us.'

It was a terrific display from United, built on solid foundations with Rio Ferdinand and Nemanja Vidić stifling danger-men Fernando Torres and Dirk Kuyt as this was their thirteenth clean sheet in all competitions. Brazilian Anderson, aged just nineteen, was not intimidated by his biggest game to date as he and Owen Hargreaves showed the green shoots of a promising central midfield partnership. While Cristiano Ronaldo was subdued, Tévez rose to the occasion, working and battling hard, and was rewarded with his ninth goal of the season but, significantly, his first on the road.

Hargreaves came to United's rescue with a goal-line clearance to deny Harry Kewell, and Patrice Evra slid in to prevent Kuyt from opening the scoring. United struck the decisive blow two minutes before half-time with their first goal attempt of the game.

Wayne Rooney's shot was deflected to Tévez, who shot into the roof of the net from close range.

The second half remained tightly contested, though United ought to have sealed victory with twelve minutes left. Ronaldo delivered a low cross to the far post and Wayne Rooney shot wide with only 'keeper Pepe Reina to beat. Ferguson held his head in his hands in disbelief as it could have proved a costly miss, especially when deep in stoppage time Steven Gerrard's free-kick dipped narrowly over the crossbar, leaving United hearts in mouths.

Liverpool: Reina, Arbeloa, Riise (Aurélio), Mascherano, Carragher, Hyypiä, Benayoun, Gerrard, Torres, Kuyt (Crouch), Kewell (Babel).
United: van der Sar, Brown, Evra, Hargreaves, Ferdinand, Vidić, Ronaldo, Anderson (O'Shea), Rooney, Tévez (Carrick), Giggs.

BIG WIN SETS UP TITLE NO. 10

23 March 2008
Premier League
United 3 (Brown, Ronaldo, Nani), Liverpool 0.

When United were eventually crowned Premier League champions, they would surely look back on the dramatic events of 'Grand Slam Sunday' as one of the defining moments of their campaign. United's comprehensive victory against ten-man Liverpool at Old

Trafford, which was followed by Chelsea's win against Arsenal, opened up a highly significant five-point lead at the top as they chased a tenth Premier League title.

Goals from Wes Brown, his first in three years, Cristiano Ronaldo and Nani also improved United's goal difference, which was vastly superior to those of Chelsea and Arsenal, who were second and third respectively. And with only seven League fixtures remaining, the title was tantalisingly within touching distance.

Sir Alex Ferguson was still erring on the side of caution, declaring, 'Chelsea and Arsenal are both playing well and it will go right to the end of the season. We cannot get carried away in this League, but it is a good morale booster and good for confidence.'

This was the sequel to 'Grand Slam Sunday' and the reverse of the mid-December fixtures involving the Premier League's 'Big Four'. With only five points separating the top three teams before the weekend's fixtures – Liverpool were too far adrift in fourth place to matter – this was a massively important double-header. Liverpool, with the least to lose, were described as dangerous opponents as they could go out at Old Trafford without the weight of expectation on their shoulders.

They were in a decent vein of form and had pulled clear of Everton in the race for the fourth and final Champions League place. Ferguson's only criticism of his team was its failure to finish off Liverpool earlier, especially after they had been given a helping hand following Javier Mascherano's sending-off late in the first half for dissent. The Argentinian, booked for a foul, continually questioned referee Steve Bennett's decisions and the patience of the match official finally snapped, ironically after Liverpool were awarded a free kick following a foul on Fernando Torres.

Mascherano, who wasn't involved, suddenly appeared on the scene to chip in with his two-penneth.

Ferguson thought his side could easily have been 3-0 ahead by half-time, pointing to an avalanche of chances which fell to Wayne Rooney and Ronaldo. It wasn't until Ronaldo, who had twice been denied by the woodwork, struck their second goal with eleven minutes left that they finally killed off Liverpool.

United had taken the lead before Mascherano's dismissal through Brown's thirty-fourth-minute headed goal, which followed a cross from Rooney, beating 'keeper Pepe Reina on the six-yard line.

In the opening period Ronaldo struck an upright while Reina made important saves to deny Rooney and Ryan Giggs. United had more of a stranglehold with their numerical advantage, though the second killer goal did not arrive until eleven minutes from time.

Reina, who had brilliantly denied Rooney, Ronaldo and substitute Carlos Tévez, was sadly at fault again as he once more lost out on the six-yard line when Ronaldo out-jumped him to head home Nani's corner, his 34th goal of the season.

Two minutes later, substitute Nani scored a stunning third. He played a return pass with Rooney and cut inside to score with an unstoppable shot.

United were duly crowned Premier League champions for a tenth time and followed that with a victory in the final of the Champions League against Chelsea in Moscow. Liverpool claimed the fourth and final Champions League place.

United: Reina, Arbeloa, Aurélio, Mascherano, Carragher, Škrtel, Alonso, Gerrard, Torres (Sissoko), Kuyt, Babel (Benanyoun).

Liverpool: van der Sar, Brown, Evra, Carrick, Ferdinand, Vidić, Ronaldo, Scholes, Rooney, Anderson (Tévez), Giggs (Nani).

LIVERPOOL'S SEVEN-YEAR WAIT

13 September 2008
Premier League
Liverpool 2 (Brown (o.g.), Babel), United 1 (Tévez).

It was a momentous victory for Liverpool, their first in a League match against United for almost four-and-a-half years. Liverpool's success was also their first on home soil against United in the League since 2001, further evidence of the monopoly of the Old Trafford side.

Rafael Benítez also savoured his first win in a League fixture against United as Sir Alex Ferguson was scathing in his criticism of his side's defending, describing it as like that of a Conference side. 'Liverpool harassed us and we couldn't cope with their tackling which was the source of their victory. They were by far the better team,' he declared.

What made Liverpool's win even more memorable was that it was achieved without Steve Gerrard and Fernando Torres, who were only substitutes as they returned from injury lay-offs.

There was no early inkling that Liverpool's dismal run against United was about to end as the visitors took the lead in the third minute. Record £30.75 million signing Dimitar Berbatov cut the ball back from the byline for Carlos Tévez to drive home from the edge of the penalty area. From the way United confidently stroked the ball about in the early stages, you couldn't see anything but another win for the Old Trafford side as they displayed a swagger you would expect from the domestic and European Champions. They played a 4-3-3 formation, with Berbatov the focal point of the attack with Wayne Rooney offering support from the flanks, where there was no place for regular wide men Ryan Giggs and Nani.

Liverpool were handed an unexpected toehold back into the game midway through the opening half following an error from 'keeper Edwin van der Sar. The Dutchman made a meal of claiming a deflected shot from Xabi Alonso and, as he over-stretched, he palmed the ball against team-mate Wes Brown, who was credited with an unfortunate own goal.

Liverpool gained in confidence in the second half as United surrendered with a whimper. The introduction of Gerrard for the final quarter of the game was a master-stroke by Benítez and provided a massive psychological lift for Liverpool. And it was another substitute, Ryan Babel, who sealed victory after another piece of dire defending in the seventy-seventh minute. Dirk Kuyt got behind the United defence and pulled the ball back for Babel to score and United's simmering frustration exploded when Nemanja Vidić was sent off in the last minute for his second booking after a crude challenge on Alonso.

Liverpool were second in the table to Chelsea, with each collecting ten points from their first four League matches while United were two thirds down the League, having collected four points from their first three League matches.

Liverpool: Reina, Arbeloa, Aurélio, Alonso, Carragher, Škrtel, Benanyoun (Gerrard),
  Mascherano (Hyypiä), Kuyt, Keane, Riera (Babel).
United: van der Sar, Brown, Evra, Carrick (Giggs), Ferdinand, Vidić, Rooney, Scholes
  (Hargreaves), Berbatov, Tévez, Anderson (Nani).

WHO SAW THIS COMING?

14 March 2009
Premier League
United 1 (Ronaldo), Liverpool 4 (Torres, Gerrard (pen.), Aurélio, Dossena).

Liverpool completed a double in spectacular style, but it was not sufficient to prevent United from later completing a hat-trick of Premier League titles. It was a defeat which was hardly forecast as United went into the derby on the back of eleven straight League victories, a run which had catapulted them from being also-rans to racing certainties for an eleventh Premier League title but, more significantly, equalled Liverpool's cherished record of eighteen championships.

And even after this defeat, United still held a four-point cushion at the top having also played one less game than their nearest challengers. Sir Alex Ferguson rather surprisingly maintained United were the better team on the day. Rafael Benítez, who had to wait over four years for his first League win against United, now celebrated two in less than six months, saying they had shown how to beat them.

He explained,

> United have been playing with so much confidence. At least people will now see that they
> can lose. The message is there for everyone. In attack they are fantastic and you can see the
> quality they have. In defence they have some weaknesses and we tried to exploit them.

It did seem an odd point to make given United had only recently lost a record of fourteen consecutive clean sheets in the Premier League. You wouldn't have guessed that given their defending against Liverpool. The warning signs were evident days earlier in the Champions League when Liverpool demolished Real Madrid 4-0 while United gained a somewhat fortuitous 2-0 home win against Inter Milan.

United were chasing the famed 'quintuple', having already won the FIFA World Club Championship and Carling Cup and still pursuing the Premier League, Champions

League and FA Cup. Could it have been fatigue as the season entered its home straight given the congested fixture list, or was it a case of over-confidence?

United actually made the better start, taking the lead midway through the opening period with a Cristiano Ronaldo penalty which followed a needless foul by Pepe Reina on Park Ji-Sung. Liverpool equalised within five minutes when Nemanja Vidić inexplicably allowed a long ball to sail over his head as Fernando Torres raced clear to score. Torres then turned provider, releasing Steve Gerrard who darted clear only to be fouled by Patrice Evra; Gerrard scored from the spot to give Liverpool a 2-1 interval lead.

Vidić was sent off in the second half following a foul on Gerrard, his second dismissal of the campaign against Liverpool. After that Liverpool sealed victory when Fabio Aurélio curled in a free kick for the third and that was followed by a fourth, a lob late on from substitute Andrea Dossena.

United ended up with three trophies and so nearly made it four after reaching the final of the Champions League, losing to Barcelona in Rome, while Liverpool achieved second place in the Premier League, their highest finish under Benítez, as they were only four points adrift of United.

United: van der Sar, O'Shea, Evra, Carrick (Giggs), Ferdinand, Vidić, Ronaldo, Anderson (Scholes), Rooney, Tévez, Park (Berbatov).
Liverpool: Reina, Carragher, Aurélio, Mascherano, Škrtel, Hyypiä, Lucas, Gerrard (El Zhar), Torres (Babel), Kuyt, Riera (Dossena).

OWEN JEERED ON ANFIELD RETURN

25 October 2009
Premier League
Liverpool 2 (Torres, N'Gog), United 0.

Liverpool fans voiced their disapproval as Michael Owen, one of their favourite sons, returned to Anfield for the first time in the colours of their deadly rivals. Owen's goalscoring exploits, which had made him a Liverpool legend, were forgotten as his entrance as a seventy-fourth-minute substitute for Dimitar Berbatov was greeted by a chorus of jeers as they voiced their displeasure at seeing him playing for United.

If ever there was a result that proved that the form book goes out of the window in derby games, then this was the one. Liverpool went into the match on the back of four successive losses in competitive matches. They were lying in eighth place in the table after back-to-back defeats against Chelsea and Sunderland and having lost four of their first nine League games.

United, by contrast, were positively flying. They had lost only one of their first nine League fixtures and only surrendered top spot the previous weekend after being held at home by Sunderland, while the Champions League was also proving a breeze. This was also Liverpool's third successive win against United as their fortunes had changed for the better after a period relatively starved of success. Indeed, in a fourteen-game sequence in 2002–8, Liverpool had managed only three victories.

Sir Alex Ferguson had no complaints after seeing his side slip to a second League defeat of the season after a performance to forget in which Nemanja Vidić was sent off for the third successive match against Liverpool, an unwanted hat-trick. 'It was a disappointing performance and Liverpool were the better team,' he conceded.

While Liverpool, desperate to end their poor run of form, enjoyed the better of the play for much of the afternoon, United were still in the contest until midway through the second half when Fernando Torres broke the deadlock. Most of the pre-match build-up concerned which players might be missing as United's Wayne Rooney and Darren Fletcher were doubts, as were key Liverpool pair Steven Gerrard and Torres. Rooney and Torres made it, but Fletcher and Gerrard were absentees.

Edwin van der Sar was the busier 'keeper, making a super double save to keep out Fabio Aurélio's free kick and Dirk Kuyt's follow-up shot with his legs. The same two players had further chances while all United produced was a header from Rooney which 'keeper Pepe Reina scrambled to safety. United improved after the restart to the point where victory looked a possibility as chances fell to Ryan Giggs and Michael Carrick.

It was Liverpool who broke the deadlock midway through the half when Torres latched on to Yossi Benayoun's through-ball, held off Rio Ferdinand and fired high into the net. Antonio Valencia came within inches of equalising in the dying minutes when his shot struck the crossbar.

In a frantic finish, both sides were reduced to ten men as Vidić and Javier Mascherano were both dismissed for second bookings. United, pressing for an equaliser, were caught at the death as Liverpool substitute David N'Gog slid in to score their second, sealing victory.

Liverpool: Reina, Johnson, Insúa, Mascherano, Carragher, Agger, Benayoun (Škrtel), Lucas, Torres (N'Gog), Kuyt, Aurélio.
United: van der Sar, O'Shea, Evra, Carrick, Ferdinand, Vidić, Valencia, Scholes (Owen), Berbatov (Nani), Rooney, Giggs.

RAFA'S RANT AT FERGIE

21 March 2010
Premier League
United 2 (Rooney, Park), Liverpool 1 (Torres).

The win which took United back to the top of the Premier League was overshadowed by a spat between Sir Alex Ferguson and Rafael Benítez. The Liverpool manager accused Ferguson of trying to influence referee Howard Webb as, on the eve of the game, he claimed the Football Association and match officials were biased against his side while favouring Liverpool.

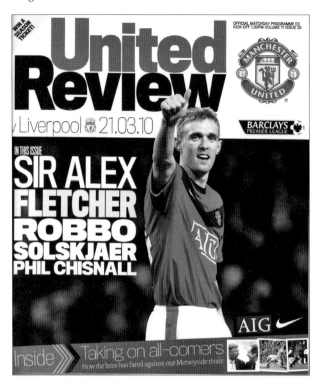

After United were awarded a controversial penalty, from which they equalised before going on to win, Benítez claimed Ferguson had tried to get inside Webb's head.

'The referees are professional, but we know of the influence of Sir Alex in everything,' explained Benítez.

This win felt even sweeter for United as it ended a run of three successive defeats against Liverpool, while also seeing them regain first place in the Premier League.

Yet it was far from a straightforward victory as Liverpool had stunned United by taking a fifth-minute lead as Fernando Torres slipped his marker to head past Edwin van der Sar. It was the first goal United had conceded in the League at Old Trafford in over 700 minutes, though that was as good as it got for the visitors.

There was controversy over the twelfth-minute penalty which saw United draw level through Rooney's spot kick. As Antonio Valencia burst through on goal, he was hauled back by Javier Mascherano with the winger falling in the penalty area.

Webb pointed to the spot and controversy raged as Benítez was adamant the contact was outside the box while Ferguson was convinced Mascherano had escaped lightly with only a yellow card. Rooney stepped forward only to see Pepe Rena deny him with a brilliant save, but the rebound fell invitingly back to United's top scorer to slot the ball home.

Park Ji-Sung, who was inspirational in the centre of midfield, Nani and Rooney all had chances to give United the lead before the break. And it was fitting that Park should score the winner as he conjured another big-match goal. His previous three goals had come against AC Milan and twice against Arsenal, including one against the Gunners in the semi finals of the Champions League. Darren Fletcher provided the cross from the right and Park ghosted in from deep to score with a diving header low past Reina.

The win extended the gap between the two teams to eighteen points, reinforcing the chasm between the two teams. While United had won eleven Premier League titles since its inception in 1992, Liverpool's last League triumph was way back in 1990.

There was also a provocative banner in the Stretford end – 'MUFC Making History – Not Living In It.'

United failed to create history by winning a nineteenth League title and eclipsing Liverpool, as Chelsea snatched the Championship by one point, while there was heartbreak for Liverpool as they missed out on Champions League football after finishing seventh.

United: van der Sar, G. Neville, Evra, Carrick, Ferdinand, Vidić, Valencia, Park
    (Scholes), Rooney, Fletcher, Nani (Giggs).
Liverpool: Reina, Johnson, Insúa, Mascherano, Carragher, Agger, Rodríguez (Babel),
    Gerrard, Torres, Kuyt (Aquilani), Lucas (Benayoun).

BRILLIANT BERBATOV

19 September 2010
Premier League
United 3 (Berbatov 3), Liverpool 2 (Gerrard 2 (1 pen.)).

Dimitar Berbatov scored the first hat-trick by a United player against Liverpool in sixty-four years on a day when Sir Alex Ferguson chose to eulogise about the brilliant Bulgarian. Ferguson focused on Berbatov's 'touch of genius' in the match-day programme, prompting the headline on the front cover, 'Off to a flier. Dimitar Berbatov has been unstoppable. More of the same is required today.'

And just to order Berbatov, who had his critics during his first two inconsistent seasons at Old Trafford, delivered again with a majestic treble. While many had doubted the £30.75 million record buy, Ferguson's support had been unwavering.

He said, 'You must persevere and trust your judgement. You must have faith and I think we are being rewarded this season for our confidence in him.'

Berbatov made it six goals in five matches – seven in six if the strike in the Community Shield is included – with an imperious display as he became the first United player since Stan Pearson in 1946 to score a hat-trick in this fixture.

Yet it so nearly didn't end in victory, which would have been a travesty, as United almost contrived to slip as new Liverpool manager Roy Hodgson experienced his first derby. They surrendered a two-goal lead but, fittingly, it was Berbatov who had the final word as he scored a late match-winner to deny Liverpool an unlikely point as this result meant it was their worst start to a season for eighteen years.

Ferguson added, 'It was a game we absolutely dominated and I was saying to myself it could have been ten. When it looked like ending 2-2, it would have been a travesty of a scoreline.' Ferguson also described it as a 'catastrophe' for Liverpool, a word Hodgson disagreed with. 'I thought United played well, but to try and undermine our performance is harsh,' he replied.

There was no inkling of the excitement in store during a lacklustre opening half in which United took the lead shortly before the break when Berbatov headed home a Ryan Giggs corner from eight yards. Nani struck the upright early in the second half before providing the assist for Berbatov's memorable second just before the hour.

Nani's cross was controlled by Berbatov's thigh as he teed himself up, finding the net with an amazing overhead kick which went in off the underside of the crossbar.

United were 2-0 ahead and there was seemingly no way back for United. How mistaken we were!

Jonny Evans handed Liverpool a lifeline and toehold back into the match midway through the second period, conceding a penalty following a foul on Fernando Torres, enabling Steve Gerrard to score from the spot. Seven minutes later and Liverpool were back on level terms as Gerrard bent a free kick around the defensive wall and low to the left of Edwin van der Sar.

Cometh the hour, cometh the man as Berbatov completed his hat-trick six minutes from time with a classy header following a cross by John O'Shea. It left Liverpool fifth bottom with only five points from their first five League matches, while United were third with eleven from the same number of games.

United: van der Sar, O'Shea, Evra, Evans, Vidić, Giggs (Macheda), Scholes, Fletcher, Nani (Gibson), Rooney, Berbatov (Anderson).
Liverpool: Reina, Johnson, Konchesky (Agger), Carragher, Škrtel, Poulsen, Meireles (Jovanovic), Gerrard, Cole, Rodríguez (N'Gog), Torres.

KING KENNY BACK AT HELM

9 January 2011
FA Cup, Third Round
United 1 (Giggs (pen.)), Liverpool 0.

The FA Cup third round tie marked Kenny Dalglish's surprise return to the managerial hot seat at Liverpool which he had vacated twenty years earlier. There could not have been a more high-profile first game, but it was not a triumphant return for King Kenny, who had just taken over from the sacked Roy Hodgson for the remainder of the season.

With Liverpool languishing in twelfth place in the Premier League, the new owners turned to Dalglish, who still had a back-room job at Anfield, to bring a feel-good factor back to the club.

Dalglish, a Liverpool legend as a player and later manager, could hardly have got off to a worse start against the League leaders. Only thirty-two seconds into his comeback game and Liverpool conceded a penalty which Dalglish branded a 'joke', as World Cup final referee Howard Webb adjudged Daniel Agger to have fouled Dimitar Berbatov on the edge of the penalty area. Subsequent television replays revealed minimal, if any, contact and it was to prove the pivotal moment of the match as it enabled Ryan Giggs to score the match-winning goal in the second minute.

Liverpool produced a spirited display, especially after they had to play for an hour with ten men. It also represented a marked improvement on performances towards the end of Hodgson's troubled reign. The other big talking point of the opening half came when Liverpool captain Steven Gerrard was sent off following a nasty challenge on Michael Carrick.

United had chances to build on their lead as Jonny Evans headed against the upright in first-half stoppage time. In the second period Javier Hernández, Berbatov, Rafael da

Silva, Patrice Evra and substitute Michael Owen all had decent goalscoring chances to put the game out of sight.

Yet there was always the threat that ten-man Liverpool might snatch a surprise equaliser and force a replay. That almost happened midway through the second half when Fabio Aurélio was denied by a super save from Tomasz Kuszczak to keep out his free kick, which was arrowing towards the top corner. Dalglish also showed he was not afraid to call big shots as he substituted Fernando Torres late on, replacing him with David N'Gog.

United: Kuszczak, Rafael, Evra, Ferdinand, Evans (Smalling), Giggs, Carrick, Fletcher (Anderson), Nani, Berbatov, Hernández (Owen).
Liverpool: Reina, Kelly, Škrtel, Agger, Aurélio, Rodríguez (Babel), Gerrard, Lucas, Meireles (Shelvey), Kuyt, Torres (N'Gog).

KUYT THE FLYING DUTCHMAN

6 March 2011
Premier League
Liverpool 3 (Kuyt 3), United 1 (Hernández).

United's bid for a record-breaking nineteenth League title experienced a wobble following defeats at Chelsea and Liverpool in the space of five days. And Liverpool did their utmost to ensure they did not see their arch-rivals overtake their total of Championship successes. It was providing to be one of the most absorbing title races for many years with United, Chelsea and Arsenal vying for glory while Liverpool were enjoying a renaissance under Kenny Dalglish, appointed caretaker manager to the end of the season.

This match belonged to one player, Dutchman Dirk Kuyt, who consigned United to defeat at Anfield, where the visitors' defence was unusually suspect in the absence of Nemanja Vidić and Rio Ferdinand through suspension and injury respectively. It was something of a makeshift back four with Chris Smalling and Wes Brown the centre-back pairing.

There was no inkling early on that Liverpool would record such a resounding victory as United were unlucky not to take the lead when Dimitar Berbatov struck an upright and Brown's deflected header was cleared off the line by Raul Meireles.

Liverpool snatched a somewhat surprising lead in the thirty-fourth minute when some delightful footwork from Uruguayan Luis Suárez set up Kuyt for a simple tap in. And it quickly got better for them as Nani's wayward header presented a gift to the Dutchman for his second.

Jamie Carragher was fortunate to escape unpunished after a late challenge which left Nani with a gashed shin and unable to play in the second period, forcing an early reshuffle of the United side. United still believed they could force their way back into the game, but those hopes were vanquished when Kuyt completed his hat-trick midway through the second period; Edwin van der Sar spilled Suárez's free kick and Kuyt was on hand to score.

Javier Hernández scored a consolation goal for United at the death, but the defeat proved to be only a minor aberration as they regained their poise to achieve their record-breaking nineteenth title while Liverpool finished sixth.

Liverpool: Reina, Johnson, Carragher, Škrtel, Aurélio (Kyrgiakos), Kuyt, Meireles (Carroll), Lucas, Gerrard, Rodríguez, Suárez (Cole).
United: van der Sar, Rafael (O'Shea), Smalling, Brown, Evra, Nani (Hernández), Carrick, Scholes (Fletcher), Giggs, Rooney, Berbatov.

SUÁREZ IN RACIST STORM

5 October 2011
Premier League
Liverpool 1 (Gerrard (pen.)), United 1 (Hernández)

The game was completely overshadowed by the accusation by United's Patrice Evra that he was racially abused by Liverpool striker Luis Suárez, and the Football Association subsequently found the Uruguayan guilty of the charge, punishing him with an eight-match ban.

It was by no means the only time Suárez had courted bad publicity because, in November 2010, he was suspended by the Dutch authorities for seven games after an allegation of biting an opponent was proven.

As for the match, it was far from memorable, only sparking to life in the final quarter, which made for compelling viewing after the remainder had been described as thoroughly underwhelming.

United went to Anfield aware that if they were defeated it would have been the first time they would have lost four consecutive trips to any club.

Sir Alex Ferguson had Wayne Rooney on the bench as Danny Welbeck was the lone front man while defender Phil Jones operated in midfield. Liverpool, meanwhile, had injury-plagued talisman Steven Gerrard making his first Premier League start since March.

And it was Gerrard who broke the deadlock in the sixty-eighth minute from a free-kick which he freely admitted was mishit. It found a hole in the defensive wall where Ryan Giggs had pulled away from Welbeck, giving goalkeeper David de Gea no chance.

Suddenly the game ignited as Rooney and Nani were introduced, owing to the need for a more adventurous approach, although Rooney was employed in midfield. The most significant change was the third and final one six minutes later, when Javier Hernández replaced Jones.

The Mexican took only four minutes to transform United's fortunes with an equalising goal, making a darting run from Nani's corner and causing defender Martin Škrtel to slip, leaving him with a free close-range header from Welbeck's decisive flick.

Liverpool might have snatched victory but for de Gea's excellent save to deny Dirk Kuyt, while at the death Škrtel and Jordan Henderson went close as the game ended all square.

Liverpool: Reina, Kelly, Carragher, Škrtel, Enrique, Lucas (Henderson), Adam, Gerrard, Downing, Suárez, Kuyt.

United: de Gea, Smalling, Ferdinand, Evans, Evra, Fletcher, Park (Rooney), Jones (Hernández), Giggs, Young (Nani), Welbeck.

LIVERPOOL'S FLYING DUTCHMAN

28 January 2012
FA Cup Fourth Round
Liverpool 2 (Agger, Kuyt), United 1 (Park)

Liverpool substitute Dirk Kuyt was again the architect of United's misery, scoring a late winner in this FA Cup fourth round tie. The Dutchman had the previous March scored a memorable hat-trick for Liverpool in a 3-1 Premier League victory against United at Anfield.

Kuyt also ended a memorable week for Liverpool, who three days earlier had beaten Manchester City in the semi-finals of the Carling Cup. It looked as though United's disciplined display would earn a replay until substitute Kuyt struck the decisive blow in the eighty-eighth minute.

Liverpool captain Steven Gerrard admitted his side was tired and both he and Reds legend Roy Keane thought United were superior in terms of possession and overall play. Television pundit Keane, however, was damning about the goals United conceded, declaring, 'The defending for both Liverpool goals was shocking. United were superior in their passing and the way they played, but that doesn't win you games.'

After all the pre-match hype about this being the first meeting between United and Liverpool in the aftermath of the Evra/Suárez racist incident, the match passed incident-free.

Evra was jeered every time he touched the ball and there were taunts, which Liverpool manager Kenny Dalglish described as 'friendly banter' as he praised both sets of fans and also the players from each team as to how they conducted themselves.

While Dalglish described it as a 'fantastic effort' from his players three days after their Carling Cup exploits, Sir Alex Ferguson referred to it as a 'devastating blow', saying he could not believe how United lost.

United had a packed five-man midfield, which included veterans Paul Scholes and Ryan Giggs, with Danny Welbeck operating as the lone front-runner, Wayne Rooney being ruled out through injury.

Liverpool took the lead in the twenty-first minute after they were gifted a goal. Goalkeeper David de Gea was beaten hands-down, failing to gather a Steven Gerrard corner as Daniel Agger had a free header into an unguarded net.

United's patient, passing game was rewarded as they drew level six minutes before the break. Rafael da Silva made a deadly burst down the right, breezing past Jose Enrique and cutting the ball back from the byline for Park Ji-Sung to fire a first-time shot from fourteen yards low to the left of 'keeper Pepe Reina.

The longer play continued, the more it became clear substitutions could provide the sway, with Liverpool bringing on Kuyt, Charlie Adam and Craig Bellamy, who provided a spark and would tilt the game their way.

The match-winning goal came in the eighty-eighth minute, when United's defence was sliced open by a long clearance from Reina which was flicked on by Andy Carroll as Kuyt breezed past Evra to shoot low past de Gea.

Liverpool could have added third goal moments later when Carroll headed against the top of the upright and Kuyt fired the rebound narrowly wide.

Liverpool: Reina, Kelly, Škrtel, Enrique, Carragher (Kuyt), Downing, Henderson, Gerrard (Bellamy), Rodríguez (Bellamy), Carroll.
United: de Gea, Rafael, Smalling, Evans, Evra, Carrick, Scholes (Hernández), Giggs (Berbatov), Valencia, Welbeck, Park.

THE HANDSHAKE THAT NEVER WAS

11 February 2012
Premier League
United 2 (Rooney 2), Liverpool 1 (Suárez).

It was described as the most toxic Premier League incident ever as the racist storm between Liverpool's Luis Suárez and United's Patrice Evra plumbed new lows.

The refusal of Suárez to shake the hand of Evra before the match contributed towards the poisonous atmosphere at Old Trafford, where there was a fracas between the two sets of players in the tunnel at half-time and another flashpoint at the final whistle.

The eyes of the world were on this match, with Suárez and Evra coming face to face for the first time since the racist storm that engulfed the Premier League match at Anfield back in October. Suárez, making his first start following the completion of his eight-match ban for the racist comments made to Evra, had earlier given Liverpool assurances that he would shake hands and let bygones be precisely that.

However, Suárez did an about-turn and snubbed the Frenchman, who reacted angrily, grabbing the arm of the Uruguayan as he went to shake hands with David de Gea, who was next in the line. Rio Ferdinand, an astonished bystander, then withdrew his hand as Suárez passed.

As the players left the field at the break there were further repercussions; a confrontation between the two sets of players in the tunnel, as stewards and police intervened to usher them to their respective dressing rooms.

At the final whistle there was a further flare-up as Evra celebrated United's victory wildly in front of Suárez. Referee Phil Dowd arrived to move United's left-back away, but other angry Liverpool players intervened.

That was by no means the end of the drama, however, as the post-match comments of rival managers Sir Alex Ferguson and Kenny Dalglish were equally explosive.

Ferguson described Suárez as a disgrace, declaring that he ought never to be allowed to play for Liverpool again and that his actions could have sparked a riot.

Dalglish, meanwhile, rounded on Sky Sports reporter Geoff Shreeves, saying he was 'bang out of order' with his questioning of the incident.

The fallout continued and the next day Liverpool issued a series of statements from a remorseful Suárez, an apologetic Dalglish and from the club itself.

There had the previous day been the little matter of the match, as United's victory, which came courtesy of two goals from former Evertonian Wayne Rooney, lifted them back ahead of City at the top of the table for just over twenty-four hours.

Rooney took centre stage in what was his 500th appearance for club and country. The twenty-five-year-old had scored 211 goals in those previous 499 games, but only two against Liverpool. However, in the space of three second-half minutes he managed to match that total.

The opening half had been a pretty tepid affair, given the intense rivalry which exists between both the clubs and the fans. That was to change through Rooney's intervention with goals after forty-seven and fifty minutes, which were to win the game for United.

Ryan Giggs' corner glanced off the head of Liverpool's Jordan Henderson and Rooney swept in an unstoppable shot from inside the six-yard box. That was quickly followed by a second as he ran on to a through-ball from Antonio Valencia and slotted a shot low past 'keeper Pepe Reina.

Rooney had a great chance to complete his hat-trick before Liverpool pulled a goal back ten minutes from time, ironically from Suárez, to set up an exciting finish as the visitors almost snatched a point in stoppage time when de Gea pulled off an acrobatic save to deny Glen Johnson.

United: de Gea, Evra, Ferdinand, Evans, Rooney, Giggs, Carrick, Welbeck, Rafael, Scholes, Valencia.
Liverpool: Reina, Johnson, Enrique, Agger, Suárez, Gerrard, Henderson, Kuyt (Adam), Downing (Carroll), Spearing (Bellamy), Škrtel.

Statistics

FOOTBALL LEAGUE 1894–1992, INCLUDING TEST MATCH

Total games: 119
Liverpool goals: 160
Manchester United goals: 163
Liverpool wins: 44
Manchester United wins: 40
Draws: 35
Anfield average attendance: 37,366
Bank Street/Old Trafford/Maine Road average attendance: 40,274

Biggest victories
Liverpool: 7-1 [1895/96]
Manchester United: 6-1 [1927/28]

PREMIERSHIP 1992–2012

Total games: 20
Liverpool wins: 11
Manchester United wins: 22
Liverpool goals: 47
Manchester United goals: 59
Anfield average attendance: 43,595
Old Trafford average attendance: 62,128

FA CUP

Total games: 17
Liverpool wins: 4
Manchester United wins: 9

Liverpool goals: 17
Manchester United goals: 25
Anfield average attendance: 37,345
Bank Street/Old Trafford/Goodison Park average attendance: 42,500

LEAGUE CUP

Total games: 4
Liverpool wins: 3
Manchester United wins: 1
Liverpool goals: 7
Manchester United goals: 5
Anfield average attendance: 41,291
Old Trafford average attendance: 42,033

CHARITY SHIELD

Total games: 5
Liverpool wins: 1
Manchester United wins: 1
Liverpool goals: 5
Manchester United goals: 6
Average attendance: 71,857

TOTAL IN COMPETITIVE MATCHES

Total matches: 187
Liverpool wins: 63
Manchester United wins: 73
Liverpool goals: 236
Manchester United goals: 258

The sides have never met in a European match.

TRANSFERS FROM LIVERPOOL TO MANCHESTER UNITED

1912: Tom Chorlton, a Stockport-born full-back, who played for Liverpool in 1904–12, making 121 appearances in which he scored 8 goals. He was a member of the First Division title-winning teams of 1904/05 and 05/06, though he played only six League matches in the second success. Chorlton played four times for United in 1913/14, only for his career at Old Trafford to be ended by the outbreak of the First World War.

1920: Tom Miller, a Scottish international striker who signed for Liverpool from Hamilton Academical in 1912. He made 146 appearances and scored 56 goals – it would have been many more but for the First World War. He signed for United in a £2,000 deal in 1920 but remained at Old Trafford for only one season, finding the net 8 times in 27 appearances.

1928: Tommy Reid, one of the most prolific forwards in pre-war football, signed for Liverpool from Clydebank in 1926. The Scot scored 38 goals in 55 appearances for Liverpool before his move to Old Trafford, where he had an even more impressive return of 67 goals in 101 matches in 1928–33. In 1930/31, when United were relegated to the Second Division, Reid was the club's leading marksman with 17 goals.

1938: Ted Savage, a half-back who signed for Liverpool from Lincoln City in 1931 who made 105 appearances, scoring twice before a move to Old Trafford where he had a brief ten-month stay in 1938, making only 4 appearances.

1938: Allenby Chilton, a half-back who only had a short stay at Liverpool as an amateur in 1938 before joining United, for whom he made his debut ten months later at Charlton, the day before the outbreak of the Second World War. By the time his career effectively kicked off at Old Trafford he was twenty-eight years of age. Incredibly, he went on to make 390 first-team appearances for United, scoring 3 times. He was a member of the 1948 FA Cup-winning team and First Division title-winning team of 1951/52 having earlier been a runner-up four times. Chilton won the first of his two England caps at the age of thirty-two.

TRANSFERS FROM MANCHESTER UNITED TO LIVERPOOL

1913: John Sheldon, a striker signed from Nuneaton in November 1909 who made 26 senior appearances in 1910–13, scoring only once. He had a better strike ratio at Liverpool, where between 1913 and 1922 he scored 30 times in 147 matches, with the First World War taking a chunk out of his career.

1921: Fred Hopkin, a winger who played for United and Tottenham during the First World War, signing for them permanently in 1919. He went on to make 74 appearances, scoring 8 times before joining Liverpool, where he achieved considerable success. He was a member of their First Division title-winning teams of 1921/22 and 22/23 and he went on to play 360 matches for Liverpool, scoring 12 times.

When a serious fire broke out in the Anfield Road stand during the game against Bolton in March 1923, it was said to be due to Hopkin scoring a rare goal.

1954: Tommy McNulty, a full-back who was a member of United's First Division Championship-winning team of 1951/52, in which he played 24 League matches. He made a total of 59 appearances without scoring before a £7,000 move in 1954 to Liverpool, where he played 36 matches in the next four years, again without scoring.

In addition, there have been players who have appeared for both clubs, but not sequentially.

Paul Ince starred for United in 1989–95, making 281 first-team appearances and scoring 29 times. He signed for Liverpool in 1997 on his return from a spell in Italy at Inter Milan. He played 81 matches for Liverpool, scoring 17 goals.

   Peter Beardsley found himself behind Frank Stapleton, Mark Hughes and Norman Whiteside for a striking spot at Old Trafford, which is why he managed only one senior appearance in the League Cup against Bournemouth in 1982. He made a breakthrough at Newcastle and later joined Liverpool, for whom he played 175 matches in 1987–91, scoring 59 goals.

   John Gidman was an apprentice at Liverpool before making his mark for Aston Villa. He became Ron Atkinson's first signing for United, making 120 appearances between 1981 and 1986, finding the net 4 times.

   Michael Owen signed for United from Newcastle on a free transfer in the summer of 2009 to the dismay of fans from Liverpool, to whom he was a legend, scoring 158 goals in 297 appearances.

Interviews

Sir Alex Ferguson argues Manchester United against Liverpool is a bigger fixture than the Manchester derby, an indication as to its importance in the football calendar.

Phil Chisnall is the last of a select group of nine players who have been transferred directly between the two teams, something which seems implausible given today's climate. Inside-forward Chisnall, whose transfer in 1964 was for the sizeable sum of £25,000, looks back on his career with two of the giants of English football and playing for Sir Matt Busby and Bill Shankly, two of the greatest-ever managers.

When I was growing up, there wasn't the often-bitter rivalry which exists today in football. As somebody growing up in Manchester in the mid-fifties, I was by no means alone in going to watch United one week and City the next.

United were the more successful side as that was the era when the Busby Babes were starting to make their mark in football, but City also had a terrific team at that time. And it was because there were two successful sides in Manchester that so many people would watch both of them.

When I joined United's ground staff in Easter 1958 shortly after the Munich air crash there certainly wasn't any great rivalry with Liverpool. That was because Liverpool were in the Second Division at the time when the Babes were the dominant team and therefore weren't perceived as a threat to them. City against United was the big derby.

When I made my debut for United in 1961/62, Liverpool were still in the Second Division, though they were promoted that season. Bill Shankly had become manager a couple of years earlier. Liverpool's incredible rise continued as they were to win the First Division title in 1963/64 when United were runners-up. And it was in April 1964 that Shankly made a bid for me and I joined Liverpool. They lifted the FA Cup in 1965 and won the League again in 1965/66 and I think that is when the rivalry began because Liverpool had started to win things. Suddenly they were the two big teams of the North.

Manchester and Liverpool are two great cities less than one hour apart. The fans are from working-class backgrounds and they are proud of their own team which is why the rivalry exists. And in recent times it has become even more intense, with United equalling and latterly overtaking Liverpool's record of eighteen League titles while both battle for supremacy in the Champions League.

There is a similar rivalry today involving Chelsea and Arsenal, though it is nowhere near as intense. And in London it has not always been Chelsea and Arsenal as Tottenham were the dominant team when they won the double in 1961 when Danny Blanchflower captained the team.

When I was transferred to Liverpool it was not the big deal it would be were it to happen today, when it would be made big to sell newspapers. You would think it is life or death the way things are portrayed today, but it is only a game. I never played for United against Liverpool which was mainly due to the two teams being in different divisions when I joined them.

Though I only made nine appearances for Liverpool, one of them was for Liverpool at Old Trafford where we lost 3-1. I cannot remember what sort of reception I received, but it was nothing out of the ordinary. It certainly wasn't like Michael Owen when he was slaughtered by a section of the Liverpool fans on his return to Anfield which I find hard to come to terms with as he was such a good player for them.

It is a completely different ball game today with a celebrity culture and players treated as Gods. When I was playing, most of us would walk up Sir Matt Busby Way after the match, have a couple of pints in The Quadrant where we would discuss the match with the fans. We would then join the queue and get the bus home from White City. And we would usually have to stand on the top deck and some frustrated window cleaner would have his two-penneth about what had gone wrong if we hadn't won.

Today you don't see the players, who are whisked away in their cars with the windows blacked out, which is ridiculous!

I came from Davyhulme, which is only a stone's throw away from Old Trafford, and went to St Mary's Secondary School, Stretford. I played for Stretford and Lancashire Boys as well as England Schoolboys and I think it was a foregone conclusion that I signed for United being a local lad, even though I could have gone to any number of clubs, the likes of City, Bolton and Aston Villa.

It was difficult arriving at Old Trafford so soon after Munich and they were forced to bring in a number of emergency players, the likes of Stan Crowther and Ernie Taylor. I had only been at the club a matter of weeks when I was taken to Wembley. I had played there for England Schoolboys but this was the first time I had been to the final of the FA Cup.

I made my debut at nineteen and that age you are not intimidated and you don't have much fear. It was great to play alongside such players and be paid for doing so. When you looked at the forward line of Law, Best and Charlton together with David Herd and Johnny Giles, it took some beating. There were also the likes of Harry Gregg, Tony Dunne and Bill Foulkes so simply to get a game was some achievement. To get one game in that company wasn't bad, but I was lucky to play just short of fifty times in the days when there were no substitutes. And I also scored in the Manchester derby, which was a highlight. David Herd also found the net in a 2-0 win at Maine Road.

The move to Liverpool came as a surprise. I was called in by Busby to be told he had received a bid from Liverpool. I didn't have to go but they were top of the League and they must have thought I could do something for them. I was only twenty-one years of age and in those days you didn't have all the advisers like they have today. You simply made up your own mind yourself.

Money wasn't an issue as I was on £35 when I went to Liverpool which was an increase from what I was earning at United. It was a good wage, probably twice the average wage at that time, but nothing like today. When I made my debut at Old Trafford I was earning £12.50 and after ten games I was given a rise to £17.50 with £2 for a draw and £4 for a win.

When I joined Liverpool there was competition from the likes of Roger Hunt, Ian St John, Peter Thompson and Ian Callaghan so it wasn't any easier getting a game.

I was lucky to play for two of the top teams in the country and accepted I wasn't going to play regularly, though that would probably be different today. I had competition from the likes of Bobby Charlton, Nobby Stiles and Roger Hunt who were all World Cup winners.

It was an amazing time to be in Liverpool in the mid-sixties as the Beatles were making their mark and there were other bands. Liverpool was buzzing and the in place to be, and it was as though everything was happening there.

I was lucky to play for three of the greatest managers of all time – Busby, Shankly and Sir Alf Ramsey for England Under-23s. They were all brilliant, though in their own ways.

Ramsey didn't show the passion and enthusiasm of Shankly and he was more like a schoolteacher though, obviously, he knew what he was doing. I was in a unique position of being in the same room as Busby and Shankly discussing my future, though in those days I was young and didn't think too much about it. Shankly had great admiration for Busby and they were in many respects like father and son. Shankly, who was just starting out in management, would often come to Old Trafford to seek Busby's advice.

I think the bond was struck because they were both Scottish and of mining stock. And because they were down-to-earth, I think that is what they made them such good managers. They knew how lucky they were to be well paid to be involved in football, and that gave a hunger to succeed and not have to return to their roots. It is similar with Ferguson, who worked in the shipyards in Glasgow. You only have to look at the success he has achieved to see how good he is.

If you looked at Busby and his assistant Jimmy Murphy, Busby was quiet and not excitable whereas Murphy was the fiery Welshman, and they complemented each other. It was a similar thing with Shankly and Bob Paisley at Liverpool where Shankly was excitable and Paisley the calming influence. Shankly would have a subtle way of saying things and one thing always sticks in my mind.

When we were playing at home, sometimes we would go to stay at a hotel at Lymm on the Friday night. If we were staying at home, Shankly would say don't forget to put your boxing gloves on when you went to bed. It was his clever way of telling you to abstain the night before a game without telling you bluntly.

And when we were going to a hotel on a Friday night, in answer to what time we would leave, he would reply what time does *The Untouchables* finish on television as he would never leave until he had watched the programme.

He loved going against convention just like gangsters do what they want. And when he was stood on the touchline in his hat and raincoat he reminded me of James Cagney. Nobody would say it, but I figured it out myself.

BEST IS THE GREATEST FOOTBALLER I EVER PLAYED GAINST – CALLAGHAN

Liverpool were still a Second Division side when Ian Callaghan signed for them. Over the next two decades, however, they became Europe's top team as an intense rivalry developed with United. Here Callaghan, who made 857 first-team appearances for Liverpool between 1959 and 1978, recalls his own personal memories of their battles.

He said,

When we won 1-0 at United in November 1963 thanks to a late goal from Ron Yeats it was certainly a big boost to our hopes of winning the title. We were only in our second season back in the First Division so to win at Old Trafford meant a bit more than just two points. To win the title you have to win at the big grounds against your potential title rivals. The victory was a big stepping-stone.

In those days I was up against United's Tony Dunne who was quick and a tough opponent. In any games my job was to get the ball and try and test out the opposing full back, take him on, get to the byline and pull the ball back for someone else to have an effort at goal. I got to know Tony very well as we played against each other many times. I'd like to think there were occasions when I got the better of him, as there were also occasions when I didn't get much of a look-in. After I retired from football I have played a lot of golf and through that have got to know Tony pretty well.

Another tough opponent was Nobby Stiles who was supposedly hated by those on the Kop. I am surprised to hear that's become accepted wisdom among people who weren't around in the sixties because my view of fans who stood on the Kop is that they were great admirers of good footballers from any side.

While they wanted Liverpool to win, they also hoped to see the side have to play at its best to do so. The spectacle, entertainment and excitement was what people paid good, hard-earned cash to see. They wanted to see United playing their very best against Liverpool, as we had to then raise our game to beat them. I am not saying the Kop loved United players, like they did with Gordon Banks who would be cheered as he ran towards either the Anfield Road or Kop. The likes of Bobby Charlton, for example, might get applauded on occasions.

In the mid-sixties George Best played and scored in a number of games against us. Best is the greatest footballer I ever played against. He had pace, perfect balance on the ball, but he could also defend. If he lost possession, you'd see him chase back to try and recover the ball. He could also head the ball as well as dribble and in front of goal he was deadly. I think it's definitely the case that no side in England has ever had three such talented players as Charlton, Law and Best in one side. Law was a great scorer of goals in the box, while Charlton was graceful on the ball. He could go past opponents either side using his pace or dribbling, and what a shot he had.

They were great players, but they wouldn't have been successful if they didn't also have other really good players alongside them, the likes of Tony Dunne, Paddy Crerand and Bill Foulkes. Alex Stepney was also a cracking 'keeper. He was fearless and, like our own Tommy Lawrence, he'd be more than willing to come out and dive at your feet to try and take the ball off you.

Later on the player I most admired was Martin Buchan, who was a very good cultured defender. He timed his tackles superbly and, in possession, he rarely wasted it.

I recall how disappointed I was when United were relegated in 1974 as you want the really great clubs in the top flight playing each other. Long may that be the case. I looked forward to any game I played in, as I loved football and to get well paid for doing something I loved was extra special. The big games, and few were bigger than playing United, were always extra special.

My roles in the games were different depending upon whether we played at home or away. When we were playing at Old Trafford and Bobby Charlton was out on the left, Bill Shankly would tell me to play further back in order to support the full-back. On the left, Peter Thompson was asked to play much more forward than me.

Were United were lucky to beat us in the 1977 FA Cup final is something I am often asked, and I have to say they were. I came on in that game when we were 2-1 down. It was disappointing to lose as the defeat denied us the treble, which United became the first club to achieve in 1999. However, four days later we did win the European Cup and, given the choice between winning that or the FA Cup, we would have picked victory in Rome.

How did the games against United during my playing career differ from those of today is also a question often posed. I would say not that much for the players who have to try and ignore the history of the occasions. That's not the case for the supporters, however, as there's now an even greater rivalry than in my days. We had a long period of success when United were very much second-best and in more recent times that's been the reverse. Due to this, the game has become the match of the season for both sets of supporters, when back in my day it was the local derbies, in our case against Everton, that were the biggest.

THEY WERE OUR BIGGEST GAMES OF THE SEASON – BUCHAN

Martin Buchan captained United for much of the seventies, appearing in three FA Cup finals and also many other massive matches. As the Scottish international argues, however, there was nothing bigger than the fixtures against Liverpool.

He reflected,

With due respect to Manchester City, the matches with Liverpool during my career were the biggest games we played each season. Since I retired Sir Alex Ferguson has gone on record as saying they are English football's biggest games because of the history attached to it.

What has changed significantly since my playing days is the attention football receives. Every game attracts the sort of publicity that we would only get for Cup finals, major European nights or big important League matches. Today, Premier League games are watched the world over and players are better known than ever was the case.

There was violence at the games I played in, but it was something that you were to a certain extent shielded from and, as players, you couldn't afford to let it affect you. The most trouble I witnessed was at, of all places, Notts County when I played there in the Second Division.

The United and Liverpool players had a mutual respect that allowed friendships to develop, especially in my case as we made up the backbone of the Scottish side in the seventies. I meet Liverpool players from that period at functions and we all get on well together. That is how it should be.

The period was a frustrating one in that in head-to-head competition we would often beat Liverpool, both at Old Trafford and Liverpool, but they were much better than us when going to places like Coventry on a miserable Tuesday night and winning. It was the difference between collecting a League title and finishing second or third. Liverpool also learned a lot about playing in Europe, especially about the need to be patient, and they would not worry if they hadn't scored early on. Also, they naturally gained confidence from winning things, and so they just kept plugging away.

The Liverpool sides of the seventies and early eighties contained some great defenders, but they could also play a bit as well. They also had some wonderful attacking players. I came up against Kevin Keegan as a full back and he was quick and constantly on the move. Later I played against Kenny Dalglish when I moved to centre-back. He wouldn't run away with you using pace. His strengths were his control of the ball and the ability to back away from you. He was also brilliant at bringing other players into action.

I played once for Scotland against Wales at Hampden Park and the Welsh forward line was John Toshack, Ron and Wyn Davies – the Welsh air-force was our nickname for them. When I was playing for United, I would leave the big man – the one good in the air – to either Jim Holton or later Gordon McQueen to look after.

I was never intimidated playing at Anfield. I remember enjoying watching the crowd in the packed Kop swaying. I found playing in front of a big noisy crowd, whether for or against you, a thrill. I can still recall playing before seventy thousand Spaniards in Valencia for Scotland and thoroughly enjoying the experience. I came on as a sub for Sandy Jardine in the World Cup qualifier at Anfield against Wales in 1977 and that, too, was marvellous.

The pitch at Liverpool wasn't that good. Most weren't during my playing career. In the winter the frost might make them bone hard and then muddy as hell if it rained while there would be a lack of grass on them come the season's end.

Here are my memories of some of the actual games. In November 1975 we lost 3-1 at Anfield and afterwards Paddy Roche in goal was heavily criticised, especially for the first goal. In fact, I blame Brian Greenhoff, who didn't get out of the way when Paddy shouted at him to do so. I feel Paddy might have had more of a chance to make it if the Doc [Tommy Docherty] hadn't decided to give 'youth a chance' by playing him at Highbury,

Anfield and Maine Road. I think it damaged his confidence. I was the captain at the time but I wouldn't have thought about saying this to the Doc, as we didn't have such a relationship.

I had a running battle with the Doc at times in my early years at Old Trafford. He would play me at full-back on the grounds that I wasn't big enough to be a centre-back. He even put me at left-back but, when it became obvious that getting up the wing and crossing with my left-foot wasn't going to work, I reverted to right-back.

It was great to beat Liverpool in the 1977 FA Cup final, although I don't personally care for having the record of being the only man to have captained sides to success in the Scottish and English Cups. A lot was made beforehand about Arthur Albiston's lack of experience. All you can do is help any new player as much as you can, but you can't play the game for them, Arthur rose to the occasion and had a very good game. It was a great pity that the Doc was sacked soon afterwards as I feel the team was just starting to come to its peak and I feel we would have done well.

In the Maine Road semi-final in March 1979, I dispute that Kenny Dalglish waltzed past me as it was reported in some papers. What happened was that Sammy McIlroy got in my way so I couldn't get towards Kenny to tackle him. In the replay I remember Mickey Thomas made a great run down the wing and, when his cross came in, Brian Greenhoff stooped down to head the ball into the net at the end where the majority of United fans were housed.

One thing that Liverpool had was a midfield in which every player contributed a good number of goals. Our midfield was a very mobile one, but we lacked crunching tacklers. I recall going to manager Dave Sexton when Jimmy Case was made available by Liverpool and suggesting he bought him. Dave, though, was set on buying Ray Wilkins. I think he could have bought both of them. Not that I am saying our midfield couldn't win the ball, it was more a matter of using pace to get to the ball first to pinch possession.

I enjoyed my career as a footballer but it is a strange job in which you get to know people fairly intimately as you're changing and showering with them each day and you also room with them on away trips. You also might be with many of the same people for a lengthy time – ten years or so. The banter is also something you have to be able to deal with. It can be cruel and you need to be able to both take it and give it in equal measure.

HOW I SIGNED FOR UNITED – LIVERPOOL LEGEND WHELAN

Ronnie Whelan became a Liverpool legend after spending fifteen years at Anfield in which he made 493 appearances and scored 73 goals for the club. He featured in the European Cup triumph of 1984, won six League titles, two FA Cups and three League Cups as well as capturing many other honours during his illustrious career.

Yet as a youngster, Whelan's dream was to play for Manchester United and it was one which he could have fulfilled had fate not intervened. Here Whelan, who is now a television pundit for Irish station RTE, tells the remarkable story of how he might easily have become a Red Devil.

Manchester United were the team I wanted to play for when I was growing up as a boy in Dublin. That was the era of Best, Law and Charlton and I was six years of age when they became the first English team to win the European Cup. I cannot remember anything of the final, though I have vague memories of seeing some of their games on television, though nowhere near as many were televised in those days compared to the modern era.

What I do recall, however, is watching United when they played in Dublin a couple of months after they won the European Cup. The pre-season match was at Dalymount Park and I got to go in their dressing room and meet the players.

My dad, also Ronnie, was an inside forward who won a couple of caps for Northern Ireland and he knew United's Irish lads Shay Brennan and Tony Dunne. It was probably because of this connection that I used to go over to United every school holiday between the ages of thirteen and sixteen and would train with other schoolboys at The Cliff.

I was a massive fan and here was I now training at United, the team I had always wanted to play for. I became an associate schoolboy and would play in some games – they would probably be for the 'B' team – and I remember beating Liverpool 5-2 at The Cliff on one occasion. Scott McGarvey and Andy Ritchie were among the group of youngsters I used to train with.

You can imagine my joy when United offered me an apprenticeship and how hard it was to turn it down. It was felt I was too young to move away so I stayed at home to complete my schooling. Whether United lost interest because of my refusal to sign, they never came back for me and Liverpool, having seen me play for Home Farm, offered me a trial at the age of seventeen and I signed for them in the summer of 1979.

It was weird growing up as a Manchester United fan and then signing for Liverpool as I knew the intense rivalry between the two clubs, even then over thirty years ago. I would have my Christmas football annuals and the rivalry was always mentioned in them. I never had any doubts, however, about signing for Liverpool as they were the best team in Europe at that time and it was always a case of signing for the best possible club. It was a no brainer that I should join Liverpool. Besides, United had not come back in for me.

I knew that if I didn't make it at Liverpool, I would get a good education at what was the best club in Europe. I always wanted to play at Old Trafford and would get to do so. The only difference is that it would be for a different team. I had watched many games at Old Trafford when I was over as a schoolboy training at the club so I knew what a special place it was. I would tend to hang around with the ball boys and would sneak down the tunnel with them before a game. It gave me a feel for the place, though obviously it is different when you are a player walking out on to the pitch.

When I stepped out at Old Trafford for the first time as a player, the only thought in my head was to win the game. I was now playing for Liverpool and the fact I had supported United meant nothing as I was a professional footballer for Liverpool. I had some great battles against United and, for me, probably the most memorable was the final of the Milk Cup in 1983 when I scored our match-winning goal in extra time when I bent a shot past 'keeper Gary Bailey.

It was a big thrill to play against United in a Cup final and to score the winning goal was an amazing feeling, even more so as it was against the team I supported as a kid.

I had appeared for Liverpool the previous year in the final of the Milk Cup against Tottenham but, though that was my first-ever final at Wembley and we won, it was nowhere near as special as playing against United.

Later I also got to score for Liverpool against United in the semi-final of the FA Cup at Goodison Park. It was a better goal than the one I scored at Wembley, though it did not mean as much as we lost the replay at Maine Road. I did get to score at Old Trafford, and it is a goal I shall never forget as I put through my own goal in March 1990. It is probably the best own goal ever scored in front of the Stretford End.

We were 2-0 ahead at the time when Glenn Hysen headed the ball out of defence. I was twenty-five yards from goal and decided to half volley it back to our 'keeper Bruce Grobbelaar. It sailed over his head and it was the most embarrassing moment I had as a player. Luckily we held on to win 2-1 and I am still reminded about it, especially by United fans when I am in the area speaking at a dinner.

While there is a rivalry between Liverpool and Everton, I would only say it became intense in the mid-eighties when Everton were winning the League, FA Cup and European Cup Winners Cup. Liverpool fans were not used to being second best and for that short period the intensity of the rivalry increased. With Liverpool and United it is as though there is always something riding on the game, even when there is seemingly nothing resting on the outcome.

Before I joined Liverpool, I remember watching the 1977 final of the FA Cup. Liverpool were going for the treble but United, who were supposed to stand no chance on current form, beat them 2-1. And it is things like that which again proves there is always more on games between the two teams.

When United were languishing behind us in my playing days or today when it is the opposite, there always seems to be something major resting on the game.

Liverpool fans certainly don't like United being talked about as one of the top clubs in Europe after they had won the European Cup so many times. When I look at what Sir Alex Ferguson has achieved at Old Trafford, I see big parallels to what Bill Shankly, Bob Paisley and later Kenny Dalglish did earlier at Liverpool.

People questioned Sir Alex at the start when things didn't go well. There must have been many times when his judgement was queried, especially in those early years when there was no success. The board of directors stuck with him and were rewarded for that. He knew changes were needed as the likes of Paul McGrath and Norman Whiteside were allowed to leave.

He did things his way and was very successful … and still is. That continuity is so important as we saw with the Boot Room at Liverpool where managers were appointed from within.

RIVALRY FRIENDLY IN MY DAY – MCDERMOTT

Terry McDermott was a key Liverpool player at the start of the most glorious chapter in the club's history, winning three European Cups, three First Division titles and two League Cups during his eight years at Anfield between 1974 and 1982. It was during this period that the rivalry between Liverpool and United began to intensify, though still not to the degree that exists today.

Midfield-man McDermott is well qualified to comment on footballing rivalries as he was brought up just outside the Liverpool boundary in Kirkby, so was used to the passion of the Merseyside derby and also the Tyne-Wear encounters when he played for Newcastle.

McDermott, a boyhood fan of the Anfield club, also argues the Liverpool/Manchester United fixtures in that period were nowhere as feisty as today. He explained:

Obviously there has always been rivalry between Liverpool and Manchester because the cities are little more than thirty miles apart. The footballing rivalry today between Liverpool and United is far more intense than in my playing days. There was never that hatred which sadly exists today, something there is no getting away from.

There was certainly no animosity between the players in my day and the likes of Bryan Robson, Kevin Moran, Paul McGrath and Ashley Grimes were friends who would meet up for a drink. There were also players like Steve Coppell who I knew from playing for England and there was never any problem involving the players.

United had a great team in the mid/late sixties when they had Best, Charlton and Law at the peak, and they were the top dogs. When Liverpool started to win the European Cup and First Division title regularly it must have started to get up the noses of the United fans, especially as they were not to have the best of times in that period.

Yet since 1990 it has been a case of United winning everything and I would say the jealousy has increased as they edged ever closer to Liverpool's record of eighteen titles which United have now surpassed.

I also saw the same scenario on Merseyside where Everton had a good spell in the mid-eighties and that was resented by Liverpool fans. Yet when Liverpool were enjoying success you never got the same degree of jealousy from Everton fans. Usually intense rivalry is between teams in the same city – Liverpool and Everton, Manchester United and City, Rangers and Celtic. I saw that from first-hand experience in Glasgow when I worked with Kenny Dalglish when he managed Celtic.

Yet the rivalry between the fans of Liverpool and Everton is nowhere near as hostile as in other cities. In the sixties, seventies and eighties you used to have reds and blues sat next to one another at derby games as they often came from the same families. It was far more close knit on Merseyside, where rival fans would live on the same street and worked side by side in the same factories.

That wasn't the case in Manchester where the joke was that all their fans came from London so there was never that same close-knit community spirit that exists in Liverpool.

That has changed since my playing days and I would say in recent times the rivalry between Liverpool and Everton fans is not as friendly as it used to be and that has also become bitter.

What makes the rivalry between Liverpool and United almost unique is that it involves teams not from the same city. In saying that, there was also the same bitter rivalry between Newcastle and Sunderland, which also bordered on hatred which was sad. I don't think there is the same degree of rivalry in London because of the large number of clubs in the capital.

During my playing days, we lost to United in the final of the FA Cup in 1977, a defeat which cost us the treble which had never been achieved before. We had won the League and went on to lift the European Cup in Rome days after the defeat at Wembley. I still believe it was a travesty and we ought to have won the FA Cup as we had the better side and were the better team on the day.

Yes it was disappointing to lose, but if you had given me the choice of two trophies to win that season I would have gone for the League and European Cup with the FA Cup the third choice.

Winning two of the three major trophies wasn't bad going, though we were greedy and wanted them all. It was not to be and the European Cup was a nice consolation prize.

I also remember meeting United in the FA Cup Semi final a couple of years later when we lost in a replay. We drew 2-2 against them at Manchester City's Maine Road ground where I missed a penalty and then lost 1-0 in the replay at Goodison Park.

I would say we probably won the highest percentage of games against United in the seventies and eighties, but United certainly won a couple of the big matches when you look back to those FA Cup matches.

It is strange how Liverpool were so dominant during the seventies and eighties and then in the nineties and noughties it has been United who have done likewise. Though United have won many more trophies than Liverpool in the last twenty years, Liverpool have still managed to win the odd big one, the European Cup and FA Cup.

When you are a boy growing up as a Liverpool fan, you always dream that one day you will play for the club, though realistically knowing it would probably never happen. I arrived late at Liverpool having first played for Bury and Newcastle, but I went on to have eight fabulous years at the club.

To win League titles and European Cups was what dreams are made of and I was lucky to live that dream. It was also a dream to play in the Merseyside derby and in Liverpool versus United games. They meant even more to me because Liverpool was my home city.

RIVALRY BECAME LESS FRIENDLY WHEN I PLAYED – MCGRATH

Paul McGrath was regarded as one of the most accomplished central defenders of his generation.

There is also no telling what McGrath, who made just shy of 200 first-team appearances for United, would have achieved but for serious knee problems and also continual off-the-field scrapes. Indeed, McGrath tested the patience of Sir Alex Ferguson once too often and he was sold to Aston Villa for a cut-price £450,000 in the summer of 1989.

Here McGrath gives his own personal insight and perspective on the rivalry between United and Liverpool. He said,

When I was back home in Ireland before I signed for United, I was aware of the rivalry given that Manchester and Liverpool are cities not that far apart.

At that time neither club was anywhere near as dominant as they were to become in later years and it was simply a healthy rivalry between the two cities. Indeed, Chelsea were the team I supported as a boy – and still do – and that was because they won the 1970 final of the FA Cup. The late Peter Osgood and Charlie Cooke were my heroes and it was great to later go to Stamford Bridge and shake Osgood's hand. Just think – had Leeds won that final, I might have started following them so would have been in serious trouble.

By the time I began playing for United, the rivalry had developed into something far less friendly. If you were an opposition fan you had to be careful where you walked. I also remember our wives were often told that may be it would be wise not to go to the game because of the risk of trouble.

I remember when the fixture list was first published each summer, United against Liverpool was the one everyone would look for first. If you ask fans which they would prefer, I am sure United against Liverpool would be the first choice, even above the derbies in their own cities. That is the game we looked forward to more than any other, and we would go out all guns blazing.

I used to love playing against Liverpool at that time against the likes of Graeme Souness, Jimmy Case and Steve McMahon. They were hard human beings but I loved going into a tackle against them as it would be full blooded and you knew they would not pull out. There was no friendship on the pitch, but there was respect and the rivalry was not vindictive. As soon as the game finished there was no animosity and twenty minutes later we would be in the bar having a drink together and enjoying a craic.

Liverpool were the team we always wanted to beat the most and, if my memory serves me right, we had a decent record against them. It was the likes of Ipswich and QPR who we struggled to beat. I am convinced if we had played Liverpool every week, we would have won the League given our record against them!

Ian Rush was one of the greatest strikers of the era in which I played the game, yet he struggled against us. I think it took twenty-odd games for him to get his first goal against us.

Yet he was one of the toughest strikers I have ever faced and had the speed of a racehorse. He never gave you a second on the ball and was one of the quickest players to close you down. You knew you could not try to be clever on the ball or he would cause you trouble and he was in a class of his own.

I was also lucky to play against Kenny Dalglish, who was also a special talent. As a footballer you want to play against best players in the world. Rush and Dalglish were two of them and, when they played together, you knew you were in for a difficult afternoon.

When we played at Anfield there were few warm receptions and you could sense the hostility the moment you stepped off the coach as most of the players will tell you. I was never worried and it was no big deal. All I wanted was to do Manchester proud and beat Liverpool. While we would always do ourselves proud against Liverpool, it was they who won all the trophies which was the frustrating thing. When you look back, they were a class outfit in that era. They held the torch for a long time and deservedly so.

I scored twice in one season at Anfield, which not many players can do. It was some feat for me as I didn't score that many goals for United. I remember one of the goals as I left Mark Lawrenson for dead and had to hit it as quick as lightning, which I did with my weaker left foot and it flashed past Bruce Grobbelaar in the Liverpool goal.

One not such happy memory was scoring an own goal in the FA Cup semi-final replay when the ball went in off the back of my head, though I seem to recall Kenny Dalglish claiming it.

I still take a keen interest when United play Liverpool and enjoyed the one when Dimitar Berbatov scored a hat-trick in the 3-2 win at Old Trafford. Though it has been a long time since I played in the fixture, one part of me still wants to put Liverpool down. That is a measure of the fierce rivalry which still exists.

I WAS BROUGHT UP TO HATE LIVERPOOL – CHAPMAN

BBC Five Live presenter and former Radio 1 DJ Mark Chapman says he was well aware of the intense rivalry between United and Liverpool from an early age.

Chapman, whose allegiance to United is no secret, was taken to his first match at Old Trafford against Wolves in 1981 for an eighth birthday treat. He said,

> I knew from the first time that I watched Manchester United play Liverpool, which was about that time, that I was meant to hate them. And I definitely feel there is a greater rivalry between United and Liverpool than between United and City.
>
> In the second leg of the Carling Cup semi final in 2009/10 at Old Trafford when Wayne Rooney scored a late winner to defeat City, the place was absolutely bouncing. It was the first time I had experienced an atmosphere like that at a derby from a United perspective.
>
> As I left Old Trafford, I said to my dad that it was like going back to 1999 and the treble year when we beat Liverpool in the fourth round of the FA Cup. United were one goal down with a couple of minutes left when Dwight Yorke and Ole Gunnar Solskjær scored and the noise was such that it could have lifted the roof off the ground. It was similar when Rooney scored the late winner against City so in that sense it was interesting that the first thing I compared that night to was United against Liverpool in 1999.

Chapman added that it will be interesting to see how the rivalry between United and City develops in forthcoming years, bearing in mind the change in City's status and standing due to the massive investment from new owner Sheikh Mansour.

He says the rivalry between United and City will always be football-related whereas with United and Liverpool there are so many more layers. Chapman said,

> That stems from the rivalry between Manchester and Liverpool which goes back to the nineteenth century and the industrial revolution. There was the fight for trade, the canals and the like. Fast forward to the twentieth century and music played a bigger part. The footballing rivalry intensified with Liverpool being so successful in the seventies and eighties while United took over in the nineties and noughties.

Chapman agreed that before that period Liverpool, who had been in the Second Division in the fifties and early sixties, were not perceived as a threat to United. He continued,

> Bobby Charlton even played in Tommy Smith's testimonial in a Liverpool shirt which is something which would be unthinkable today. Matt Busby also had Liverpool connections so the rivalry wasn't there in that area.
>
> By the late seventies, however, Liverpool had won back-to-back European Cups and several First Division titles and that is when the rivalry kicked in. And when you layer in all the other social and economic factors, that only serves to crank up the rivalry even further. You only have to look at music and we will still want to champion Oasis over the Beatles which is again Mancunian versus Scouse.

Chapman added that since 1990 the footballing power base has shifted from Liverpool to Manchester, where United have dominated for two decades just as the previous two saw the Anfield club have a stranglehold and monopoly on the honours.

While the 1999 FA Cup fourth round tie between United and Liverpool is a game he will never forget, there are also other memorable contests between the two teams.

Chapman can recall the League match on New Year's Day 1989 at Old Trafford when United won 3-1 in a hostile atmosphere. He said,

> John Barnes scored for Liverpool and we were sat in K Stand and the away fans were in the lower tier and home ones above them, something which would not happen today.
>
> When Barnes scored the Liverpool fans fired a flare into our section and it landed on the knee of a mate's dad who was sitting three seats away. He managed to get it off before anything more serious happened. That sticks in my mind partly because of the firecracker and partly because some of Fergie's fledglings like Russell Beardsmore, who scored that day, were breaking into the team.

The 1996 final of the FA Cup between the two teams is also a stand-out match, especially as it completed the domestic double for a second time. Chapman continued,

> Eric Cantona scored the winner and that was the season he had returned from his nine-month ban and the final remembered for Liverpool wearing their white suits. Cantona's

first match back after his ban was against Liverpool at Old Trafford and he scored a dubious penalty which Ryan Giggs won in front of K Stand.

That match finished 2-2 and the atmosphere that day was amazing. I saw it on a television programme recently and it brought goosebumps back just watching it back on the television.

Delving further back to his school days, Chapman also remembers the FA Cup semi final and replay against Liverpool in 1985.

He recalled, 'Bryan Robson was cheered off by fans after we won the replay at Maine Road. When I look back, there have been some very good Cup games between the two teams.'

Chapman says the treble-winning campaign remains the highlight of his time watching United. He continued,

I remember leaving the Nou Camp in Barcelona after we had beaten Bayern Munich in the dramatic finish to the final of the Champions League and turning to my dad and saying it will never get better than that.

Nothing will ever beat that night in terms of the way we won the final in the same way Liverpool fans will never get any better than coming back from 3-0 in the final against AC Milan in Istanbul. It is strange how the two clubs are linked like that and I don't think it will get any better for Liverpool than that night, just as I cannot envisage anything beating our win against Bayern Munich in 1999.

ALSO AVAILABLE FROM AMBERLEY PUBLISHING

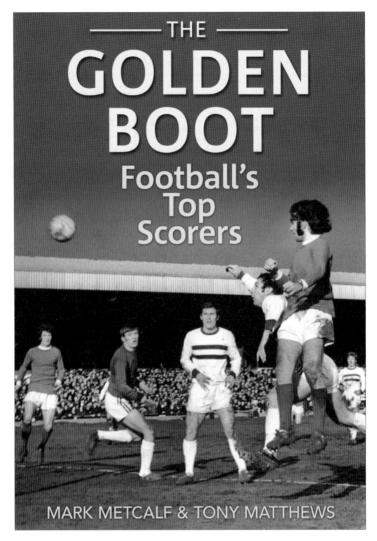

THE GOLDEN BOOT
FOOTBALL'S Top Scorers

MARK METCALF & TONY MATTHEWS

The Golden Boot: Football's Top Scorers

Mark Metcalf and Tony Matthews

The first history of the Golden Boot – from 1888 to the present day.

978 1 4456 0532 6
256 pages

Available from all good bookshops or order direct
from our website www.amberleybooks.com